Berliner Chic

Berliner Chic
A Locational History of Berlin Fashion

Susan Ingram and Katrina Sark

intellect Bristol, UK / Chicago, USA

First published in the UK in 2011 by
Intellect, The Mill, Parnall Road, Fishponds, Bristol, BS16 3JG, UK

First published in the USA in 2011 by
Intellect, The University of Chicago Press, 1427 E. 60th Street,
Chicago, IL 60637, USA

A catalogue record for this book is available from the
British Library.

Library of Congress Cataloging-in-Publication Data

Ingram, Susan (Susan V.)
    Berliner chic : a locational history of Berlin fashion / Susan Ingram
and Katrina Sark.
        p. cm.
    Includes bibliographical references.
    ISBN 978-1-84150-369-1 (pbk.) -- ISBN 978-1-84150-432-2 (e-book)
1. Fashion--Germany--Berlin--History. 2. Clothing--Germany--Berlin-
-History. 3. Women designers--Germany--Berlin--History. I. Sark,
Katrina. II. Title.
    GT931.B47I54 2011
    391.00943'155--dc22
                            2010030866

Cover designer: Holly Rose
Copy-editor: Jennifer Alluisi
Typesetting: Mac Style, Beverley, E. Yorkshire

ISBN 978-1-84150-369-1

Printed and bound by Gutenberg Press, Malta.

Contents

List of Illustrations

We have gone to great effort to trace and contact the copyright holders of all images in this book. We regret that the rights to some images, like those by Helmut Newton, proved beyond our means, but are all the more grateful to those copyright owners who have granted permission, and provided us with reasonable terms, to reproduce their works. We would especially like to acknowledge the generosity of the Stiftung F.C. Gundlach in this regard. If any copyright holders of images have not been properly credited, please contact the publishers, who will be happy to rectify future editions.

Cover:
Heinrich Zille, Linienstraße 34. (Heinrich-Zille-Gesellschaft Berlin E.V.)

Introduction:
0.1. Berlin, 1995. (Photo: Rico Puhlmann, Archive Rico Puhlmann)
0.2. Linienstraße 34, November 2009. (Photo: K. Sark)
0.3. Window of the Zille Destille restaurant, Propststrasse 10. (Photo: K. Sark)
0.4. *Textil Report* cover, Rico Puhlmann. (Archive Rico Puhlmann)
0.5. Berliner Chic postcard stand on Unter den Linden. (Photo: S. Ingram)

Chapter One:
1.1. Altes Museum. (Photo: S. Ingram)
1.2. Franz Defregger: Portrait of Franz Lipperheide, 1905. (Staatliche Museen zu Berlin, Kunstbibliothek)
1.3. Frieda Lipperheide, after a photo by E. Encke, 1885. (Staatliche Museen zu Berlin, Kunstbibliothek)
1.4. *Lehrbücher der Modenwelt* 1897. (Staatliche Museen zu Berlin, Kunstbibliothek)
1.5. First exhibition of the Lipperheide Costume Library, March 1900 in the Lichthof of the Kunstgewerbemuseums. (Staatliche Museen zu Berlin, Kunstbibliothek)
1.6. *A Century of Fashion, 1796–1896.* (Staatliche Museen zu Berlin, Kunstbibliothek)
1.7. Cover, "1920s Fashion" exhibition catalogue. (Stadtmuseum Berlin)

5.3. Trabi Safari in front of the Memorial to the Murdered Jews of Europe. (Photo: S. Ingram)

5.4. Trabi Safari down the street from Checkpoint Charlie. (Photo: S. Ingram)

5.5. Trabis from the Zoo Tour at the Rock and Roll Hall of Fame and Museum, Cleveland. (Photo: S. Ingram)

5.6. Ramones Museum founder, Flo Hayler. (F. Hayler)

5.7. Ramones Museum, Krausnickstraße 23. (F. Hayler)

5.8. Ramones Museum, Krausnickstraße 23. (Photo: S. Ingram)

Chapter Six:

6.1. The Palace of the Republic, viewed from the Spree, 2005. (Photo: S. Ingram)

6.2. The razed site where the Palace of the Republic once stood, November 2009. (Photo: K. Sark)

6.3. Corner of Unter den Linden and Friedrichstraße after *Hotel Unter den Linden*; was torn down to make room for the Upper East Side shopping mall, June 2006. (Photo: K. Sark)

6.4. Bebelplatz, Fashion Week 2009. (Photo: S. Ingram)

6.5. Be Berlin poster. (Photo: S. Ingram)

6.6. Be Berlin as a sponsor of Fashion Week 2008. (Photo: S. Ingram)

6.7. Black Roses Berlin, Alte Schönhauser Strasse 39. (Photo: K. Sark)

6.8. Shoes Berlin, Rosenthaler Strasse 50. (Photo: K. Sark)

6.9. Interior of Made in Berlin, Neue Schönhauser Strasse 19. (Photo: K. Sark)

6.10. Interior of Skunk Funk Berlin, Kastanienallee 19. (Photo: K. Sark)

6.11. Interior of Berlinomat, Frankfurter Allee 89. (Photo: K. Sark)

6.12. Waahnsinn Berlin, Rosenthaler Strasse 17. (Photo: K. Sark)

6.13. Eastberlin, Alte Schönhauser Strasse 33–34. (Photo: K. Sark)

6.14. Sophienhof with sewing machine. (Photo: K. Sark)

6.15. All Saints display with sewing machines, Rosenthalerstrasse 52. (Photo: K. Sark)

6.16. Interior of Cube, Schönhauser Arkaden mall. (Photo: K. Sark)

Chapter Seven

7.1. "Nice that we were there," graffiti on Prinzenstrasse, August 2009. (Photo: S. Ingram)

Dedication

The story of Berliner Chic is, in the first instance, the story of the women of Berlin, the *Berlinerinnen*. Even more than the male designers, manufacturers (*Konfektionäre*), middle-men (*Zwischenmeister*), illustrators, photographers, collectors, museum directors, corporate executives and creative entrepreneurs, it is the women of Berlin who have given Berliner Chic its lasting significance.

Berlinerinnen have always made clothes: from the nineteenth-century home seamstresses, whose hard, underpaid work made the ready-to-wear industry not only possible but highly successful, to designers like Sabine von Oettingen, who made clothes for underground fashion shows in the GDR out of shower curtains and plastic used by farmers to cover strawberries.

In clothing themselves, *Berlinerinnen* have always pushed the limits of not only their imaginations but also their means: from the glamorous flappers of the golden twenties, who popularized the stylish Berlin look by parading along Kurfürstendamm and prided themselves on being able to distinguish between real and artificial silk; to the rubble women among the ruins of Berlin in the post-WWII years, who sewed clothes out of dish rags (*Lumpenkleider*) and army blankets, and who, like Fassbinder's Maria Braun, traded American cigarettes for a rare new dress on the black market; to the *Botschafterinnen der Mode* (female fashion ambassadors) models of the economic-miracle-years, who became the faces of German post-war fashion.

Berlinerinnen have also done much to preserve and collect clothes: women like Dorit Lücke, who worked at the GDR Fashion Institute for over twenty years until its dissolution in 1991 and fought for its collections and archive to remain intact until it became a part of the *Stadtmuseum*; women like Christine Waidenschlager, fashion curator at the Berlin Museum since the beginnings of its fashion collection in the 1980s, who organized the "Berliner Chic" exhibition for the *Stadtmuseum*, along with many other fashion exhibitions and publications, and who now works at the *Kunstgewerbemuseum*; women like Dagmar Neuland-Kitzerow, who is in charge of the fashion collection at the Museum of European Cultures in Dahlem, curated its *Stunde Null* exhibition and has done much work on the history of Berlin fashion; women like Adelheid Rasche, director of the Lipperheide Costume Library, who has published numerous books on fashion, curated exhibitions, and organized an ongoing lecture series on fashion at the *Kulturforum*. These are the women who have made Berliner Chic what it is today.

Berlinerinnen also continue to reinvent Berlin fashion. Women like Claudia Skoda, c. neeon (Clara Kraetsch and Doreen Schulz), *Stadtkluft* (Claudine Brignot of *urbanspeed* and Sandra Siewert of *s.wert*) and Natascha Loch carry on the tradition of Berliner Chic and carry its meanings into today's fashion. *Berlinerinnen* will always be ready to wear: the women who live in the city, are photographed in its streets, wear local brands and give Berlin fashion its reputation as *exigéant* and *schräg*. Without all of these women, there would be no Berliner Chic, and so it is to them that this project is dedicated.

Acknowledgements

"No one can tell where art begins and where the work of daily life ends."

Rudolf Virchow (cited in Karasek 5)

This seminal quote by Virchow fit too well for too many sections of this book to make it the epigram of only one. Rather, because it captures perfectly the spirit of "Benjaminian Bildung" we see Berliner Chic standing for and because it served us as a kind of leitmotif, it belongs here.[1] The forces of modernization that refuse to recognize any but economic value turn texts like *Werther* and the Lipperheides' *Modejournal* into pearls offering illumination of key aspects of modernity. There are places, and academies, that confront one with such lessons, and it is little wonder that comparatists in such places have found in Benjamin a congenial guide. The contributions of James Donald, Ackbar Abbas and Esther Cheung to the study of urban culture have been particularly inspiring for us in this regard.

This volume was aided enormously by a number of institutions and people to whom we owe our deep gratitude. In addition to the wonderful women in Berlin, who generously took time from their demanding schedules to meet with us, to answer our questions and our emails, and to go over our work with exemplary thoroughness and thoughtfulness (Dagmar Neuland-Kitzerow, Dorit Lücke, Adelheid Rasche, and Christine Waidenschlager), we would also like to acknowledge Hans-Jörg Fahtke and his colleagues, who made working in the Lipperheide Costume Library and the neighboring *Kunstbibliothek* an enjoyable, rewarding experience.

Funding provided by the Social Science and Humanities Research Council of Canada (SSHRC) made this volume possible; the encouragement of Klaus Rupprecht, during his tenure as Director of the Canadian Centre of German and European Studies (CCGES) at York University, was instrumental in securing that funding; and CCGES Centre Coordinator, John Paul Kleiner, in addition to fuelling our curiosity for, and appreciation of, the connections between and pleasures of industrial and socialist chic, made sure the paperwork required to access it was taken care of in a timely and (at least for us) painless fashion. CCGES also generously funded one of Katrina's research stays in Berlin.

Our funding allowed us to attend a number of conferences, where we had the chance to present material that went into the making of this book and to receive much important feedback: a joint Congress session of the CAUTG (Canadian Association of University Teachers of German) and the CCLA (Canadian Comparative Literature Association) held at York University in Toronto in May 2006; "Berlin's Culturescape in the 20th Century" (Regina, September 2006); "Ethnonationalism, Transnationalism and Media Culture," an international symposium (York, March 2007); "Cinema and Social Change in Germany and Austria" (University of Waterloo, May 2008); "Crossroads in Cultural Studies" (University of the West Indies, Jamaica, July 2008); the CCLA Congress held at Carleton in May 2009; the Popular Culture Association and American Culture Association International Conference (Turku, Finland, July 2009); the seminar on "Berlin's Imagined Geographies" at the ACLA in New Orleans in April 2010; and the "Exhibiting Capital(s): Berlin and Beyond" panel at the NeMLA in Montreal in April 2010. Our thanks to the organizers of these sessions and all of the engaging interlocutors we encountered at them.

Special thanks are due Gisela Argyle, Marlene Kadar, Lee Kuhnle, Peter McIsaac, Elena Siemens and editor extraordinaire James Ingram, who all read over chapters at various stages of completion and provided us with valuable feedback. Our anonymous peer reviewer at Intellect was extremely helpful in offering suggestions for refining our focus and polishing our prose, while May at Intellect kept us on track and on time.

We would also like to thank our families for their continuous unconditional support, encouragement, generosity and kindness. Katrina also would like to acknowledge her wonderful support network in Montreal and beyond: Carolyn Miller, Aletta Vanderheyden, Zoë Constantinides, Heather Gibb, Diane Dechief, Lina Shoumarova, Valerie Habra, Andrea Archibald, Laure Juilliard, Phil Miresco, Nav Jagpal, Lucas van Lierop, Jonas and Justin Badiyan-Eyford and Boris Sark. Finally, this project would never have been realized without the unstinting support – technical and editorial as well as intellectual and emotional – of Markus Reisenleitner. If we have learned anything from him, and from this project, it is the benefits and pleasures of working together.

Note

1. For more on "Benjaminian Bildung" and how it contrasts with "Kantian Bildung," see Ingram.

Introduction: Locating Berliner Chic

"A location, in the perspective of this book, is an itinerary rather than a bounded site – a series of encounters and translations."

(Clifford 11)

"Get a good costume, that's half the battle."

(Peter Falk, *Wings of Desire/ Der Himmel über Berlin*)

Berlin is back in fashion. Emerging first from the decades of relative obscurity it fell into as a divided city and then from the dust of the reconstruction it underwent preparing to resume its status as capital of the reunified Germany, Berlin enters the second decade of the twenty-first century with renewed vigor and flair. Berlin's fortunes have always ebbed and flowed with the tides of historical circumstance. Once home to emperors and dictators, peddlers and spies, the city seems now to have managed in the age of

Fig. 0.1: Berlin, 1995. (Photo: Rico Puhlmann, Archive Rico Puhlmann)

globalised turbo-capitalism to turn its image as "poor but sexy" into a successful brand and to become, in the process, a fashion showplace that attracts the young, hip, and creatively industrious as well as increasing numbers of tourists. The city owes the felicitous phrasing of "poor by sexy" to its colorful mayor, Klaus Wowereit, who in an interview with the *FOCUS-Money* magazine in November 2003 declared that one didn't need money to have sex appeal: "One sees that with Berlin. We're poor but still sexy."[1] In other words, Berlin is not a typical European museal city the way Paris, Vienna, Florence, Venice, Rome and Athens are, filled with buildings posterity has come to regard as great works of art. Rather, Berlin is filled with historical significance – in Svetlana Boym's phrasing, it is "a city of monuments and unintentional memorializations" (180); in Brian Ladd's, a city of ghosts. Nor is Berlin a Koolhaasian generic city that radiates a fashionable global coolness,[2] which is not to say it hasn't developed its own form of chic – that it has is the subject of this book.

The questions motivating this study – why the "poor but sexy" label seems to so adequately capture the city's character and how it so masterfully sums up the multifacetedness of the city's image – direct us to the importance of fashion as a determining component of that image. When it comes to fashion, Berlin is not any city whatever. It may not be recognized as a global center of fashion the way London, Paris, New York, Tokyo and Milan are; it may rate barely a mention in Breward and Gilbert's 2006 *Fashion's World Cities*. Nonetheless, as this volume seeks to establish, Berlin is the ideal place from which to learn about and appreciate fashion as a cultural-historical phenomenon and as an integral component in the success of city images. Berlin may not have been the capital of the nineteenth century – that honor belongs to Paris and endeared Paris to the Berliner who bestowed it with that title, Walter Benjamin. However, as a crucible of modernity, a city that came of age thanks to nineteenth-century modernization, suffered great trauma in the twentieth and continues to be haunted by the onslaughts of the modernity Jameson has shown is becoming increasing late and ever more global, Berlin is the spiritual home of a particular kind of fashion. Not luxurious haute couture, trendsetting avant-garde radical fashion "at the edge," nor fashion with aesthetic roots in a past that draw on an artisanal tradition and taste for beautiful things (Quinn 2002; Evans; Frisa et al.), in Berlin one rather finds the fashion of industrialization; that is, fashion understood as a modern culture industry that has been formative for both Berlin's history and its image.

Berlin is, to put it another way, literally "ready to wear." Its sense of identity has been predicated on its ability to make things: clothes, history and much more. It is a city on the make, a gritty city, Chicago on the Spree (its Weimar nickname). The home of Franz Biberkopf, the "hero" of Alfred Döblin's 1929 novel *Berlin Alexanderplatz*, Berlin's cultural imaginary hosts a panoply of less than savory characters, or highly savory – depending on your taste. From Marlene Dietrich to Franka Potente, the actresses associated with Berlin settings are anything but dainty, while the sounds and lyrics produced in the city by bands like U2 and Depeche Mode have been described as "tough, coarse and complex" (Wurtzel 97). Even Goethe, after his one and only visit to the city in May 1778, found the city best summed up by the word "crude" (Richie xv). Grime and a distinct lack of highbrow sophistication have been Berlin's lucky charm and have given it a particular caché. The birthplace of the Love Parade, Berlin is not the city of love but the city of tough love, the city of the whips, chains, slings and arrows of outrageous fortune – in a word, *the* city of modernity.

The relations between modernity and fashion are well established. In her pioneering 1985 study *Adorned in Dreams: Fashion and Modernity*, Elizabeth Wilson defines fashion as "dress in which the key feature is rapid and continual changing of styles" (3) and notes that fashion "speeded up and proliferated to keep pace with modern life" (35). In *Fashion at the Edge: Spectacle, Modernity and Deathliness* (2003), Caroline Evans expands on Wilson's discussion of the problems but also the merits of the term modernity as a way of understanding fashion, and relates it to Marshall Berman's triumvirate of modernization, modernity and modernism, with modernization referring to "the processes of scientific, technological, industrial, economic and political innovation that also become urban, social and artistic in their impact" (7), modernity referring to "the way that modernisation infiltrates everyday life and permeates sensibilities" (7–8), and modernism referring to "the wave of avant-garde artistic movements that, from early in the twentieth century, in some way responded to or represented these changes in sensibility and experience" (8). Like Evans, we use these terms respectfully but advisedly, mindful of their shortcomings and the predominantly literary form of criticism they were intended to inform. However, the impact of modernization on Berlin cannot be overstated. The way it infiltrated everyday life and permeated sensibilities there is the essence of the industrialization of fashion, and Berlin's urban imaginary cannot be understood in the absence of these terms.

Berlin figures neither in Wilson's and Evans' accounts, which concentrate on the London-Paris nexus of high fashion, nor in *Fashion and Modernity*, the 2005 volume Breward and Evans edited, which "scrutinises the relationship of fashion to technology, industrialization and consumption from the court masques of seventeenth-century London to the forensic laboratories of late-twentieth-century Washington" (3). To find Berlin in a discussion of fashion and modernity, one turns to Ulrich Lehmann's readings of Simmel and Benjamin in his 2000 *Tigersprung: Fashion in Modernity*. For Lehmann, who studied in Frankfurt (as well as Paris and London), the distinctiveness of places matters. Paris is not Berlin is not Prague. He notes at one point, for example, "Max Ernst, at that time working far away in Cologne" (348), that is, working far away from André Breton, who in 1919 was also writing on the corset "far away" in Paris. Lehmann finds it integral to understanding the importance of class in Simmel that Simmel's ideas were based on the Berlin society of the 1900s in which they were developed (155), the implication being that had his theories been based on Parisian society of the 1900s or Berlin society of the 1950s, they would have taken a rather different form. Lehmann also finds it noteworthy that Benjamin and Simmel were writing in the same city and were thus influenced by its cultural life (205).

We go further. We find in the specific style of Berlin's modernity a rubric to understand changing cultural manifestations and class constellations that have proven capable time and again of providing challenges to the bourgeois-led *Kulturnation*. One of the hallmarks of German modernity, "culture" (that is, *Kultur* in the sense of nationalist-oriented, bourgeois-dominated, distinction-producing high culture, rather than aristocratic French *civilization* with its universalizing aspirations) was the central girder of the national sensibility that took hold there in the nineteenth century and gave rise to a *Bildungsbürgertum*, educated middle-classes responsible for making society not just civil but civilized (cf. Elias). As the nature of culture changed over the course of the twentieth and into the twenty-first century, so too, as Barbara Kosta has pointed out, has the nature of the *Bildungsbürgertum* (16) changed, and so have the challenges to it. Rather than rejecting the trampish character Marlene Dietrich played in *The Blue Angel* as the Weimar *Bildungsbürgertum* did, one could argue, as Kosta has, "that a new *Bildungsbürgertum* emerges in the twenty-first century, one that embraces select exemplars of popular culture, with film literacy figuring as a sign of the 'educated' citizen" (16; Fig. 0.1). This in turn has led to the emergence of new trampish characters. Focusing on the urban rather than the national thus helps us to recognize and account for a pattern of fashion-related counter-hegemonic challenges transcending the city's own cultural imaginary, receiving global recognition and being adopted by changed local hegemonies as a badge of honor, a component of the increasingly definable brand Berlin.

When seeking to understand fashion's relation to this incessantly modernizing city, what comes most strongly into focus are a number of modern institutions – the museum, historiography, photography, film, alternative music scenes and strategizing corporations – that have been able, for reasons we explore, to foster relatively successful, or at least not completely unsuccessful, counter-hegemonic challenges to authoritative powers. These institutions, formed by and making possible new kinds of cultural practices, may not have been invented in Berlin, but it was there that they were able to be established in ways that made fashion-related formations workable and that constituted "outsides" to the inside of the hegemonic power they countered. That outside could be within Berlin itself, as in the case of the Lipperheides and the challenge their costume library represented to the hegemonic "old" art collected on the Museum Island, which we detail in Chapter One. The outside could be outside of traditional academic practice, as was the case with the new understanding of historiography, which, as we show in Chapter Two, arose as a challenge to imperial models and shifted historians' focus to nations and their capitals. It could also be Berlin itself that played the role of outside, as in the prominently craftsmanly and commercial approach to fashion photography cultivated there vis-à-vis the more aesthetic and avant-garde tendencies of the fashion capitals (Chapter Three), the case of the UFA studios vis-à-vis Hollywood (Chapter Four), or as a place of musical escape (Chapter Five) – both for musicians (David Bowie, Iggy Pop, U2, etc.) and fans (especially of techno). Finally, it could be the hegemonic challenge that came from the outside in the form of global capital and was resisted internally, as in the case of new Berlin-branded fashion retail (Chapter Six). In all cases, the success of these challenges is not to be measured by any kind of Gramscian overthrowing of the "inside," the ruling class, but rather in the formation of new kinds of cultural practices with a degree of autonomy and the ability to reach beyond Berlin and influence how the city now exists as an imagined environment, that is, one that "embraces not just the cities created by the 'wagging tongues' of architects, planners and builders, sociologists and novelists, poets and politicians, but also the translation of the places they have made into the imaginary reality of our mental life" (Donald 8). As James Donald has demonstrated, recognizing the imaginative component of a city – that it is as much a "state of mind," as Robert Park wrote in 1915, as it is physical materiality – encourages one not to merely live in a city but rather to "live the city" (8), a process with ethical and political as well as aesthetic implications. To draw attention to the importance of global influences in forming urban imaginaries, our approach might be best understood not as strictly urban but rather as "glurban."

* * *

This project began with, and takes its name from, an exhibition and a photograph. The opening of the "Berliner Chic: Mode von 1820 bis 1990" exhibition in November 2001 was proudly declared to be adding a fashion museum to the Berlin museal landscape in the form of a permanent exhibition (*Dauerausstellung*) of the *Stadtmuseum*'s collection of authentic Berlin clothes and historical artifacts from the Berlin fashion industry (Waidenschlager 2001, 7). This announcement echoed throughout the German press, with headlines such as the one in the *Märkische Oderzeitung* in Frankfurt an der Oder declaring: "Now Berlin also has a fashion museum." However, when we went to see it in the fall of 2005, we discovered that the exhibition had been prematurely dismantled; *Stadtmuseum* management had in the meantime decided the Museum Ephraim Palais in Berlin's oldest quarter, the Nikolaiviertel, was better used as a space for rotating exhibitions. While the Berliner Chic exhibition may not have succeeded in becoming a permanent fashion museum, via its catalogue it was formative in providing a historical narrative of Berlin fashion that stretched back to 1820. We were intrigued by the exhibition's disappearance, a state of mind fed by the chance discovery of a photograph – of an early twentieth-century storefront at Linienstraße 34, a building which has also since disappeared (Fig. 0.2). It graced the front cover of a collection of photographs by Heinrich Zille and also graces ours. One of Berlin's favorite sons, Zille gave Berlin, as Michael Kimmelman noted on the occasion of Zille's sesquicentenary in March 2008, "an enduring image of itself, a psychic imprint that went beyond depicting what the buildings and streets looked like" (Fig. 0.3). The exhibition and the photograph suggested to us that Berliner Chic was a more enduring link between Berlin and fashion than any thus far recognized in scholarship, something subsequent references to Berliner Chic we encountered seemed to confirm (Figs. 0.4 and 0.5). They were vivid demonstrations to us of the extent to which place, and Berlin, matter in the history, and study, of fashion, just as fashion matters in the history, and study, of Berlin.

These references to Berliner Chic also point to one of the hallmarks of modernity, part of the epistemic shift that took place over the course of the turn to the nineteenth century that Foucault has been so helpful in getting us to think through: namely, the rising significance of visuality.[3] Drawing on Jonathan Crary's work on the historical construction of vision, *Techniques of the Observer: On Vision and Modernity in the Nineteenth Century*, we note that the shift from what he terms the "geometrical" optics of the seventeenth and eighteenth

Fig. 0.2: Linienstraße 34, November 2009. (Photo: K. Sark)

centuries, i.e. the "stable and fixed relations incarnated in the camera obscura" (14) to the "physiological" optics, which exposed the "idiosyncrasies of the 'normal' eye" and "dominated both scientific and philosophical discussion of vision in the nineteenth century" (16), was part of a much larger historical process that involved not only the emergence of a new kind of observer-subject-consumer, as Crary has detailed. It also required the implementation and institutionalization of new cultural practices, for which all roads seems to have led to Berlin.

It was in Berlin that the first museum "for which the historically complete representation of different artistic periods was explicitly made part of its mission," something, as we note in Chapter One, Charlotte Klonk attributes to "the German emphasis on distinctiveness and individuality thus led to the abandonment of the eighteenth-century canon of art and a new appreciation of the diversity of styles in the different periods of the history of art" (343).

Fig. 0.3: Window of the Zille Destille restaurant, Propststrasse 10. (Photo: K. Sark)

It was also in Berlin that a growing historical consciousness took hold, something, as we follow up in Chapter Two, Theodore Ziolkowski attributes to the intellectual environment permeating the new university Humboldt founded there in 1810. In Berlin, urban art took on forms that directly reflected the contradictions and heterogeneity specific to the city's rapid growth, something which led Eberhard Roters to conclude that "[n]ot only photomontage, but montage as a whole, is Berlin's specific contribution to twentieth-century art" (10). This leads us in Chapter Three to re-examine the nexus of fashion and photography that emerges from Berlin, and in Chapter Four to move from photography to the next new technology to feature montage, namely film, on which, we find, Berlin had a similarly influential impact. While no city has been able to compete with Hollywood since WWI, there was, as Tom Saunders has detailed, "a fleeting moment in the first half of the postwar decade" when the almost monopolistic power wielded by UFA from Berlin's outskirts over the entirety

Fig. 0.4: *Textil Report* cover, Rico Puhlmann. (Archive Rico Puhlmann)

of the German cinematic process from production through to distribution "even appeared to mount a frontal assault on American hegemony. For a comparably brief period in the second half of the decade it became the rallying point of a pan-European movement aimed at checking American inroads. However beleaguered, it thus presented a commercial as well as artistic alternative to American domination" (6) and, as we see in Chapter Four, provided the infrastructure for filmmaking to again rise to global prominence more recently. The situation in the alternative music scene, subject of Chapter Five, again establishes Berlin as home to new anti-institutions, such as the Hansa Studios and the opening provided by reunification for rave culture, something we follow Dietrich Dieterichsen in seeing as having emerged from punk and which we connect with Jon Stratton's understanding of punk as expressing "the inchoate agony of the experience of the cultural trauma that ended the confidence, and hope, of Euro-American modernity" (2007, 149). Finally, in Chapter Six, we take as

Fig. 0.5: Berliner Chic postcard stand on Unter den Linden. (Photo: S. Ingram)

our point of departure Mark Rectanus' sentiment that Berlin "at the outset of the twenty-first century…is an ideal place to observe the forces of corporate globalization, corporate politics of spaces, and debates over national identity or postnational identity" (8). Rectanus bases this conclusion on "the expansive building projects by Daimler (DaimlerChrysler) at Potsdamer Platz or in the Sony Center," which he sees as "reflecting the material interests of corporate real estate development" (8). In light of Sony's and Daimler's recent decisions to abandon this strategy, which, as Rectanus notes, went "[b]eyond deploying their corporate images within the urban center, these projects establish the corporation's political, economic, and social interests in 'real' spaces, in Germany's new capital and in the center of the 'new Europe's' crossroads between east and west" (8–9), we look at Daimler's attempt via its luxury brand Mercedes-Benz to maintain a presence in the capital via Fashion Week.

These processes of institutionalization – museums, historiography, photography, film, alternative music scenes and corporate strategizing – are part of the larger struggle over visuality that Janet Ward (2001) identifies in *Weimar Surfaces* as one of the hallmarks of modernizing Berlin:

> Because, however, modernist thought was both obsessed with and repelled by visuality's rapid expansion into the social imaginary, modernism was also host to an uncomfortable rivalry between visuality and textuality, resulting in a schizoid (antimimetic) condition of representation. As Jay points out in *Downcast Eyes,* modernism brought with it not just a scopic fascination but also its opposite, namely 'visual spleen as well as visual euphoria.' (13)

Wilhelmine Berlin in the nineteenth century may have been in the first instance, as Peter Fritzsche has convincingly established, a "word city," dominated by newspapers, announcements, posters and the like, but it was also in Wilhelmine Berlin that "the modern city first became *bildwürdig*, worthy of representation" (Czaplicka 11), literally, worthy of being represented in a picture, a trend that Fritzsche notes at the end of his study:

> [T]he city had become visually compelling, inviting crowds and thus providing the basis for urban spectatorship. Newspaper readers encountered the city more and more as spectators and as such, they grew more and more alike. Given the emphasis the print media placed on the production of visual pleasure and the transformation of readers into consumers, they anticipated the widespread influence of film and television. (247)

Contemporaries also noted this shift:

> In a lecture in 1912 at the inauguration of a movie theatre in Berlin, Egon Friedell attacked the pseudo-ideals of enemies of movies: 'This brings us to the main objection commonly made to movies: That they lack words and, therefore, can only portray crude and primitive things. But it is my belief that words no longer enjoy some absolute hegemony

nowadays… Words are gradually losing their reputation. Something like a regression of the spoken word is taking place…' (cited in Roters 173).

The so-called "Kinodebatte," which ensued as cinema's increasing popularity "threatened literature's monopoly and destabilized the contemporary cultural system" (Kaes 7), has come to be seen as embodying a key problematic of the twentieth century. Timothy Corrigan, for example, sees twentieth-century history situated "between the 'traditional word' and 'technological image,'" and he finds that tracing the directions of this battle throughout the twentieth century "as it works through movies, books, and culture dramatizes one of the most pressing motifs of these times" (cited in Kosta 14). *Berliner Chic* offers further substantiation of this motif and its persistence.

A key aspect of the shift to visuality involved the evolving status and publicness of women. As Katharina von Ankum points out in her introduction to *Women in the Metropolis*, the role of "women's multifaceted presence and participation in the public sphere was as central to their emancipatory vision of modernity as their increased visibility was to men's fears of modernization" (11). Our aim was to be attentive to the gendered significance of visuality's rather tempered victory as modernity has become increasingly late and global. While women are not explicitly our focus, it is impossible to ignore the key role they have played in organizing and maintaining Berlin's fashion exhibitions and collections, providing comprehensive historical research on fashion with Berlin components and doing much of the manufacturing of fashion in Berlin.

Finally, in constellating Berlin with fashion, we kept stumbling across something that rather surprised us: the difficulty fashion has had in establishing a permanent residence, in finding a durable home for itself, in Berlin. Like generations of migrants, fashion has had to struggle to make a go of it in the city. Berlin fashion comprises an urban milieu fled both to and from, made up of turbulent stories of entrepreneurially savvy manufacturers and cultural workers striving to establish themselves in their city, and to establish their city as a fashion capital, and being repeatedly interrupted by politics, ideologies and war. More than merely descriptive of Berlin's fashion industry and its ready-to-wear clothing, *Berliner Chic* evokes histories of elsewhereness, in the first instance of Paris, but also of a myriad of homes left behind. Where in the midst of all this flux has Berlin fashion been able to make space for itself? What traces remain of Berlin fashion that allow its history to now be written? What have been the media of its transmission? What forces have kept it from being forgotten and allow it now to flourish? How is the history of a city's fashion different from the history of a nation's fashion? In wrestling with and trying to provide answers to these questions, we can only acknowledge the radical depths and gendered implications of Benjamin's insight that while fashion may be, as Werner Sombart suggested, the midwife of capital, it is also the handmaiden of history, one which encourages reflection on the many histories that have, and have not, been written about fashion in Berlin. Keeping in mind both the partiality of all approaches to history and Doreen Massey's important insight that "[t]he identity of places is very much bound up with the histories which are told of them, how those histories are told, and which history turns out to be dominant" (186), we knew better than to try to write *the* definitive history of Berlin fashion.[4] But we do hope that in locating the formative, fashion-related influences on the making of Berlin's poor-but-sexy image, we will encourage similarly historically informed accounts to be written of the formative institutions that have helped to give shape to the imagined environments of other cities.

The specificity of a city's histories and locations gives each city the potential to turn itself into its own kind of fashion space. Bradley Quinn developed the concept of fashion space to analyze the consistency of the vision informing fashion-designed spaces, such as a label's flagship stores and website, but, as we have been able to ascertain in our study, it is also useful for the analysis of cities. Since entering the twentieth-first century, Berlin has transformed itself into a hip, technologically savvy, new media and marketing mecca for youthful and creative entrepreneurs, who, in their still affordable apartments, studios, and coffee shops, have been forging a new urban infrastructure of different scenes and industries, which the city's marketers have recognized and mobilized. There is a rich historical dimension to the components that have gone into the making of this multifaceted twenty-first-century image, and it is uncovered in the following chapters, which attempt to reveal what all has gone into making Berlin chic.

Notes

1. See the "Politik" section of *Focus*, 19.10.2006, http://www.focus.de/politik/deutschland/wowereits-berlin-slogan_aid_117712.html: Erstmals stellte Wowereit diesen Zusammenhang in einem Interview des Magazins FOCUS-Money im November 2003 her. Er wurde gefragt: „Macht Geld sexy?" und verneinte daraufhin einen Zusammenhang zwischen erotischer Ausstrahlung und Reichtum: „Nein. Das sieht man an Berlin. Wir sind zwar arm, aber trotzdem sexy."
2. See the essay "The Generic City" in Koolhaas and Mau.
3. If Jessica Dubow is right in arguing that "Benjamin's city contests the assertion of territory as a largely optical experience of the world" (266), then we should be clear here that our approach to Berlin is not Benjamin's, which does not mean that they do not overlap and intersect in interesting ways.
4. Thanks to Anna Zimmer for making us aware of this work of Massey's.

Chapter 1

Berliner Chic in Museums

"The very project of modernity is born out of the desire for a world without surprises, a safe world, a world without fear."

(Bauman and Galecki)

"The museal gaze thus may be said to revoke the Weberian disenchantment of the world in modernity and to reclaim a sense of non-synchronicity and the past."

(Huyssen 1995, 34)

Museums have been much maligned. Since their revolutionary beginnings in late eighteenth-century Paris, they have been accused of rendering objects inauthentic and crepuscular, of disciplining or interpellating class-based (but not class-conscious) national subjects, of showcasing the trophies of imperial war and conquest, and, more recently, of succumbing to the seductive forces of the market.[1] Given that the museum has become an increasingly important site for fashion (Steele 8), it is perhaps to be expected that fashion would be implicated in these critiques. In 1983, Yves Saint-Laurent became the first living fashion designer to be honored by the Metropolitan Museum of Art with a solo exhibition, and Diana Vreeland's exhibition became a lightning rod for controversy, a fate shared by subsequent blockbuster exhibits, such as the Armani exhibit organized by the Guggenheim, designed by Robert Wilson and sponsored by Mercedes-Benz, which opened in New York in 2000, travelled to Bilbao in 2001 and the *Neue Nationalgalerie* in Berlin in 2003 before proceeding on to London, Rome, Tokyo, and Las Vegas, garnering criticism as well as kudos along the way.[2]

As this chapter reveals, fashion has not only been implicated in but has also provided the impetus for a particular strand of this criticism. Since entering the Berlin landscape towards the end of the nineteenth century, fashion has served to work against the prevailing assumptions about museums as the proper public places for the display of art treasures, i.e., precisely those items that have drawn the wrath of the older sociological critiques of the museum "as an institution that saw its function as reinforcing 'among some people the feeling of belonging and among others the feeling of exclusion'" (Huyssen 1995, 15). Adorno once noted that museum and mausoleum are connected by more than phonetic association (175), but as Andreas Huyssen points out in *Twilight Memories*, museums have also acted as iterations or translations that promote the living-on (the survival) of objects and the memories they carry with them, as "a life-enhancing rather than mummifying institution in an age bent on the destructive denial of death: the museum thus as a site and testing ground for reflections on temporality and subjectivity, identity and alterity" (16). Moreover, it is not only that this older critique "does not seem to be quite pertinent any longer for the current museum scene which has buried the museum as temple for the muses in order to resurrect it as a hybrid space somewhere between public fair and department store" (15). As we hope to establish here, the conjugation of fashion (in which, as laid out in the Introduction, we follow Elizabeth Wilson in understanding in terms of rapidly changing styles of dress) and Berlin museum culture establishes a much longer historical trajectory for this type of hybridity than previously assumed and encourages a thoroughgoing rethinking of the relationship between fashion and the museum. Huyssen may have thought it was hyperbolic to claim in *Twilight Memories* that "the museum is no longer simply the guardian of treasures and artifacts from the past discreetly exhibited for a the select group of experts and connoisseurs; no longer is its position in the eye of the storm, nor do its walls provide a barrier against the world outside" (21). The history of Berlin's fashion collections and exhibitions shows that museums were never solely guardians but also educators and equalizers, providing historical support for Ursula Link-Heer's argument that fashion itself operates museally (146). It is not only, as Huyssen argues, that "[t]he quality argument collapses once the documentation of everyday life and of regional cultures, the collecting of industrial and technological artifacts, furniture, toys, clothes and so forth becomes an ever more legitimate museal project" (22); fashion in Berlin has long given itself the mission of revaluing musealizing practices and underscoring the questioning of who has been in a position to determine what counts as legitimate. As we trace its history here, first laying out the Berlin museum landscape and then turning to the city's main fashion-related collections – the *Lipperheidesche Kostümbibliothek* (Lipperheide Costume Library); an early twentieth-century attempt by the Berlin Fashion Museum Society to establish a fashion museum; another, similarly unsuccessful attempt toward the century's end by the Fashion Department of the *Stadtmuseum* to do the same thing; and the prestigious Kamer/Ruf collection, acquired in 2003 – we draw specific attention to the locations, both social and geographic, of the legitimacy that was being challenged.[3]

The Establishment of the Berlin Museum Landscape

The museal tradition in which Berlin fashion has been able to provide a counter-hegemonic challenge to traditional high-culture aspirations is bound up in one of those endearingly untranslatable concepts that Germany seems to take pride in producing: *Kunstgewerbe*.[4] Like *Bildung*, "whose range of meanings includes (and combines) formal education, aesthetic cultivation and character formation" (Sheehan 115), *Kunstgewerbe* also covers a particular spectrum, in its case, of handiwork practices that include (and combine) a range of skills and talents that have their roots in the medieval guild system but that had to readjust to modern developments in aesthetics (artistic autonomy) and industrial production. As late as the 1873 Grimm *Dictionary* and the 1908 Meyer's *Konversationslexikon*, it was considered a synonym of "art industry" (*Kunstindustrie*) and deemed to be an "abomination" (*Unding*) that didn't exist: "These days there is no such thing as 'art-craft,' there are those who work, who are at the same time artists; there are also artists, who understand how to do a good business with their art! Alone an 'art-craft' is an abomination" (Franke 167).[5] John Maciuika has also lamented this "confusing array of terms," noting that the terminological slipperiness reflects "the chaotic state of the relationship between crafts and industry in the nineteenth and early twentieth centuries" (112). Evers attributes the blossoming of *Kunstgewerbe* museums in the middle of the nineteenth century to "an optimistic trust in their ability to overcome the division of art and craft that was experienced by some as painful and felt to have led to a decline in taste and a loss of craft-oriented abilities" (8), and as we will see in this chapter, *Kunstgewerbe* in Berlin provided a unique terrain on which fashion has been able to assert itself ever since.

The "confusing," "chaotic," generally intense and intimate relations between art, crafts and industry in the nineteenth century spilled over into and helped to shape Berlin's museum landscape. Some see this tradition stretching back to Friedrich the Great (1712–1786), the enlightened absolutist monarch who transformed Prussia from a European backwater into a politically reformed and economically and militarily strong state and first made some of the Prussian art treasures available by opening the picture galleries at Sanssouci, his summer palace in Potsdam, to the public (Gaehtgens 14). However, to get a sense of the early struggles to institutionally delimit this area, it is better to go back to his grandfather, Friedrich III Elector of Brandenburg, who in 1696 founded both a Prussian Academy of Arts as well as an *Akademie der bildenden Künste und der mechanischen Wissenschaften* (Academy of Fine Arts and Mechanical Sciences) (Mislin 41), and who, five short years later, became the first king in and of Prussia and moved the Prussian capital from Königsberg to Berlin. The Prussian Academy of Arts followed the model of the French *académie des beaux-arts*, provided training in the fine arts of painting, sculpture and architecture (but, unlike the French, not music)[6] and led to the development of similar academies "for painting, sculpture and architecture" in Munich (1770), Düsseldorf (1773) and Kassel (1777). In contrast, the *Akademie der bildenden Künste und der mechanischen Wissenschaften* brings out the root meaning of the *bildende* arts, shifting it away from its usual translation of "fine" in the direction of "formative" or "forming/molding." While the failure of this academy was perhaps to be expected, given the disjunctive nature of its undertaking, it led to the founding, in 1799, of the *Bauakademie*, which took over the education of architects and engineers and established a Prussian tradition of conveying institutional value to the industrial arts in the manner of the British. Upon its founding in 1754, the British institution that went on to be known as the Royal Society of Arts after 1847 was called "The Society for the Encouragement of Arts, Manufactures and Commerce," and at the exhibitions the Society began holding in 1760 "paintings, sculptures, architectural models, pumps, ploughshares and weaving looms were displayed together under the communal heading of 'inventions,' for the edification of the membership and the enlightenment of farmers, manufacturers and businessmen. Experimentation was encouraged, as was the ideal of making the various branches of intellectual endeavour work in harmony" (Greenhalgh 7–8).[7]

The imperially influenced kernels that went into Berlin museum-making were thus already in place by the time of the French Revolution. What ended up sprouting first was a series of art museums, aided considerably by the French precedent for an art museum (the Louvre) and the fact that, by 1796, each of the other German-speaking states already had a public collection "in which art could be visited, copied, and discussed; should not Berlin be on a list that included Dresden, Vienna, Munich, Mannheim, Düsseldorf, and many lesser capitals?" (Sheehan 54). This mounting interest in art museums among European powers received a further boost with the return, in 1815, of the Prussian artworks that had been looted by Napoleon.[8] Because these had come to be seen, in the wars against Napoleon, as German treasures and not merely the Prussian king's possessions, Friedrich Wilhelm III was pressured to make them available to the public and to erect a suitable building for this purpose (cf. Sheehan 70–80; Crimp).

This building, the first of five museums to be erected on the northern part of the island formed by the Spree in the center of Berlin, was decisive for the shape that art museums took in the nineteenth and twentieth centuries (Vogtherr). Previously, as Klonk has shown in her work on the National Gallery in London, museum visitors were encouraged by presentation techniques to attend to "a universal standard of art that transcended whatever was presented to the senses" (343). Now, however, "the autonomy of subjective experience came to be emphasised both in the production of art and in its reception… Instead of fixed ideals, what was now valued was the expression of distinctness and individuality, be it in individual artists, periods, or countries" (343–4). Moreover, this new form of cultural space did not only develop parallel to "the roughly contemporary emergence of the prison, the asylum and the clinic" but rather, as Tony Bennett corrects Douglas Crimp, reversed it, aiming "not at the sequestration of populations but, precisely, at the mixing and intermingling of publics – elite and popular – which had hitherto tended towards separate forms of assembly" (Bennett 93). The debate that ensued over what to call the new structure is indicative of this aim. While the Romantic poet Ludwig Tieck proposed "a monument of peace for works of fine art" to immortalize the peace that had returned to Europe with the Congress of Vienna, and philologist Friedrich Schleiermacher favored "a treasury for sculptures and painting distinguished by their age and their art" (Crimp 262), the suggestion to win favor and be inscribed in the new building was by an archeologist and member of the Academy of Arts who had been active in the 1799 founding of the *Bauakademie*, Alois Hirt.[9] Rather than a monument or a treasury, Hirt chose to call the building a "museum" and to designate its purpose with the word "studio," which recollected "the so-called original museum of Ptolemy of Alexandria, which was indeed a place of study, […a] residence for scholars, containing a library and collections of artifacts…as one of the memoranda about the inscription stated, 'a kind of academy'" (Crimp 262). Hirt's inscription (Fig. 1.1), the grammaticality of which has become the source of some contention,[10] reflected the initial plans for the structure, which "called for building a new wing on the Academy of Sciences that would house a study collection for artists and scholars" (Crimp 263). Many objected, however, because, in Crimp's analysis, they understood public in Hegel's sense of universal rather than Marx's

Figure 1.1: Altes Museum. (Photo: S. Ingram)

sense of fractured by class divisions and therefore thought the name of the new institution should reflect that it was open to the general public and not merely to a specialized elite. The most influential objection came from the architect Karl Friedrich Schinkel, who had plans of his own, namely for an entirely new structure to be built directly across Unter den Linden from the Palace that would initiate "a complete renewal of the very heart of Berlin, diverting the river Spree, improving shipping facilities, and rebuilding the loading docks and warehouse at the north end of what would later become the Museumsinsel" (Crimp 263). The growth of the Museum Island over the course of the next century indicates the support Schinkel's plan met with, something spurred on, on the one hand, by the solidification of the *Kulturnation*, its increasingly developed bourgeois historical consciousness (the subject of the next chapter), appreciation of *Bildung*, and desire for access to collections of antiquities and other treasures from which it could be educated and in the process amass cultural capital; and, on the other, by the severe case of collecting fever that imperial Prussia came down with as the nineteenth century "progressed."[11]

While the growth of the Museum Island proceeded in fits and starts and not always in a Schinkelian vein,[12] it demonstrates the ongoing need for buildings to house the expanding Prussian collections. The first, one of Schinkel's many masterpieces in Berlin, was erected between 1823 and 1830 and called the Royal Museum until 1845, when the building of a *Neues Museum* was well under way, resulting in the original structure being renamed the *Altes Museum*. It now houses the antique collection of the Berlin State Museums. The New

Museum was designed by Schinkel student Friedrich August Stüler when it became clear that the capacity of the old museum would not be adequate. Constructed between 1837 and 1859, it was severely damaged during WWII and restored only well after reunification. Re-opened in October 2009, it again houses the Egyptian and early history collections it was originally built for. The *Nationalgalerie*, which Stüler designed for Joachim H. W. Wagener's collection of nineteenth-century art and whose construction took place between 1869 and 1876, was the third museum to be erected on the Museum Island. It was also severely damaged during WWII, but was somewhat reconstructed after the war and renovated between 1998 and 2001. Its focus is primarily the nineteenth century, and its collection includes noteworthy Classical, Romantic, Biedermeier, Impressionist and modernist paintings as well as sculptures.[13] The fourth museum to be built on the island was designed by Ernst von Ihne, built between 1897 and 1904, and it now houses a collection of sculptures, Byzantine art, and coins and medals. Originally called the Kaiser Friederich Museum after the ill-fated, liberal-minded Friedrich III, who reigned for only a little more than three months in 1888 due to his father's longevity and his own contracting of cancer of the larynx, it was renamed in 1956 after its curator-extraordinaire, Wilhelm von Bode. The final museum on the Museum Island is the Pergamon Museum, which Bode planned before WWI when it was clear that the material collected from the archeological excavations in the Near East would not be able to be housed in the existing buildings, but which was not completed until 1930. It is named after the second-century BCE Pergamon Altar, one of the monumental structures it houses that was transported back from an excavation site, the ancient Greek city of Pergamon (now in northwestern Anatolia). Currently being redesigned, the Pergamon Museum will become the lynchpin of the Museum Island, connecting all five museums.

We have outlined the Museum Island in such detail not because any of its museums had strong connections to fashion but rather, precisely because they did not, while at the same time developing a hegemony over the Berlin museum landscape during its formative period to which the fashion collections were forced to respond. Bode, for example, by the time he became the general director of Berlin's museums in 1905, was "one of the most famous museum officials in Europe, widely known for his extraordinary knowledge, energy, and dedication" (Sheehan 157); during his tenure as director of all Berlin museums (from 1905 to 1920), the museums went from "provincial backwater to world-class art center" (McIsaac 373). While more traditional museum historians credit him with inflecting the Kaiser Friedrich Museum with the martial, imperial aspect of modern Germany and turning it into "a monument to Prussian might" (Eisler 31), more contemporary scholars, such as Sheehan and McIsaac, have begun attending to the complex social relations involved in the museum's collecting and display practices. There is strong evidence to suggest, for example, that Bode was less beholden to a simplistic notion of top-down, militaristic imperialism than traditional museum historians have tended to assume. McIsaac emphasizes his non-aristocratic background: "From the 1860s on, members of the educated middle classes (*Bildungsbürgertum*) such as Bode increasingly entered governmental ranks. In the process, they displaced aristocratic administrators whose appointments had been motivated more often by nepotism than by professional qualification… When Bode began his service, for instance, the Berlin museums were headed by Count Guido von Usedom, a failed diplomat whose relationship to the royal family led to his subsequent museum appointment" (375). McIsaac further points out that the innovative mode of display Bode initiated was directly tied to his relations to the wealthy middle classes, whose donations and other forms of support were at least as important for making Berlin's collections world class as the support of the Emperors; he gives as an example James Simon, who brought, among other items, the bust of Nefertiti to Berlin.[14] These monied members of the *Besitzbürgertum* literally bought into the sophistication and learning that Bode exuded, reinforcing the hegemonic position of the Museum Island's high culture approach to art that fashion has repeatedly challenged from upstart locations slightly removed from Unter den Linden, the city's central monarchical avenue.

The Lipperheidesche Kostümbibliothek

The *Lipperheidesche Kostümbibliothek* was the first fashion-related challenge to Berlin's museal establishment.[15] It has gone on to become, in its own self-description, "the world's largest special collection focusing on the cultural history of clothing and fashion," containing some 40,000 volumes of books, journals and magazines from the sixteenth century to the present, as well as manuscripts, paintings and around 150,000 individual sheets of drawings, prints and photographs.[16] Taking its name from its benefactors, Franz Joseph Lipperheide (1838–1906, Fig. 1.2) and Wilhelmine Amalie Friederike Lipperheide, née Gestefeld (1840–1896, Fig. 1.3), the Lipperheide collection was founded as the formative period of musealizing was reaching its peak and beginning to encounter resistance from avant-garde reformers who rejected what they saw as ossified eighteenth-century definitions of art and beauty (Sheehan 143–8).[17] From educated backgrounds – Franz's father was a secretary of the court (*Gerichtsaktuars*) in Berleburg, Westphalia; Frieda's a district judge (*Amtsvogt*) in Lüchow bei Hannover –,[18] both made their way to Berlin, where they met while working in the fashion department of the Louis Shäfer publishing house in Berlin on one of the leading fashion magazines of the day, the *Bazar*. They quickly discovered a shared sensibility and set of ambitions, and decided to marry and start up their own publishing house in order to publish a new kind of fashion magazine. In September 1865, the biweekly *Die Modenwelt, Illustrirte Zeitung für Toilette und Handarbeiten* (*The Fashion World, an Illustrated Magazine for Dressing and Handiwork*) appeared under Frieda's editorship, a position she maintained until her death at the age of 56.[19] Unlike the *Bazar* and other popular contemporary fashion magazines, the *Modenwelt* contained no literary content but only articles about fashion and craftwork, which made it less expensive than its competitors. Also popular was the practical nature of the fashion reports and advice for making one's own clothes (Wagner 1964, 140). The extent of its success can be gauged by the villa the Lipperheides built in the Tirolian Alps, which was on the market in November 2008 for 2.85 million Euros. Their residence in Berlin, Potsdamer Straße 38 (now 96), became a well-known address among late nineteenth-century Berlin society. The Lipperheides had no need

of Bode's sophistication or learning. They rejected his valorizing of "old" art and browbeating of collectors (cf. Lindemann). Rather, the popularity of their pragmatic publishing strategy allowed them to set their own priorities, which involved establishing resources for doing solid work in costume design ("fundierte Kostümkunde") (Mayerhofer-Llanes 261). Lipperheide's passion for collecting was, as reported by friends and colleagues, a personal one: "He was loathe to rely on the learned and not only purchased from firms with good reputations but also from small, unknown dealers. Experts meant nothing to him; through hard work and devotion he tried himself to be knowledgeable in a wide range of areas" (Wagner 1964, 141). In other words, Lipperheide not only rejected depending on others for expertise but his preference for self-cultivation carried over to his publishing and collecting practice, making available to as wide an audience as possible materials related to a cultural practice everyone in one way or another followed, namely dress (Fig. 1.4). Unlike Bode's strict policing of the art world, the Lipperheides published and collected material on the history and the international scope of clothing practices that opened up a variety of possible clothing styles for readers to choose among, a move whose enormous success was reflected in their elevation in 1892 into the nobility (they were granted the titles of Baron and Baroness). Seven years later, and three years after Frieda's death, when their extensive collection became property of the Crown, it did not go to the Museum Island, but found a home not too far from the Lipperheides' fashionable residence

Figure 1.3: Frieda Lipperheide, after a photo by E. Encke, 1885.
(Staatliche Museen zu Berlin, Kunstbibliothek)

in the *Bibliothek des Kunst-Gewerbemuseums*, which had been elevated to the rank of museum in 1894 with Peter Jessen appointed as its director (Rasche 1995b, 66). The Lipperheides thus do not fit neatly into the *Bildungsbürgertum/Besitzbürgertum* dichotomy that historians and museum scholars use to map the rising German middle classes in the nineteenth century. There may have been, as Alexandra Richie claims, a "distinct line" that existed between "the aristocrats and everyone else" (207), but the fact that "new rich Berliners" were a more varied and contentious lot than credited even in comprehensive, nuanced accounts like McIsaac's or Richie's is demonstrated by an institution like the *Kunstgewerbemuseum*.

When the *Deutsches-Gewerbe-Museum zu Berlin* opened in 1868, it was following in the footsteps of London's South Kensington complex (now the V&A), which opened in 1852 in the aftermath of the Great Exhibition, and of Vienna's Museum for Art and Industry (now the MAK – *Museum für angewandte Kunst*, Museum for Applied Arts), which opened in 1863.[20] The *Gewerbe-Museum*'s founding director, Julius Lessing, a good friend of the Lipperheides, was responsible for its acquisitions and organized a successful exhibition of crafts from Berliners' private collections that took place in 1872 in the *Zeughaus* and led to the key acquisition in 1875 of 6,570 historical crafts from the Prussian *Kunstkammer*.[21] With the success of this exhibition, the *Gewerbe-Museum* earned itself a permanent home, the Martin Gropius Bau, which it moved into in 1881; Lessing earned himself the undying enmity of

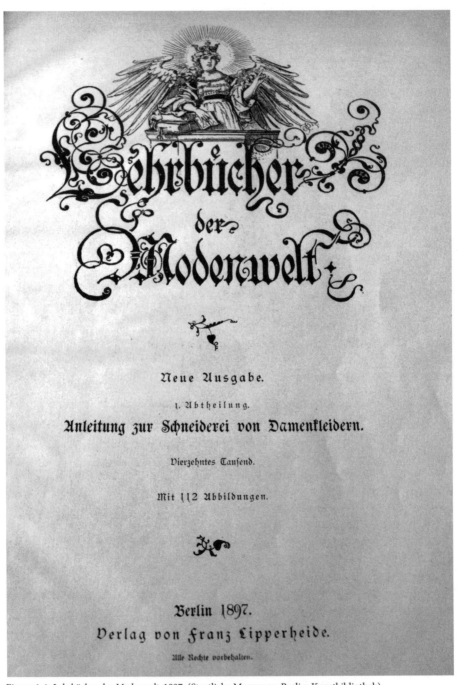

Figure 1.4: *Lehrbücher der Modenwelt*, 1897. (Staatliche Museen zu Berlin, Kunstbibliothek)

Bode (Mundt 1992, 175); and a space opened up for fashion to infiltrate, complicate and decorate "this upstart capital," whose nouveau pretensions had begun to make it an object of ridicule in the older European capitals, a state of affairs reflecting its increasing importance (see Richie 211–12).

The focus of the Lipperheide collection reflects its donors' disdain of pretension as well as the scope of their cosmopolitan, scientific interests.[22] As Lipperheide wrote in the introduction to the 1896 catalogue of his collection, "For more than a half century the study of dress has enjoyed a constantly growing interest: how appropriate for it now to properly become the object of scientific study" (Rasche 1999a, 114). The collection's enormous range is reflected in the exhibitions that have been mounted of material from the collection, which reflect historical vicissitudes. First displayed in March 1900 after having been acquired the previous year (Fig. 1.5), it was not presented again to the public for another twenty years, until after the WWI.[23] (It was not the first fashion-themed exhibition in the city; that honor belongs to the 1896 Industrial Exhibition [cf. von Heyden, Fig. 1.6]).[24] None of the

Figure 1.5: First exhibition of the Lipperheide Costume Library, March 1900 in the Lichthof of the Kunstgewerbemuseums. (Staatliche Museen zu Berlin, Kunstbibliothek)

Figure 1.6: *A Century of Fashion, 1796–1896*. (Staatliche Museen zu Berlin, Kunstbibliothek)

Lipperheides' collection was displayed during the WWI, but after a May 1922 exhibition of the fashion journal *Styl*, there were five exhibitions between 1926 and 1928, reflecting an increasing interest in fashion as well as the extraordinary energy and organizing acumen of Wolfgang Bruhm, who intermittently filled the Director position left vacant by the death of Heinrich Doege in 1922 and who did much to ensure that fashion was on display in this period of enormous financial uncertainty. In 1934 Bruhm was appointed curator (*Kustos*) of the Lipperheide collection, a position he maintained until his death in 1945 (Rasche 1999a, 120–1). During this period, he organized exhibitions on "New German Fashion Drawings" (1933), picking up on the growing nationalist sentiments, and on "From the New Acquisitions of the Baron von Lipperheide's Costume Library and Related Collections" (1936–7). In the fall of 1939, Bruhm began safeguarding the most valuable items in the Art Library, first moving them into the basement and then, between 1942 and 1943, arranging their storage in various bunkers and storage areas in and around Berlin. It took several years to determine the extent of the wartime losses. Eva Nienholdt, who was appointed to head the collection in 1951, after it had been moved into the Dahlem museum complex, reported that of the 9,433 books before 1943, 1,439 (mostly more recent ones) had gone lost, including all of the almanacs (Rasche 1999a, 122). In 1954 the Art Library was reopened in the rebuilt *Landwehrkasino* (Jebenstraße 2, what is now the Museum of Photography), and the Costume Library received a reading room on the main floor (Rasche 1999a, 123). Since starting up again in 1955, the collection has been showcased regularly. The flourish of activity in the early 1980s – seven exhibits in three years – is nicely captured by the title of the 1982 "Fashionable Extravaganzas." This was followed by another spurt at the decade's end, with exhibitions on haute couture from the 1920s, fashion in miniature, and fashion photography in Paris and Berlin. There was another short lull in the period following the fall of the Wall and reunification, during which the collection was resettled to its new home in the *Kulturforum*, where the collection has been regularly displayed in exhibitions – from local favorites like costume designers William Budzinski, Charlotte Josephsen and Regina May to international icons like Christian Dior, Max Mara, Yves Saint Laurent and fashion photographer Peter Lindbergh – that highlight the collection's range as well as the *Kunstgewerbemuseum*'s good relations with other museums.

Some of the more recent exhibitions have also begun to reveal the Lipperheide collection's impressive range of fashion photography, which was displayed for the first time in 1979, the same year the International Museum of Photography at the George Eastman House in Rochester, New York, USA, staged a "groundbreaking and ambitious survey of fashion photography from the nineteenth century to the (then) present, with a large-scale catalogue, written by Nancy Hall-Duncan" (Williams 198). The Berlin exhibition featured primarily French material (Wagner 1979), as did the two exhibitions that followed after reunification: "Paris – Berlin, Fashion Photos from 1900 to 1988" and "Early Fashion Photography from Parisian Ateliers in the Lipperheide Costume Library." One notes that the Berlin curators do not seem to have shared Hall-Duncan's sense of "wariness" about displaying something as "sinful," that is, something produced "not only for love but for money," in a museum (cited in Williams 198). Rather than seeing fashion photographs and the people who made them as "something to be critiqued, even apologized for," Gretel Wagner, who succeeded Eva Nienholdt as head of the Costume Library in 1964, and Adelheid Rasche, who succeeded Wagner in 1990, are more like Roy Strong at the V&A: clearly proud to curate such valuable material and keen to raise its profile (cf. Williams 205–6). In 2005, for example, Rasche put on an exhibition to raise the profile of fashion photographs from the 1930s, a comparatively obscure period of Berlin fashion photography history. The exhibit featured approximately one hundred photographs by the eleven photographers she saw as both having set the tone for the period's fashion photography as well as capturing the diversity of approaches at the decade's beginning: "experimental exposures stand next to traditional studio portraits, the influences of the Surrealists contrast with strict backgrounds whose architectural style owes much to the new objectivity, photographs with a low horizon and a worm's eye view stand next to close-up, almost intimate fashion portraits" (Rasche 2001, 43). At the same time, the exhibit documented the encroachments of the Nazis and the shifts in style from the sporty "garçonne" type at the end of the 1920s to more traditionally feminine figures and more dowdy styles as the decade wore on (44). The trilingual (Italian, French, German) volume also includes the biographies of the photographers, including the tragic deportation of Yva to Majdanek in 1942, where she is presumed to have perished.

First Attempt to Build a Fashion Museum in Berlin

While path-breaking and of international renown, the Lipperheide collection only scratches the surface of the fashion riches in Berlin's museum collections. The first attempt to establish a fashion museum resulted in a well-visited exhibition of the items collected but did not leave a lasting imprint on the museum landscape.[25] The initial impetus for this venture came with the rising nationalism that accompanied WW1. In 1914, the French, led by Paul Poiret, had founded the *Syndicat de Défence de la Haute Couture Française* to counter the piracy and "rash of unlicensed department-store copies bearing his name" that Poiret had discovered during his travels to the United States (Breward 2003, 352). After the outbreak of war, the German fashion industry, led by the hat makers, decided to follow suit and founded a *Verband zur Förderung der deutschen Hutmode* (Association for the Furthering of German Hat Fashion). With anti-French sentiment fulminating as WWI descended into horrific trench warfare, an influential article appeared in the 8 April 1915 *Berliner Tageblatt* calling for a German fashion museum. Ernst Friedmann, an architect and the owner of Friedmann & Weber, a Decorative Arts shop for furniture, arts and crafts, and antiques, tried, successfully, to arouse interest in a museum devoted to clothing and accessories. Not only would such a collection nicely complement the Lipperheide's library and allow for the historical development of fashion to be studied, it would also provide a basis for Berlin to challenge Paris's status as leading fashion capital (Rasche 1995b, 67); its extraordinary nineteenth-century economic growth had already seen it overtake its "formidable" rivals, Paris and London, in industrial output (Richie 152). Debate around the issue swirled, as indicated by a commentary in the 1 August 1915 *Vossische Zeitung*: "Some see in such an institute an undertaking of the highest levity, others of scientific value and deep seriousness, for yet others, however, it is the stuff of an op-ed piece" (cited in Rasche 1995b, 67). The forces in favor of the museum gained momentum, and on 11 December 1915, at an assembly in the great hall of the *Künstlerhaus* that was open to the public, the *Verein Moden-Museum e. V. Berlin* (Berlin Fashion Museum Society) was founded, something "[t]he mayor of Berlin, Georg Reicke, viewed… as particularly auspicious, since 'Germany is now extensively uncoupled from French fashion and the German Volk is more sensitized to national interests'" (Guenther 44). The board was chaired by Peter Jessen and included representatives from the prestigious fashion firm Hermann Gerson as well as the mayor. It opened an office at Potsdamer Straße 134b and set about building up a collection of exemplary pieces of historical clothing, the considerable success of which is reflected in the "Two Hundred Years of Clothing Art 1700–1900" exhibition it put on between November 1917 and the end of February 1918 (Rasche 1995a, 16).

Also impressive was the location the society was able to arrange for the exhibition: the Ermelerhaus. Originally built in 1761 as a residence for Peter Friedrich Damm, it had become the property of the city of Berlin in 1915 and was opened to the public for the first time for the exhibition.[26] Eighteenth-century dresses were displayed in the Rococo-styled main hall on the upper level, while fashion from the Empire period, Biedermeier and turn-of-the-century followed. A "room of glass cases" completed the collection, with 237 items in total on display (Rasche 1995a, 17). The exhibition demonstrated the historical development of changing clothing styles in order to develop a sensibility in the public for the importance of historical clothing and of the competitive value of contemporary clothing in a historical perspective. It was hoped that collectors with possible pieces for the collection would be won over by the exhibition and moved to make donations that would culminate in a museum (Rasche 1995b, 68). While contemporary reviews reveal its success in attracting an unexpected 6,000 visitors (Rasche 1995b, 71; Guenther 18), history was to take a different course and the Fashion Museum Society was not able to reach all of its goals, not only of "collecting outstanding examples of clothing from the past and the present…[and] educat[ing] experts and consumers on the demands of technology, taste, and organization" (Guenther 44–5) but of creating a museum that would guarantee that these goals continue to be met in perpetuity.[27]

Like the "Berliner Chic" exhibition over eighty years later, the "Two Hundred Years of Clothing Art 1700–1900" exhibition was not able to find a permanent home. The piece of property that the city of Berlin had promised to earmark for the construction of a new museum in 1916 became unavailable, and so the Association of Women's Fashion and Its Industry, which had taken over the Society in 1918 (the idea of "German fashion" was one of the many casualties of the war [Wagner 1993, 122]), had to settle for organizing temporary exhibits and fashion shows (Waidenschlager 1993, 23). In a 1921 essay by Hans Mützel in the *Zeitschrift für Historische Waffen- und Kostümkunde* (*Journal for the Study of Historical Weapons and Costumes*), the hope is expressed that the state will assume responsibility for the collection and unite it with the textile collection in a *Kunstgewerbe- und Völkerkundemuseum* (Decorative Arts and Ethnography Museum). Rasche presumes individual pieces were integrated into its permanent exhibition on display in the Berlin Palace. She then follows the collection's fate as it, together with the entire textile collection, fell into Soviet possession at the end of the war and was then housed in the *Kunstgewerbemuseum* annex in Schloß Köpenick, which became the permanent home for items in the east of the city in 1963; those in the west were temporarily accommodated in Schloß Charlottenburg and moved to the *Kulturforum* complex near Potsdamer Platz when it opened in 1985. After inventory clearances in 1958 and during the 1970s, these clothes seem to have ended up in the Museum for German History, now the *Deutsches Historisches Museum*. The fashion and textile collection in the everyday culture collection (*Sammlung Alltagskultur II*) of the *Deutsches Historisches Museum* comprises, according to its website, 15,000 pieces of "civilian" clothing from the mid-eighteenth century to the present that elucidate themes of everyday life and cultural history from eighteenth-century corsets and flapper dresses to children's clothes from the former East German Pioneers and the Hitler Youth and velvet jackets worn by hippies and bomber-jackets worn by skinheads.[28] According to Rasche's research, at least some of the Fashion Museum Society's collection would seem to be among these items.

Berlin Fashion Museum: Take Two

Another major source of Berlin fashion can be traced back to the Fashion Department that was established in 1981 by Rolf Bothe, then Director of the Berlin Museum, to accommodate gifts the Museum had been given. From 1981 until 1993, the Berlin Museum's fashion collection was displayed on the second floor of the Collegienhaus at Lindenstrasse 14.[29] Built in 1734–1735, the former home of various public authorities was badly damaged during WWII, rebuilt in the 1960s and made home to a museum intended to complement the offerings in the Märkisches Museum in East Berlin. Dedicated to recounting Berlin history, it opened in 1969. New additions to the fashion collection and thematic displays were featured in the museum until the major reorganization brought about by reunification.

The Fashion Department's collection was first showcased in an exhibition curated by Christine Waidenschlager on "Couture – Ready-to-Wear – Vaudeville, 1920s Fashion from the Berlin Museum" (*Couture, Konfektion, Varieté: Mode der 20er Jahre aus dem Berlin Museum*). The first substantial exhibition the Berlin Museum's Fashion Department mounted after ten years of collection activity, the exhibition was on display in the Grundkredit Bank from 8 November to 29 December 1991, and one can imagine that it was in some way indebted to Barbara Mundt's groundbreaking 1977 "Metropoles Make Fashion: Haute Couture of the 20s" (*Metropolen Machen Mode. Haute Couture der Zwanziger Jahre*) exhibition at the *Kunstgewerbemuseum*. One need not assume that reunification was a factor in the "Couture – Ready-to-Wear – Vaudeville" exhibition's conception. Waidenschlager makes clear that it was indeed intended to make visible the work that the Fashion Department had been engaged in during the past decade, something "which seems especially important against the background of the political changes since 1989. The makers of Berlin fashion and ready-to-wear have justified hopes that Berlin – looking to the markets of Eastern Europe – will once again in a united Germany become the fashion centre of Germany" (10). The exhibition was thus designed to strengthen the Fashion Department's identity as a place which preserved historical costumes, provided information to all those interested in and working with fashion, and collected and documented contemporary developments (10). The choice of 1920s fashion can thus be seen to be an astute calculation to foreground the sexiest, most "glittering" (8) period in Berlin's fashion history – the period of its heyday before being systematically decimated during National Socialism – at a time when the Department's fate was uncertain and under review. The catalogue for "Couture – Ready-to-Wear – Vaudeville" is a stroke of genius in this regard. The clothes are photographed on mannequins dynamically placed against typical 1920s backgrounds, both interiors and exteriors. One's head is turned to look at a painting; another, wearing a summer dress, stretches out both arms as though directing traffic; the same one in a sand-brown sleeveless knee-length beaded evening dress looks like it is leaning against an art-deco wall. Good effect is made of period pieces, with mannequins posed waiting at both the bottom and top of photogenic staircases.[30] The image chosen for the cover features a mannequin dressed in a sleeveless red-crepe three-quarters length evening dress who is turned away from a silver-rimmed mirror as though she had been caught looking at herself (Fig. 1.7).[31]

Figure 1.7: Cover, "1920s Fashion" exhibition catalogue. (Stadtmuseum Berlin)

Following up on the success of "Couture – Ready-to-Wear – Vaudeville," the Berlin Museum's Fashion Department mounted "Heinz Oestergaard: Fashion for the Millions, Inventory from the Berlin Museum" (*Heinz Oestergaard: Mode für Millionen: Bestände aus dem Berlin Museum*). Taking place between 4 July and 30 August 1992, also in the Grundkredit Bank, this exhibition featured the work of the oldest of the most prominent post-war German fashion designers. Born in 1916 in Berlin, Heinz Oestergaard became renowned after WWII for his ingenuity and style. He was able to balance an appreciation of luxury with a "reality check" sense of the possible, something often attributed to his having spent the last two years of WWII in a Russian POW camp. Returning to Berlin in 1945, his first items of women's clothing were made of "old uniforms, curtains, blankets and flags" (Waidenschlager 1992, 17). The following year he opened "Schröder-Eggeringhaus & Oestergaard" and became, at age 30, the youngest fashion designer in Berlin. As Christine Waidenschlager details in her portrait of Oestergaard, it was his inspired realization (while traveling through West German cities in the late 1940s) that Parisian haute couture – and the German ready-to-wear versions that took their cues from it – did not have enough of a customer base to draw on for the long term. To survive, he was convinced a designer needed partners in industry, and his own personal solution was to work with ones developing new

Figure 1.8: Heinz Oestergaard, at a showing of Cupresa-Cuprama items, 1952. The model on the left is Irmgard Kunde; on the right is Marina Ottens. Unknown photographer.

washable synthetic fabrics (Fig. 1.8). The 48 items of the fashion-democratizer's work on display in the exhibition demonstrated his talent with fabrics, from the earliest – a black wool gabardine suit from 1952–53 on loan from the Krefeld Textile Museum – to a pleated negligee from 1968, the year after Oestergaard left Berlin for Munich, where he designed the green German police uniforms for which he is perhaps most renowned. Seventy-five years-old at the time of the exhibition, which closed two weeks after his birthday, Oestergaard remained artistically active for another decade, passing away in 2003.

With the expansion of Daniel Libeskind's extension onto the Collegienhaus, the Fashion Department's collection, as well as the theatre collection, became homeless. As Waidenschlager relates in the introduction to the "Berliner Chic" exhibition catalogue, "with the decision in fall 1999 to give the Collegienhaus entirely over to the Jewish Museum, those optimal exhibition rooms were lost for the fashion collection" (Waidenschlager 2001, 8). All the happier, she continued, that as of November 2001, two months after the Jewish Museum's opening, the fashion collection would be getting quarters in one of the *Stadtmuseum* buildings: namely, the Ephraim Palais, one of the late Baroque palaces still remaining, and beautifully restored, in the Nikolaiviertel, the historic kernel of Berlin. Veitel Heine Ephraim, Friedrich the Great's banker whose investments did much to stoke the city's manufacturing sector, had bought the property in 1762 and had it rebuilt for his son Benjamin, who liked to entertain distinguished guests. By 1806 Benjamin Ephraim had been bankrupted by the war with Napoleon, and the Palais was used in the nineteenth century as a registration office and also to house police officers. In 1936, it was taken down by Hitler's architects but fortunately not destroyed. When its reconstruction was decided on, on the occasion of Berlin's 750th anniversary in 1987, it was possible for it to be returned to nearly its original form and location. Like the Ermelerhaus in 1917, it reopened to house a fashion exhibition. Rococo would seem to be the preferred choice for housing fashion exhibits that are intended to be permanent.

The "Berliner Chic" exhibition originated when Christine Waidenschlager, who had been curating fashion exhibitions at the Berlin Museum since the mid-1980s and who was in charge of expanding the fashion collection, had the idea to do a project in collaboration with the Jewish department of the Berlin Museum that focused on the Jewish *Konfektionshäuser*. The emphasis was to be placed on the nineteenth century as that was the collection's greatest strength. However, with the relocation of the project from the Collegienhaus to the Ephraim Palais, and the final decision, in December 2000, to present an exhibition that included 43 original gowns, Waidenschlager and her team found themselves with eleven months to renovate the new venue, conceptualize a way to connect the historical exhibition not only with the city itself but with the current fashion world of Berlin, and put together a catalogue that featured articles on the history of fashion in Berlin, graphics, illustrations and photographs from archival collections of the *Stadtmuseum*, as well as photographs of the period gowns on display. Waidenschlager's approach to curating the exhibition was to make it personal, encouraging visitors to personify the labor that went into the making of the garments by connecting them with their own family histories; instead of seeing old clothes, she wanted them to see someone's mother or grandmother at work (Fig. 1.9). As she noted in an interview, "in almost every family there was an aunt, an uncle, a grandmother or a mother who had worked in the fashion manufacturing industry and identified with that industry. Berliners, and especially female Berliners, identify with this fashion collection; it evokes their personal historical identity because one identifies with clothing much more than with industrial machines. It was always my impression that fashion was particularly important to the identity of the city."[32] Understanding Berliners' history and their sensitivity to it, she put on display items in a way that would connect them to it.

The nine rooms on the Ephraim Palais's upper floor encouraged conceptualizing the exhibition in terms of epochs: each room represented a period from Biedermeier to reunification. Period furniture, photographs, and other historical items were used to provide an atmosphere of authenticity. Windows were covered with light projections of paintings or photographs (from the *Stadtmuseum* collections) so that visitors could look out at the historical Berlin, which simultaneously solved the problem of dealing with light-sensitive garments that could only be exposed to 50-volt light bulbs. A dimmed, blue corridor allowed visitors to adjust to the low lighting before entering the exhibition rooms, which

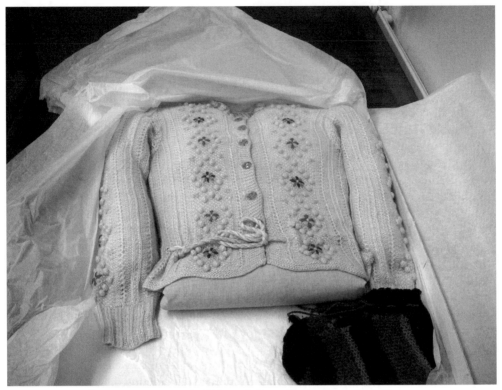

Figure 1.9: Sweater from Museum Europäischer Kulturen fashion collection. (Photo: K. Sark)

then unfolded chronologically. The color concept reflected a historical dimension as well. The closer one got to the present time, the warmer the colors.

The first room spanned the decades of the Biedermeier era (1820 to 1850), the formative period during which the first Berlin fashion manufacturers were founded. The light projection of a painting by Johann Wilhelm Brücke covering the window showed a view of a Berlin street and the City Hall tower from 1840. The next room displayed the industrial metropolis of the Kaiserreich from 1850 to 1890. Industrialization and Berlin's rise to capital status were captured in Julius Jacob's painting projection of a busy city square in Wilhelmplatz in spring 1886. In the third room, entitled "Die Berliner Konfektion," the painting projection by Paul Andorff revealed a view of Berlin fashion production in the Kurstrasse in 1877. The fourth room presented the Wilhelmine era from 1890 to 1914, with its opulent parade uniforms and capital grandeur, captured by M. Zieseler in his painting "Wilhelm II und Begleitung nehmen eine Parade ab" (William II and his Followers Take a Salute), from 1896. The fifth, oval-shaped, room at the center of the Palais was dedicated to the Weimar Republic and commemorated the rise of Berlin as a fashionable world-class metropolis with vibrant commercial, art and nightlife scenes. Fashion magazines were displayed throughout the room. After the vibrancy and glamour of the oval room came a somber grey, almost entirely empty room, which symbolized the destruction of the Jewish fashion manufacturing industry during the Nazi epoch. A board hung on the wall with the names of Jewish fashion manufacturers, whose fate could be looked up in archival files. The seventh room presented Berlin rising from the ruins of its "Stunde Null;" a photograph by Albert Kolbe from 1947 showed several rubble women pushing a large iron cart on rails and clearing the rubble in the Behrenstrasse. Room eight showed the development of fashion and the different approaches to work in the divided city from 1950 to 1970. While the GDR Fashion Institute was established in the East in 1952, the West saw the rise of independent fashion designers, like Detlev Albers, Heinz Oestergaard and Uli Richter. A photograph by Albert Kolbe of the Karl-Marx-Allee from around 1965 was juxtaposed with Henry Croner's 1965 photograph of its West Berlin equivalent, the Europacenter. The chronological stroll ended with a democratization of fashion and the fall of the Wall. In this final room, in warmer, brighter colors, the work of young designers from East and West Berlin was displayed together, and Rolf Zoller's photograph of the Brandenburg Gate on 10 November 1989 set the tone of reunification. One hundred and seventy years of fashion history ended on a positive and celebratory note. The entire display was changed once a year to exhibit a greater variety of dresses and articles from the collection and to prevent the dresses from overexposure to light. Bridging Berlin's fashion past with its present and future, the Ephraim Palais also featured, from November to February 2002, designs, fashion shows and installations by contemporary Berlin designers Claudia Skoda, Maria Tembrink, Janet Knaack, Anna von Griesheim, and the label Herz + Stöhr.

The Fashion Department expanded its stock in the 1990s to over 5000 dresses and just as many accessories, which makes its subsequent closure all the more regrettable (Figs. 1.10 and 1.11).[33] The estate of the Berlin illustrator Lieselotte Friedlaender was acquired in 1989 with the help of the *Stiftung Deutsche Klassenlotterie*. Clothing from the years 1820 to 1880 was acquired in 1993 with the help of the *Preußischen Seehandlung* (Prussian Maritime Trade). The archive of the doyen of Berlin fashion illustrators Gerd Hartung was acquired in 1995 with the help of the *Klassenlotterie*. The artistic estate of the fashion photographer Kim (Gerd Krommick) was donated to the Museum in 1997. The work of the fashion designer known as 'WKS,' Wulf Konrad Schwertfeger, was also privately donated, as were the company archives of H. W. Claussen and the Mandel Company, as well as the press and image archive of the Fashion Exhibition Society, which was founded in 1983 by Berlin's economic senator and disbanded in 1994. Perhaps most importantly, the extensive inventory of the archive of the GDR Fashion Institute was donated to the Museum in 1991 by the Fashion Institute's successor organization. These treasures, which Dorit Lücke details in her contribution to the "Berliner Chic" exhibition catalogue and which are now stored in Spandau, include primarily women's clothing and accessories as well as books, fashion journals, travel reports, Comecon documents (Council for Mutual Economic Assistance, in German: RGW, *Rat für gegenseitige Wirtschaftshilfe*), academic work and all of the documents regarding the industry and its trade in the GDR (92–7).

Figure 1.10: Boxes of the fashion collection of the Stadtmuseum Fashion Department. (Photo: K. Sark)

When Berlin's municipal museums were reorganized in 1995, the Fashion Department became part of a new administrative arrangement called the *Stadtmuseum* and "Berliner Chic" became the most prominent of what has turned out to be a series of exhibitions put on at the Ephraim Palais connected to the institutions of fashion in Berlin.[34] Work of contemporary designers was exhibited in conjunction with the "Berliner Chic" exhibition in 2003, while an exhibition on children's clothing from the Wilhelminian period opened the same day as "Berliner Chic," 23 November 2001, but only ran until 9 January 2002. The Gerd Hartung collection that the Fashion Department had acquired in 1995 was exhibited during the second half of 2004. Erna Schmidt-Caroll's Weimar sketches and the work of costume and stage designer Wolf Leder were exhibited in the first half of 2006. The summer of 2007 featured an exhibition on the styles of Berlin sunbathing, while the work of Heinrich Zille and of costume and stage designer Martin Rupprecht were exhibited during the first half of 2008. Finally, Gisèle Freund's photographs of Berlin taken during her return to the city from 1957–1962 were shown from 22 November 2008–8 February 2009. The work of "local heroes" deserving of prominence in the historical pantheon of Berlin fashion is thus slowly but surely being registered through the efforts of *Stadtmuseum* curators.[35]

Figure 1.11: Hanging clothes from the fashion collection of Museum Europäischer Kulturen. (Photo: K. Sark)

There are also several clothing-textile collections in Berlin that make no claims to fashion but contain items that are very fashionable indeed. In addition to the already mentioned *Deutsches Historisches Museum*, the Museum of European Cultures (currently in Dahlem but to be relocated to the planned Humboldt Forum at Schlossplatz) owns a large collection of clothing made and collected in Berlin. Originally opened in 1889 as the *Museum für deutsche Volkstrachten und Erzeugnisse des Hausgewerbes* (Museum for German Folk Costumes and Household Products), it suffered great losses during WWII but still became one of the leading museums in the former GDR thanks to the interest of the Institute for German Folk Culture of the GDR's Academy of Sciences (Karasek 4). Many of the municipal *Bezirksmuseen* (district museums), such as the Charlottenburg Heimatmuseum, own collections of local clothing and textiles as well as articles and documents from their clothing manufacturing industry. There is also, as will be discussed further in Chapter Five, the Marlene Dietrich collection at the Film Museum in the Sony Centre. While a deliberate emphasis on collecting fashion articles as such is a relatively recent museal venture, it has certainly grown in importance since the 1970s and '80s,[36] and, as becomes evident from the above-mentioned collections, there is substantial material available in Berlin collections waiting to mobilized to this effect.

The Kamer/Ruf Collection

These "Davidian" efforts need to be understood in relation to the acquisition in February 2003 by the *Kunstgewerbemuseum* of the one of the largest costume and couture collections ever to go on the market: the 1572-piece Kamer/Ruf collection. The collection takes its name from London-based Martin Kamer, who was born in Zug in Switzerland and developed a keen knowledge of the history of costume and theatre history from studies and work in costume and theatre design in Europe, America and Australia, and Wolfgang Ruf, who founded the Galerie Ruf AG in Rastatt, Germany, in 1981, moved to Beckenried bei Luzern in 1998 and is recognized as one of the foremost experts on European textiles and costumes from the thirteenth through the twentieth centuries (Schönberger 11–12). Kamer specialized in opera and ballet, worked with Rudolf Nureyev from 1974 to 1986, and established the collection's reputation by providing pieces for fashion exhibitions at the Metropolitan Museum of Art in New York, such as "The Eighteenth Century Woman," "Dance," "Man and Horse" and "Orientalism," for the "Revolution in Fashion: European Clothing, 1715–1815" at the Kyoto

Figure 1.12: Kamer/Ruf Collection on display at the Kunstgewerbemuseum. (Photo: K. Sark)

Costume Institute in Japan, and for "Addressing the Century: 100 Years of Art and Fashion" at the Hayward Gallery in London (11–12). In acquiring the Kamer/Ruf collection, the *Kunstgewerbemuseum* enriched its holdings with 660 pieces of clothing and 912 accessories, including rare items of male clothing in the style of the French court dating back to the eighteenth century, and 280 women's dresses by designers who constitute a who's who of the fashion world, beginning with Charles Frederick Worth and including Paul Poiret, Mariano Fortuny, Coco Chanel, Madeleine Vionnet, Elsa Schiaparelli, Cristóbel Balenciaga, Madame Grès, Christian Dior, Yves Saint Laurent, Rudi Gernreich, Paco Rabanne and Gianni Versace (13). Restoration expert Waltraut Berner-Laschinski needed two years to treat and inventory the collection (Böker 2005).

Just as the Lipperheide Costume Library was displayed to the public shortly after its acquisition, so too was the Kamer/Ruf. Between 5 November 2005 and 5 February 2006, an exhibition entitled "Runway Fashion: The Kamer/Ruf Collection – Fashion from the 18th to the 20th Century" (*Laufsteg Mode: Die Sammlung Kamer/Ruf – Mode vom 18. bis 20. Jahrhundert*) was held at the *Kulturforum*. A selection of approximately 50 pieces of

Figure 1.13: Warhol dresses from the Kamer/Ruf Collection on display. (Photo: K. Sark)

clothing and 30 accessories tried to give visitors an appreciation of the collection's riches by presenting the items not chronologically but rather in groupings according to keywords: opulence, geometry, sculpture and print. The effect was to make the vastness of the collection palpable (Fig. 1.12). Not only were there recognizable designer pieces, iconic prints (Warhol's (Fig. 1.13) and Mondrian's mini dresses) and historical pieces, it was all accompanied by hats and shoes. Unlike the "Berliner Chic" exhibit, the collection did not tell a story of Berlin or of its people. Rather, it told the story of Kamer's collecting prowess and how fortunate the museum, the city and the country were to have his collection.

The *Sammlung Kamer/Ruf* catalogue reveals an interesting repositioning of the *Kunstgewerbemuseum* in the Berlin museum landscape. From the laudatory remarks of the General Director of the *Staatliche Museen zu Berlin*, Peter-Klaus Schuster, it is apparent that the acquisition of this Goliath of fashion collections was intended to bring a new dynamic into that landscape by setting the *Kulturforum* on a course to become "a second Museum Island, to develop into a Museum Island of the Modern Arts of the 20th and 21st century" (9). Barbara Mundt, former director of the *Kunstgewerbemuseum*, also stresses in her contribution to the catalogue that the *Kunstgewerbemuseum* had built up a respectable collection of textiles, estimated at around 11,000 objects in 1890, ten years after it had become part of the Royal Museums (2005, 15). She neatly glosses over the fact that the *Kunstgewerbemuseum*, which is now part of the prestigious *Staatliche Museen zu Berlin* that belong to the Foundation of Prussian Cultural Heritage (*Stiftung Preußischer Kulturbesitz*, founded by a West German federal law passed in 1957), does not enjoy the same status as the Museum Island, either in the eyes of tourists or scholars: Bode's canonical status in Berlin history merits him an entire page in Richie's monumental history of Berlin (227), while the only Lessing she mentions is the Enlightenment author of *Emilia Galotti* and *Nathan der Weise*. Julius, the first director of the *Kunstgewerbemuseum*, is conspicuously absent.

Building Momentum

Acquiring the Kamer/Ruf collection may not have allowed the *Kunstgewerbemuseum* to dominate the Berlin museal scene, but it helped to reassert its, and Berlin's, presence in the realm of fashion. The acquisition also had the domino effect of bringing another prestigious collection to the *Kunstgewerbemuseum*: that of Uli Richter, the post-WWII "ambassador of German fashion." Exhibited at the *Kulturforum* from 13 September 2007 to 6 January 2008 to celebrate Richter's eightieth birthday, the exhibition honored the designer, whose presence in the international centers of fashion from the 1960s through the 1980s helped to resurrect Germany's status. The global, and national, thrust of the exhibition is unmistakable in the catalogue's introduction: "After Gianni Versace, Giorgio Armani, Max Mara and Christian Dior, now for the first time a German fashion designer is honored in such a prominent place" (Waidenschager and Kessemeier 8).[37] Efforts also continued to be made to establish the *Kunstgewerbemuseum*'s centrality: "To show Uli Richter and his fashion collection in the *Kulturforum* at Potsdamer Platz is a program for the future of the *Kulturforum* as the central location of the *Staatliche Museum zu Berlin* for modernity, for the concentration of its 20th-century art and art history collections at a historic location where modernity in all of its facets realised itself in Berlin" (8). The *Kunstgewerbemuseum*'s choice to position itself in Berlin's museum landscape in this way is forward-looking, historically justified, and resembles that of the shopping complexes developed during the post-reunification building spree, which we discuss in Chapter Six. By tapping into the city's branding process in the way that it has, the *Kunstgewerbemuseum* reveals that it has recognized the value of its proximity to Potsdamer Platz and accepted the responsibilities and marketing realities that come with being one of the main European fashion authorities.

Recent exhibitions at the *Kunstgewerbemuseum* are further signs of this acceptance. In the build-up in the summer of 2009 to the November celebrations of the twentieth anniversary of the fall of the Wall, it was one of several Berlin museums to stage an exhibition about the former East Germany (Böhlke 2009). "Free within Limits/Borders: Fashion, Photography, Underground, GDR 1979–89" (*In Grenzen frei: Mode, Fotografie, Underground, DDR 1979–89*) took upon itself the task of disproving the common assumption that there had been no counterculture in East Germany simply because it had not been sanctioned by the state (Fig. 1.14). In addition to sections on the official fashion magazine *Sibylle* and the German Fashion Institute, the exhibition also featured the work of photographers who had

Figure 1.14: "Free Within Limits/Border" exhibition at the *Kunstgewerbemuseum*. (Photo: S. Ingram)

Figure 1.15: Frieda von Wild, Berlin 1988. (Photo: Sybille Bergemann, Sybille Bergemann/Ostkreuz)

Figure 1.16: Tribute to Yves Saint Laurent at the *Kunstgewerbemuseum*. (Photo: S. Ingram)

documented the underground and underground fashion: Robert Zayd Paris, Roger Melis, Helga Paris, Michael Biedowicz, Harald Hauswald, Jürgen Hohmuth, Werner Mahler, Ute Mahler, Tina Bara, Sven Marquardt, Frieda von Wild and Sybille Bergemann. The exhibition was co-curated by von Wild (Fig. 1.15), who got an early start to modeling thanks to her mother, Sybille Bergemann, and first appeared in *Sibylle* at age 12 in one of Bergemann's photos. Much of the work was on public display for the first time.

Upon the passing of Yves Saint-Laurent on 1 June 2008, the *Kunstgewerbemuseum* paid its respects to the designer with a spontaneous tribute consisting of a dozen Kamer/Ruf dresses assembled among the vitrines on the lower level of the *Kunstgewerbemuseum* and a digitally projected screening on one of the walls of the fashion show staged in Paris to honor his retiring from his fashion house in 2002 (Fig. 1.16). Unlike the thematically organized blockbuster exhibition that was designed and developed by the Montreal Museum of Fine Arts and the Fine Arts Museums of San Francisco, in partnership with the Fondation Pierre Bergé, and which opened in Montreal two days before Saint Laurent's death,[38] this show was organized quickly and without any budget.

The *Kunstgewerbemuseum* has also taken to promoting the work of promising young designers, such as c.neeon, whose colorful clothes were exhibited in the summer of 2006, and Stephan Hann, whose work has been described by curator Angela Völker at the MAK in Vienna as "a kind of visualized hip-hop."[39] Around 50 of Hann's striking dresses made of unexpected materials like Tetra Paks, photo negatives, light bulbs, medication blister packs

Figure 1.17: c.neeon fashion show in front of the *Kunstgewerbemuseum*, July 2008. (Photo: S. Ingram)

and the foil caps of champagne bottles were on display in the winter of 2009. The museum also hosts fashion shows by designers like c.neeon during Fashion Week (Fig. 1.17).

* * *

The history of collecting and exhibiting fashion in Berlin, as laid out in this chapter, supports a broader understanding of collectible modernity than the traditional one that takes art history as its focus. Berlin's fashion collections have been, and continue to be, displayed and made accessible in catalogue form due to great curatorial effort on the part of, among others, Barbara Mundt, Gretel Wagner, Adelheid Rasche, Christine Waidenschlager, Angela Schönberger and their staffs. These preservational efforts should not be viewed in terms of exclusion and marginalization, as one could interpret Huyssen tending to in comments such as "[t]he former exclusions and marginalizations have entered into our present and are restructuring our past" (1995, 28). As the material collected in this chapter establishes, the presence of fashion in Berlin's museum landscape has since its beginnings provided that landscape with an artisanal quality that continues to draw attention to the mechanisms involved in the prestige-making machinery of the hegemonic institutions on the Museum Island and that more generally mitigates the unquestioned acceptance of high art, or mass art, as an ultimate standard. In Berlin, "*Kunst*" has since its institutionalized beginnings in a royal academy been confronted with challenging presences, first of "mechanical sciences" and then of "*Gewerbe*," and the result has provided alternative models of what the parameters and role of culture should be. The friendship of the Lipperheides and Julius Lessing ensured that resources related to the changing nature of dress were available to the public that expanded their horizons. In giving the public the ability to make informed choices about, and indeed the ability to make, their own clothing, the Lipperheides' work in publishing and collecting valorized dress as a field of aesthetic as well as industrial endeavor. Despite a pattern of cesuras, beginning with the decimation of WWII and repeated by the reorganizations following the division of the city in 1961 and its reunification in 1990, and despite the Museum Island's reassertion of its dominance in reunified Berlin, once again becoming the primary focus of the city's tourist gaze,[40] fashion-related musealizing work continues to appear beyond its hegemonic shadow. Aided by the acquisition of the glamorous, internationally recognized Kamer/Ruf collection, whose designer brands demonstrate how the old modern high-low culture split has to a great extent been superseded and resignified by market-driven, niche-oriented global forces, fashion continues to provide important impetus to the shaping of Berlin's museal landscape.

Notes

1. A Decree issued by the Revolutionary Convention in Paris on 27 July 1793 ordered the creation of the "Museum of the Republic" at the Louvre, which then opened on 9 November 1793 (Ameri 61). Elaboration of these critiques can be found in Sheehan 49–50, Maleuvre 13–21, Adorno, Bennett, Clifford and Huyssen.
2. For an account of the Yves Saint Laurent exhibit, see Steele; for Armani, see Potvin 2007, 2009.
3. We are greatly indebted to Peter McIsaac for sharing his expertise in the field of German Museum Studies with us and for generously helping us to find our way through the following material. We would have been far less likely to venture as far as we have into this field without his encouragement and support, and without his collegially sharing with us his exhibition catalogues on Bode and *Kunstgewerbe*.
4. As discussed later in the section, the term has been variously translated into English as "arts and crafts" and "decorative arts." The lack of a standardized, one-to-one translation points to the inability of any term in English to capture the jarring dissonance that is produced by the original's combining *Kunst* (art) and *Gewerbe* (which can, in addition to "craft," be rendered as "industry," "trade" "business" and even "art" – as in "graphisches Gewerbe"/graphic art).
5. The original is: "Es giebt heutzutage gar keine Kunstgewerbe, es giebt Gewerbetreibende, welche zugleich Künstler sind; es giebt auch Künstler, welche aus ihrer Kunst ein sehr lucratives Gewerbe zu machen verstehen! Allein ein Kunstgewerbe ist ein Unding" (Franke 167). Unless otherwise indicated, all translations are ours.
6. The French academies – the *Académie de peinture et de sculpture* (founded 1648), *Académie de musique* (founded in 1669), *Académie d'architecture* (founded in 1671) – were founded separately from the *Académie royale des sciences*, which was the responsibility of the Minister of Economy, Colbert (Mislin 41).
7. One should note that this is not the British equivalent of an academy of sciences. That organization is known simply as the Royal Society, not the Royal Society for Arts, and was founded in 1660 as the Royal Society of London for the Improvement of Natural Knowledge with the mandate to support scientific research, rather than work in the arts and/or crafts.

8. That this trend was Europe-wide is indicated by the 1820 opening of the Prado in Madrid, while Britain's National Gallery followed in 1824.

9. Hirt is also known for having written treatises on *Die Baukunst nach den Grundsätzen der Alten* (The Art of Building According to the Principles of the Ancients, 1809), *Die Geschichte der bildenden Künste bei den Alten* (History of the Fine Arts in Antiquity, 1833) and the three-volume *Geschichte der Baukunst bei den Alten* (History of the Art of Building in Antiquity, 1820–1827).

10. Crimp translates "Hirt's own German rendering of what he intended by the Latin (FRIDERICVS GVILELMVS III STVDIO ANTIQVITATIS OMNIGENAE ET ARTIVM LIBERALIVM MVSEVM CONSTITVIT MDCCCXXIII): "Friedrich Wilhelm III. stiftete das Museum für das Studium alterthümlicher Gegenstande jeder Gattung und der freien Künste" as "Friedrich Wilhelm III founded this museum for the study of antique objects of all kinds and the fine arts" (Fn 18, 266) and offers the following gloss of the grammatical issues: "As one now reads it, one naturally connects the genitives *antiquitatis omnegenae et liberalium artium* with *studio*, and one is very surprised later to encounter *museum*. One is unsure whether the former genitives belong to it or to studio or should be divided between the two, or if, as appears to be intended, *studio* should be dependent upon *museum*…. Moreover, if *antiquitatis* is here supposed to mean the antique alone, then *omni-genae* cannot follow it. If one is to understand by this term, instead, antique objects, then one must employ the plural *antiquitates*, the singular *antiquitas* being incorrect" (Fn 21, 266). While inscriptions can do funny things with the laws of Latin, as Classicist Sarah Blake confirmed (and we would like to thank Sarah for providing her expertise in this matter), there is no obvious problem with this inscription beyond the awkwardness of the adjective *omnigenae*. According to Blake, "*Museum* can go at the end…. And I think that it's clear that the genitives are dependent on *studio*, which is dependent on *museum*….[T]here are two things to say about the phrase *antiquitatis omnigenae*. The commentator is right that *antiquitas* (here *antiquitatis* in the genitive) in the singular means 'antiquity' generally and really only in the plural, antiquitates (or, *antiquitatum* in the genitive plural) should it be taken to mean 'antique objects'. *Omnigenae* (which is a rare word in the classical period so I'm not very familiar with it) can have two meanings: all types; every kind, or all-begetting; all-producing. So the whole thing could mean: Friedrich Wilhelm III founded this museum for the study of all (types of) antiquity and the fine arts. 1823. – *Omnigenae* here maybe meaning all periods of antiquity, not just the Greeks? This is where *omnigenae* is awkward; OR: Friedrich Wilhelm III founded this museum for the study of all-generating antiquity and the fine arts. 1823. – which I think may be overly poetic but…. The inscription is not wrong, but it reads awkwardly. I know that *omnigenus* was an adjective used more commonly in post-classical prose, so it is possible that it seems wrong to a strictly classical eye, but that it sounded just right to later ears" (Email correspondence of 30/11/08).

11. For the *Kulturnation*, see Elias; for the development of the *Bildungsbürgertum*'s historical consciousness, see Crane; and for cultural capital, see Bourdieu.

12. This is Peter McIsaac's felicitous turn of phrase.

13. The presence of French impressionist and modernist art in the *Nationalgalerie* underscores that Paris had indeed become by this time, as Walter Benjamin claimed, the "Capital of the Nineteenth Century."

14. The new visitor pavilion on the island is named after Simon.

15. Information for this section is distilled from the following internet sources: http://www.smb.museum/smb/news/details.php?lang=en&objID=13023;http://tibs.at/burgen/burgen_schlosser_tirol/lipperheide.htm; http://www.europeanrealestate.org/property/ref/SH20513-441; http://www.diegeschichteberlins.de/. For more on the Lipperheides and their collection, see Wagner 1964, Mayerhofer-Llanes, and Rasche's 1999 publications, which are catalogues of exhibitions organized to celebrate the collection's hundredth anniversary.

16. This self-description is available on the library's website (http://www.ifskb.de/modebild).
17. As Sheehan notes, Nietzsche's exhortation "I want to set against the art of artworks a higher art – the art of inventing festivals" was very much part of this backlash (141).
18. The first translation is from the MWB Mijnwoordenboek online German-English dictionary (http://www.mijnwoordenboek.nl/EN/theme/JU/EN/DE/C/5). The second translation is from Oliver Weiss' "Old German Professions" website (http://www.rootsweb.ancestry.com/~romban/misc/germanjobs.html).
19. The cause of her death is subject to debate; however, whether a stroke, as reported in the *Modenwelt*, or a heart attack as reported in the letters of her close friend Hugo Wolf, it was in any case unexpected and sudden (cf. Rasche 1999b, 16).
20. It has subsequently been known in English as the Museum of Industrial and, more currently, Decorative Arts. For a historical overview of the museum and the intentions of its founder, Julius Lessing, see Mundt 1992.
21. These acquisitions consisted of "works of glass and ceramic, wood and leather, stone, ivory, amber, enamel, gold, silver, bronze, brass, tin, lead and iron, of clocks and instruments, jewelry, musical instruments, stained glass windows and textiles" (Mundt 1992, 175). Mundt details the *Kunstgewerbemuseum*'s three-pronged approach to collecting in her contribution to the Kamer/Ruf catalogue; the three areas are fabrics and needlework, carpets and tapestries, and costumes. We should also note that the *Gewerbe-Museum* is to be distinguished from the Ethnological Museum, although both collections have roots in the Royal Prussian *Kunstkammer*. The ethnographic collection was moved into the *Neues Museum* on the Museum Island in 1856, then into the *Museum für Völkerkunde*, which was founded in 1873 (its first director was Adolf Bastian), and in 1886 into its own building in what was then called the Königgrätzerstraße near Potsdamer Platz (today: Stresemannstraße). This building was completely destroyed during WWII and what could be saved of the collection was moved into their warehouse in Dahlem (this museum complex was Bode's dream-child, but the first buildings didn't appear until the 1970s). In 1999 this museum was given its current name – the Ethnological Museum.
22. The collection includes "pictorial and written sources on all aspects of the international history of clothing and fashion and covers a variety of subjects such as travel and festivity, sports and leisure, dance and theatre, etiquette and table manners, caricature and dress code. The collection of graphic art focuses on costume and fashion designs from the Renaissance to the contemporary, international fashion illustrations and 20th century fashion photography" (http://www.ifskb.de/modebild).
23. A complete listing of all the exhibitions based on the Lipperheide collection is as follows:

March 1900: "Special Exhibit of the Contents of the Lipperheidsche Costume Library" (*Sonderausstellung aus den Beständen der Freiherrlichen Lipperheid'schen Kostümbibliothek*)
May 1922: "*Styl*, the Journal, Pages on Fashion and the Nice Things in Life, Hand-Drawings and Prints" (*Zeitschrift »Styl«, Blätter für Mode und die angenehmen Dinge des Lebens Handzeichnungen und Drucke*)
5–28 September 1926: "Women's Dress in Fashion and Painting, Changes and Development of Fashionable Taste from 1750–1925" (*Das Frauenkleid in Mode und Malerei. Wandlung und Entwicklung modischen Geschmacks von 1750–1925*)
1927: "Paris Fashion in Lithographs from the First Half of the 19th Century" (*Die Pariser Mode in der Lithographie der 1. Hälfte des XIX. Jahrhunderts*)
1928: "Women's Dress in Fashion and Painting from the 18th Century to the Present" (*Das Frauenkleid in Mode und Malerei vom 18. Jahrhundert bis zur Gegenwart*), "German Fashion Pictures and Illustrations of Today" (*Deutsches Modebild und Mode Illustration von heute*), and "Fashion of Yesterday" (*Mode von gestern*)

1933: "New German Fashion Drawings" (*Neue deutsche Modezeichnungen*)

December 1955–February 1956: "Fashion Advertising Then and Now" (*Modewerbung einst und jetzt*)

30 July–31 October 1956: Exhibition of the Lipperheide Costume Library to mark the 50th anniversary of Franz von Lipperheide (*Ausstellung der Lipperheideschen Kostümbibliothek*)

March–April 1959: "19th-Century French Caricatures in the Lipperheide Costume Library" (*Französische Karikaturen des 19. Jahrhunderts in der Lipperheideschen Kostümbibliothek*)

February–March 1960: "Masks and Masquerades in the Graphics Works in the Possession of the Lipperheide Costume Library" (*Masken und Mumereien aus vier Jahrhunderten. Aquarelle und graphische Blätter aus dem Besitz der Lipperheideschen Kostümbibliothek*)

September–November 1962: "The Elegant Berlin Woman: Drawings and Fashionable Accessories from Two Centuries" (*Die elegante Berlinerin. Graphik und modisches Beiwerk aus zwei Jahrhunderten*)

1 August–8 October 1967: "New Acquisitions of the Lipperheide Costume Library" (*Neuerwerbungen der Lipperheideschen Kostümbibliothek*)

11 September–30 November 1968: "Dutch Fashions: Drawings from the Lipperheide's Costume Library" (*Holländische Moden. Graphik aus der Kostümbibliothek Lipperheide*)

28 September–7 October 1972: another general exhibition (*Die Lipperheidesche Kostümbibliothek*)

27 September–5 November 1977: "The Graphic Artist Gerd Hartung: Fashion Drawings and Sketches for the Theatre" (*Modezeichnungen und Theaterskizzen*)

17 July–15 October 1979: "Work Apparel in the Service of Fashion" (*Im Dienste der Mode. Berufsdarstellungen*)

16 September–15 November 1981: "The Bright Jacket in Prussia: Military and Civil Uniforms of the 17th to 20th Centuries in Drawings, Engravings and Photographs" (*Der bunte Rock in Preußen. Militär- und Ziviluniformen 17. bis 20. Jahrhundert in Zeichnungen, Stichen und Photographien*)

11 January–24 April 1982: "Fashionable Extravaganzas 1786–1860" (*Modische Extravaganzen 1786–1860*);

1 July–30 October 1982: "French Folk Costumes from the 19th Century" (*Französische Volkstrachten aus dem 19. Jahrhundert*)

March–May 1983: "Fez and Pleated Skirts: Folk Costumes from the Balkans" (*Fez und Faltenrock. Volkstrachten aus dem Balkan*)

December 1983: "Fashion Designs from the 1920s" (*Modeentwürfe der 1920er Jahre*)

June–September 1983: "The Beautiful Woman" (*Die schöne Frau*)

October–November 1983: "Man is Man" (*Mann ist Mann*)

18 December 1986–10 May 1987: "Fashion in Miniature" (*Mode en miniature*)

15 March–1 July 1988: "Haute Couture from the 1920s" (*Haute Couture der zwanziger Jahre*)

6 November 1989–20 February 1990: "Paris – Berlin, Fashion Photography from 1900 to 1988" (*PARIS – BERLIN, Modefotos von 1900 bis 1988*)

15 September–15 November 1994: "Early Fashion Photography from Parisian Ateliers in the Lipperheide Costume Library" (*Frühe Modefotografie aus Pariser Ateliers in der Lipperheideschen Kostümbibliothek*)

25 August 1994–1 October 1995: "Pictures of Fashion – Fashion Pictures: German Fashion Photography from 1945 to 1995" (*Bildermode – Modebilder: Deutsche Modephotographien von 1945–1995*)

4 September–12 October 1997: "Peter Lindbergh – Fashion Photographs" (*Peter Lindbergh: Modefotografie*)

16 March–2 May 1999: "Varieté and Revue: The Costume Maker and Collector William Budzinski" (*Varieté und Revue. Der Kostümbildner und Kostümsammler William Budzinski*)

28 July–12 September 1999: "Fashion Drawings from Berlin: For Charlotte Josephsen's 90th Birthday" (*Modezeichnungen aus Berlin – Charlotte Josephsen zum 90. Geburtstag*)
15 July–20 September 2000: "Regina May and the Fashion-Drawings of the Time" (*Regina May und die Mode-Zeichen der Zeit*)
15 July–10 September 2000: "Growth II: New Acquisitions to the Lipperheide Costume Library" (*Zuwachs II. Neuerwerbungen der Lipperheideschen Kostümbibliothek*)
29 May–29 July 2001: "Female Ambassadors of Fashion: Star Models and Photo Models from the 1950s in International Fashion Photography" (*Botschafterinnen der Mode: Star-Mannequins und Fotomodelle der Fünfziger Jahre in internationaler Modefotografie*)
11 January–10 March 2002: "Fashion from the Berlin Press-Ball" (*Mode auf dem Berliner Presseball*)
5 December 2003–15 February 2004: "Ridicule! Fashion in Caricatures: 1600–1900" (*Ridikül! Mode in der Karikatur, 1600 bis 1900*)
13 May–24 July 2005: "Berlin Fashion Photography of the 1930s" (*Berliner Modefotografie der Dreißiger Jahre*)
30 November 2006–4 March 2007: "COATS! Max Mara, 55 Years of Fashion from Italy" (*Max Mara: 55 Jahre Mode aus Italien*)
20 October 2006–7 January 2007: "Napoleon's New Clothes – Parisian and London Caricatures in Classical Weimar" (*Napoleons Neue Kleider – Pariser und Londoner Karikaturen im Klassischen Weimar*)
13 February–28 May 2007: "Christian Dior and Germany 1947 to 1957" (*Christian Dior und Deutschland, 1947 bis 1957*)
7 May–9 August 2009: "Sequins, Poses, Compacts: Fashion Drawings and Objects from the 1920s" (*Pailletten – Posen – Puderdosen, Modezeichnungen und Objekte der Zwanziger Jahre*).

24. There were also earlier ethnological displays of clothing, such as the ones at the *Museum für deutsche Volkstrachten*, but these involved folk-oriented items, which were part of a society that understood itself to be feudal, that is, predominantly pre-modern and relatively unaffected by industrialization (Karasek 4–5).
25. This account draws heavily on Rasche's valuable 1995 articles.
26. In the exhibition catalogue, Damm is described as a manufacturer who provided Friedrich the Great's army with leather goods and uniforms and who profited handsomely from the Prussian war machine (*Führer*).
27. A record of the Society's acquisitions was kept between 1917 and 1925; available in the Art Library, it offers a detailed record of the objects' material, cut, color, provenance, purchase price and value, and thus of the scope of the collection, which ranged from the eighteenth to early twentieth century, included men's, women's and children's clothing as well as accessories and, conspicuously, a number of historical costumes that had been acquired from portrait painters (Rasche 1995a, 18).
28. Dr. Regine Falkenberg is in charge of this collection. We regret that she was not able to meet with us. More details about the collection are available online at: http://www.dhm.de/sammlungen/alltag2/textilien/index.html.
29. The collection was also occasionally displayed at fashion shows, such as one held in the foyer of the Grundkredit Bank Berlin on Friday, 4 March and Sunday, 6 March 1988, to which Bothe invited the members and friends of the museum.
30. The following locations are thanked in the credits for their help with the photos: *Bröhan Museum, Hebbeltheater, Museum für Verkehr und Technik, Renaissancetheater,* and *Sender Freies Berlin*.
31. The mannequin was photographed by Nicolas von Saft in the *Bröhan Museum*.

32. Waidenschlager, Interview, 2 December 2005.
33. The Fashion Department of Munich's *Stadtmuseum* has also been closed, cf. http://www.goethe.de/kue/des/prj/mod/ain/en3720675.htm.
34. These are archived on the *Stadtmuseum*'s website: http://www.stadtmuseum.de/php/archiv/archivi.htm:

"Wilhelminian Children's Dress, 1871–1918, A Special Presentation of the Collection of Childhood and Youth" (*Das wilhelminische Kinderkleid, 1871–1918 Sonderpräsentation der Sammlung Kindheit und Jugend*), 23.11.01–1.9.02;
"Working Models/Autonomous Couture, Kratzert/Pahnke Present their Fashion in the Museum Ephraim Palais" (*Arbeitsproben/couture autonome Kratzert/Pahnke präsentieren ihre Mode im Museum Ephraim-Palais*), 4.3.03–30.3.03;
"Gerd Hartung 1913–2003: Chronicler of Berlin Fashion" (*Gerd Hartung 1913–2003: Chronist der Berliner Mode*), 23.06.04–09.01.05;
"The Costume and Theatre Designer Wolf Leder: A Life for the Stage" (*Der Kostüm- und Bühnenbildner Wolf Leder: Ein Leben für die Bühne*), 22.01.06–21.05.06;
"In the Whirl of the Big City: Erna Schmidt-Caroll: Berlin Sketches 1920–1938" (*Im Getriebe der großen Stadt Erna Schmidt-Caroll: Berliner Zeichnungen 1920–1938*), 17.03.06–25.06.06;
"Berlin Goes Swimming...Beach Dreams and Dream Beaches" (*BERLIN GEHT BADEN...von Strandträumen und Traumstränden*), 24.6.07–14.10.07;
"Heinrich Zille: Children of the Street" (*Heinrich Zille. Kinder der Straße*), 11.01.2008–02.03.2008;
"Martin Rupprecht: Stage Designs and Costumes" (*Martin Rupprecht | Bühnenbilder und Kostüme*), 8.3.08–1.6.08;
"Gisèle Freund: Seeing Berlin Again, 1957–1962" (*Gisèle Freund. Wiedersehen mit Berlin 1957–1962*), 22.11.2008 – 08.02.2009.
35. There have also been fashion-related exhibitions at other *Stadtmuseum* sites, such as the exhibition "She Clothes the Rich, She Sews For the Poor: Berlin Silk and Its Silk Trade" (*Sie kleidet den Reichen, sie naehret den Armen: Berliner Seide und Seidenhandel*) at the *Museum Knoblauchhaus* May 1996 to January 1997. See Bolz.
36. Waidenschlager, Interview, November 2009.
37. These comments would seem to be erasing from memory the Oestergaard exhibition at the Kunstforum in 1992, or perhaps it is not seen to count because it was part of the Berlin Museum's (now *Stadtmuseum*'s) collection.
38. The exhibition was, according to its catalogue, "the first retrospective spanning the forty years of creation of the Maison de haute couture Yves Saint Laurent." It was shown at the Musée des Beaux-Arts in Montréal from May 29 to September 28, 2008, and the de Young Museum of San Francisco, from November 1, 2008, to March 1, 2009. The exhibition website is at: http://www.mbam.qc.ca/micro_sites/ysl/index.html.
39. On the website of the Museum of Applied Arts: http://www.mak.at/mysql/ausstellungen_show_page.php?a_id=772&lang=en.
40. The long queues in front of the *Neues Museum* when it opened in the fall of 2009 were a match for those to get into the Foster dome of the *Reichstag,* demonstrating that the Museum Island has become a form of mass tourism.

Chapter 2

Berliner Chic and Historiography

"[T]hat is what Berlin is all about: just as in Jerusalem, you step to the side and find yourself entrapped in someone else's history."

(Zinik)

"The only constant is change."

(Moritz and Hartung 127)

C lio, the Greek muse of history, is not only a Romantic. As Theodore Ziolkowski implicitly established in his work on German academic historiography, she is also a *Berlinerin*:

The reasoning behind establishing Berlin as the seat of the new history and its permeation of the other disciplines is almost syllogistic in its rigor. Germany, according to the belief of many young Germans of the revolutionary age, was destined to be the new intellectual center of Europe. Prussia had proved itself to be the center of Germany. Berlin as its capital was the center of Prussia, and the university as its mind was the center of Berlin. The reorganization of the faculties had moved philosophy to the center of the university. And history, as Schiller, Fichte, Hegel and others were in the process of demonstrating, was the new center of philosophy. Q.E.D. (Ziolkowski 21)

The museal development that we traced in the previous chapter is thus part of a much larger epistemic shift whose spiritual seat was in Berlin. Parallel to the process of historicizing that Michel Foucault identified in *The Order of Things* as marking a rupture at the end of the eighteenth century and leading to the formation of modern science in the nineteenth, Ziolkowski identifies in the changes in the early nineteenth-century Berlin academy a pronounced historicization, not only in the development of history as its own discipline, but also in Hegel's historical approach to philosophy, Schleiermacher's historical approach to theology, Savigny's historical approach to law and Schubert's historical approach to medicine. In short, "[t]he sense of history had the effect of temporalizing every facet of human thought, within the faculties and without… [and] neither in England nor in France did this process have the same impact on the disciplines of philosophy, law, and theology as was the case in the faculties of German universities – first in Berlin and gradually elsewhere" (Ziolkowski 181). The city's profoundly historical sensibilities can thus be seen to have their roots here.

A striking amount of material on fashion in Berlin has been excavated by German- and English-speaking historians in response to critical events and periods in the city's history. The standard work on the subject, Uwe Westphal's *Berliner Konfektion und Mode 1836–1939: Die Zerstörung einer Tradition* (*Berlin Ready-to-Wear and Fashion 1836–1939: The Destruction of a Tradition*) was researched and written in the two years building up to 1986, the *aetas horribilis* in the context of German historiography for reasons not unrelated to Adorno and Horkheimer's argument about the destructive inevitabilities inherent in the becoming enlightened of (implicitly German) history. The fortieth anniversary celebrations of the end of WWII resulted in an eruption of controversy over how to work through the legacies of the Nazi atrocities, one of the more important moments of "German national self-interrogation" (Maier 2) or "Holocaust moments," as Atina Grossmann has called them. After the Germans were not invited to some D-Day festivities in June 1984, the mismanaging of the ones marking VE Day in May 1985 was all the more unfortunate. To mark the occasion, Helmut Kohl's government invited Ronald Reagan to a ceremony intended to reestablish Germany's normalcy among nations. Unfortunately it turned out that 49 SS troops were also interred in the German military cemetery at Bitburg where the ceremony was to take place, putting Reagan in the uncomfortable position of either declining, and rejecting German overtures to reenter the pantheon of what one could term memorially capable nations, or accept and face censure for his attendance, which he did. On this already uncomfortable terrain, a debate broke out among German public intellectuals the following summer (the so-called *Historikerstreit*) over the question of whether the German path should be considered unique (the *Sonderweg* thesis) or rather mitigated by the context of other reprehensible conduct in the twentieth century, specifically Stalin's.[1]

It is against this contentious historical backdrop that Westphal's groundbreaking study on the Berlin ready-to-wear industry appeared, right in time for the celebrations of the city's 750th anniversary in 1987. Westphal, who went on to write accounts of the Bauhaus's fate, of advertising in the Third Reich, and of German, Czech and Austrian Jews in English publishing, and to become the Secretary of the PEN Club London, where he lives, was interested in the question of whether the Berlin ready-to-wear industry was really as Jewish as anti-Semitic propaganda had made it out to be, and he secured funding from the Foundation of the Prussian Maritime Trade, which supports work on Brandenburgian-Prussian history ("Schwerpunkt der Förderung ist die Aufarbeitung der brandenburgisch-preußischen Geschichte") to find out. Approaching the topic as a historian, Westphal was perplexed at both the lack of available material and the doggedness with which the Nazis' label of "Jewish ready-to-wear" stuck to the fashion industry: "to the present day the idea of 'Jewish ready-to-wear' affixed by the Nazis is still prominent. And it is not only many experts in the field who thoughtlessly promulgate the old lies about the seemingly preponderant position of Jews in ready-to-wear. Even the associations in the field, the Association of Women's Outerwear in Cologne and the Association of Berlin's Clothing Industry, allow these untruths to stand without questioning in their publications" (12). Up until the publication of his book in 1986, Westphal was unable to find an industry representative in a position to make any clear statements about the history of the industry and either the actual number of Jews involved in the founding of the industry or the number active in the industry who perished at the hands of the Nazis, something which his final, admittedly incomplete, listing of 180 ladies-wear companies that no longer existed in 1940 and the fate of their owners was intended to address.

That Westphal's book became the standard work on the subject is made clear in Rolf Bothe's foreword to the second edition, which was published in 1992. Bothe, the Director of the Berlin Museum responsible for establishing the museum's Fashion Department in 1981, details the shocking belittling of the fate of the Jewish entrepreneurs during the National Socialist period in the previous works on the subject: Moritz Loeb's 1906 *Berliner Konfektion* (*Berlin Ready-to-Wear*), Erwin Wittkowski's 1928 *Die Berliner Damenkonfektion* (*Berlin Women's Ready-to-Wear*), Werner Dopp's 1962 *125 Jahre Berliner Konfektion* (*125 Years of Berlin Ready-to-Wear*), Brunhilde Dähn's 1968 *Berlin Hausvogteiplatz* (the square on the southern part of the Museum Island around which ready-to-wear industrialists established themselves in the nineteenth century – something we detail later in the chapter), which before Westphal's was regarded as the standard work on the subject, and Heinz Mohr's 1982 edited volume *DOB Mode in Deutschland von 1945 bis Heute* (*Women's Outerwear Manufacturing Fashion in Germany from 1945 to the Present*). Westphal's work, on the other hand, comes in for praise for providing evidence that disproves the Nazi propaganda claim that 90% of ready-to-wear companies were owned by Jews with a thorough analysis of existing documentation as well as interviews with Jews involved in the ready-to-wear industry in the 1930s who had been forced to emigrate (9). That the original publication created something of an uproar is made clear in Westphal's afterword, in which he marvels that the deferred effects of the history he dredged up would include his having to temporarily vacate his apartment because of anonymous telephone harassment at night. By 1992 Westphal's work had taken on further contemporaneity. Not only does he liken accounts of the plundering that occurred in Berlin in 1938 with the race riots in Los Angeles, but he also mentions recent visits to places in the former east, such as Leipzig, where cases concerning property expropriated by the Nazis were in the process of being decided.

Westphal begins his account of Berlin fashion almost 550 years before the founding of the first Berlin ready-to-wear firms, with the 10 April 1288 awarding to a tailors' guild of a foundation document (*Stiftungsurkunde*) by the government of the Margrave Otto V. and Albrecht from the House of Askanier, which affected the "dear fellow citizens" of Berlin by forbidding any unregulated purchasing or production of clothing (13), but he moves quickly to the nineteenth century and his topic, Berlin's ready-to-wear industry. This half-a-millennium gap has in the meantime begun to be filled by cultural and literary historians: Daniel Purdy's 1998 *The Tyranny of Elegance: Consumer Cosmopolitanism in the Era of Goethe*, Karin Wurst's 2005 *Fabricating Pleasure: Fashion, Entertainment, and Cultural Consumption in Germany, 1780–1830*, Julia Bertschik's 2005 *Mode und Moderne: Kleidung als Spiegel des Zeitgeistes in der deutschsprachigen Literatur* (*Fashion and Modernity: Clothing as a Mirror of the Zeitgeist in German-Language Literature*), Astrid Ackermann's 2005 *Paris,*

London und die europäische Provinz: die frühen Modejournale 1770–1830 (*Paris, London and the European Backwaters: The Early Fashion Journals 1770–1830*) and Anna Zika's 2006 *Ist Alles Eitel? Zur Kulturgeschichte deutschsprachiger Modejournale zwischen Aufklärung und Zerstreuung, 1750–1950* (*Is All Vanity? Towards a Cultural History of German-Language Fashion Journals between Enlightenment and Distraction, 1750–1950*). Purdy's thesis is that "eighteenth-century German consumer culture began within the readerly imagination and that an elaborate and self-critical discourse on consumption existed in Germany well before any portion of that diverse Central European region approached industrialization on the scale of England or France" (2), and his main supporting source is Friedrich Justin Bertuch's *Journal des Luxus und der Moden*, "known to contemporaries simply as the *Mode Journal*" (Fn 1, 245), a work Wurst, Bertschik, Ackermann and Zika all address: Wurst mines it for material on the national costume debates and the emergence of the middle-class in the territory of what is now known as Germany, Bertschik examines it in conjunction with Berlin-born Caroline de la Motte Fouqué's (1773–1831) writings on fashion, while Zika offers a detailed account of its production.[2] Given that the *Mode Journal* ran from 1786 to 1827 and that Bertuch was the wealthiest entrepreneur in not Berlin but Weimar, where he served as Duke Karl August's treasurer from 1785 to 1796, it is not surprising it is of little interest to Westphal, whose focus is resolutely Berlin.

While Berlin receives only occasional mention in passing in the other historical fashion-related monographs, usually in comparison with Hamburg or Weimar, in Purdy's it is the scene of Chapter 9. "The Uniform's Tactical Control: Execution over Performance" delves into the history of Prussia's uniform culture, beginning with Friedrich Wilhelm I of Prussia's edicts of 1719 prohibiting his subjects from wearing anything but local clothing (Purdy 196, cf. Westphal 14, Guenther 78). By the eighteenth century, Berlin had become one of the largest garrison cities in Europe. According to Purdy's sources, "For most of the century, 20–24 percent of Berlin's inhabitants (including women and children) were attached to the army" (199). He further cites Johann Kaspar Riesbeck's 1783 *Briefe eines reisenden Franzosen über Deutschland* (*Letters of a Travelling Frenchman about Germany*): "With the exception of Constantinople, no city in Europe has so large a garrison as Berlin. Around 26,000 men are stationed here" (199). There can be no doubt that the military presence in Berlin set the fashion tone in the city: "By the turn of the nineteenth century, the spring review and the fall exercises had become regular events in the Berlin fashion season. *Die Zeitung für die elegante Welt* reported in 1801 that the May review was the crowning event of spring" (Purdy 207–8). However, the influence of Friedrich the Great's tattered, and often dirty, wardrobe on that scene was less direct. Purdy reads it not as "a collapse of military rigor; rather, it memorialized its historical accomplishments" (216). He further notes the similarities between it and the attitude Werther is depicted as having towards his clothing in Goethe's 1774 *The Sufferings of Young Werther*. Purdy cites a letter published in the *Mode Journal* in April 1791, from which he deduces the influence of the *Werthermode* as a signifying system which allowed young men to challenge "the very mechanisms by which bodies were regulated within corporate society":

The young fashionable Berliner of the distinguished and largest class wears, from morning until night, boots, a round hat, a blue coat with a red collar, in a very militarist style and very often with dirty linen. Dressed in this manner, he goes to lectures, to Unter den Linden, to coffeehouses, a meal, again to Unter den Linden, to the theater, and very often into society. He enters polite society only when parents, a love affair, or some other convenience brings him there, and under no circumstances can he be bothered to change his attire. He is hardly concerned whether his clothes fit the colors or ornaments of the season.... What is formal attire to him? That would seem fussy. And why adorn himself? For whom? He simply has no need to. (166, translation modified)

Purdy is astute in linking Werther's sentimentalism as revealed by the novel's form, its "fragmented and private epistolary monologue," and the militarist masculinity on display throughout Berlin to the same interpretative paradigm: "one that sought to correlate knowledge of an interior consciousness with exterior bodily signs" (178), and he knows better than to claim that either Friedrich or Werther were more than trendsetters for a relatively small, if nonetheless influential, segment of the population.

Purdy thus helpfully identifies several factors that slowed Berlin's track to fashion until the 1800s. Based on an account in the *Mode Journal*, the arduous physical distance from the fashion centers of London and Paris has to top the list:

The shortest route, by which we receive ladies' fashions, runs over Frankfurt and Leipzig. The French merchant packs up the newest fashions in a box, some of which were never worn in Paris, others no one wants to wear anymore. He consigns the whole lot to the barbarians of the North and sends it to the Frankfurt and Leipzig fairs – that already takes time. From there, our merchants bring it to Berlin, but only after another two months have passed. (120–1)

More debatable is the extent to which the development of the ready-to-wear industry in Berlin can be attributed to the military. Purdy establishes that "[b]y 1782, Berlin had become one of Europe's largest wool-producing cities, with 300 weavers and roughly 3,000 looms producing 113,104 garments for both soldiers and civilians" (197), but he refuses to take sides in the debate about its effects: "According to Werner Sombart, the 19th-century ready-to-wear clothing industry developed from the economies of scale required by the manufacture of uniforms, and guild tailors were increasingly employed as wage workers by textile entrepreneurs. Krause disagreed with the point but did support Sombart's overall thesis that Prussian demand for uniforms brought about innovations in the textile industry fundamental to the emergence of a fashion clothing industry in Berlin" (Purdy Fn 10, 275, cf. Sombart 170–3, Krause 204–5). Purdy then refers his readers to Westphal, where one finds that Westphal's interest is in the situation of the Jews under Friedrich, the bettering of which is attributed not as much to any humanistic leanings on Friedrich's part but rather to his interest in them as taxpayers and a potentially effective economic factor for the state

(Westphal 14). The rise of the ready-to-wear industry results, in Westphal's view, from a confluence of favorable conditions, especially new transport and trade routes, which helped to enlarge local markets, as well as the approximately 800 newspapers in circulation by 1840, many of which with features on fashion (travel reports on Parisian fashion seem to have been particularly popular) (16). Up until that point, the circumstances which Purdy outlines seems to have prevailed: "The demand that enabled large-scale producers to organize themselves as industrial enterprises was…provided primarily by the military and the court. A wider market of middle-class consumers had not yet developed in Berlin/Brandenburg" (4). The influence of the military has to be seen therefore as substantial, if debatable, and in any case not wholly responsible for the rise of the ready-to-wear industry in the nineteenth century; its presence was already determinative in the early eighteenth century, and yet the city was at that point not ready for ready-to-wear.

The negative influence of the Prussian court on the rise of fashion in Berlin, on the other hand, was unquestionable, given its rejection of any and all forms of wasteful frippery: "the Hohenzollerns, renowned for their frugality, were held up as having eschewed representational ostentation in favor of an ideology of individual worth" (Purdy 110). An article in the December 1787 *Mode Journal* confirms that the popular reaction to the royal family's walk in a Berlin park was indeed influenced by royal sentiment: "The worthiness of the monarchical personage subsists in himself, not in borrowed splendor, which is why everyone present bowed before them and not their clothes. Very little Asiatic or French luxury is to be found at the Prussian court; hence its power and wealth" (Purdy Fn 59, 266). It was not the case, however, that subjects may not have desired fashionable goods, but rather that they had been properly disciplined to reject them. Purdy underscores the effectiveness of police laws and other state measures to control consumption. In praising Prussian control of foreign luxury goods, the anonymous female author also implicitly mapped the limitations of economic and criminal disincentives to consume (115):

> Actually, many Berliners would do more in the way of luxury; some charming foreign fashion ware would certainly tempt the ordinary Berliner for once to not let his left hand know what his right is doing; however, the excise taxes and customs charges applied to everything foreign are out of proportion compared to other countries. The Berliner thinks it over, resignedly turns his desiring eyes from the alluring object, and falls back into formation with his dear old sense of economy. His wife reads in the *Mode Journal* that her sisters along the Danube and the Rhine are wearing French linen and English muslin – "O dearest husband, I would so very much like a little muslin dress!" "Of course, dear child, but the custom duties!" And Madame continues to wear Silesian linen. (Jan. 1791, cited in Purdy, 12)

Berliners, like other Germans, may have developed quite a fashion sense in the eighteenth century, mainly but not exclusively due to texts like the *Mode Journal* and *Werther*. Purdy offers a key qualification on this point: "This is not to say that German consumer culture was entirely based on the simulation of real products through textual and imagistic representations; however, a considerable proportion of what counted as material reality in London and Paris passed as a literary reconstruction among the German *Bildungsbürgertum*" (xiv). What his study usefully explains is why German cities, including Berlin, did not matter much as far as fashion was concerned before the nineteenth century. Well into the 1800s, fashion remained for them something one expected to read about but not encounter in one's surroundings.

The fate of the *Mode Journal* underscores the end of the textual era Purdy so ably demarcates: "In its final year, 1827, the title was changed once more to *Journal für Literatur, Kunst, und geselliges Zusammenleben (Journal for Literature, Art and Sociability)*. The increasing de-emphasis on the words *Mode* and *Luxus* reflected the increasing self-confidence of German readers in their own fashion judgments as well as the journal's increasingly futile attempt to keep up with its competition. Fashion prints began to disappear from the journal after 1823. The few that did appear accompanied literary references" (Purdy Fn 27, 247), a trend that continued, as we saw in the previous chapter, until the Lipperheides' *Modenwelt* began publishing in 1865 with a strict focus on the practicalities of fashion.[3]

Westphal picks up the story at this point with the founding of several highly successful and influential firms: in 1815 by Nathan Israel of a textile-trade business; in 1836 by Hermann Gerson, born Hirsch Gerson Levin in Königsberg, of a business which traded in silk, needlework, lace and French linen in the Königliche Bauakademie No. 3 (Fig. 2.1); in 1837 by the Manheimer brothers David, Moritz and Valentin of a company that made men's coats;[4] in 1839 by Rudolph Hertzog of a ready-to-wear shop in the Breitegasse (Fig. 2.2); and in 1840 by David Leib Levin of a business that manufactured women's coats at Gertraudenstrasse 11; these addresses are all at the southern (i.e., non-museum) end of the Museum Island (Fig. 2.3). As Westphal documents, ready-to-wear soon became the most important branch of Berlin's economy, thanks in no small part to thriving exports, and he gives readers a flavor of an average day in the life of a ready-to-wear industrialist by including a lengthy excerpt from Moritz Loeb's 1906 *Berliner Konfektion. Großstadt-Dokumente (Berlin Ready-to-Wear, Documents from a Metropolis)* (32–7), a rather different focus than, for example, Alexandra Richie's, whose account of industrializing Berlin includes the following:

The clothing industry was particularly repugnant. Women were forced to work in sweat shops for starvation wages in utterly degrading conditions; one presser, Ottilie Baader, described her life as endless grey drudgery in which years passed without her noticing that she had 'once been young.' Cheap labour kept German textiles competitive and there were nearly 500 wholesale garment dealers in Berlin in 1895 which exported goods all over the world, but the price was high. The women sewing and pressing in the Berlin sweat shops lived to an average age of twenty-six. (169)

Both the Franco-Prussian War of 1870 and WWI served to nationalize as well as further spur on the industry. As Westphal notes, the Association of Women's Fashion and Its Industry

Figure 2.1: The large sales room, lighted from above, of House Hermann Gerson at Werdersche Markt 5. (Stadtmuseum Berlin)

(*Verband der Damenmode und ihrer Industrie*), founded in 1916, had as its main goals to make Germany independent of French fashion, to unify German fashion guidelines and to enhance Berlin as a central fashion hub (46). The purpose of the first Fashion Week it organized in 1917 was to prove that German fashion could stand up to the "French fashion policies" (46). That standing up to could also mean adapting to is evident in the Berliner Chic of the interwar period: women's couture and ready-to-wear clothing made in Berlin following Parisian models (49) and a distinctive local arrangement of highly competitive companies unwilling to form cartels (62), who farmed out their production to thousands of small homeworker-factories located mostly in the working-class districts in northern and eastern Berlin (66). Westphal marshals together the relevant statistics to provide a snapshot of the industry that was then systematically eradicated by the Nazis, in a process he documents with equal exactitude.

The approach of Roberta Kremer's *Broken Threads: From Aryanization to Cultural Loss – The Destruction of the Jewish Fashion Industry in Germany and Austria* collection is precisely the opposite of Westphal's. While Westphal was trying to establish that the ready-to-wear industry in Berlin was not as Jewish as it had been made out to be, *Broken Threads* showcases

Figure 2.2: The sales room of Rudolph Hertzog's, around the year 1850. (Stadtmuseum Berlin)

the pre-Holocaust work of fashion designers and manufacturers in Germany and Austria as explicitly Jewish and documents the destruction of the Jewish fashion industry in Germany and Austria. Based on an exhibition of original German and Austrian clothing collected by Vancouver-based collector and fashion historian Claus Jahnke, which was put on in 1999 by the Vancouver Holocaust Education Centre in partnership with the Original Costume Museum Society of Vancouver, *Broken Threads* framed the work of "the Jewish designers, retailers and manufacturers who played an important role in the German-Austrian fashion scene prior to World War II" with images of "Nazi propaganda, boycotts, humiliation, and Aryanization" (Kremer 3). The sumptuously illustrated catalogue contains short articles by leading scholars that provide a solid overview of the history of Jewish fashion production and display in Germany and Austria before the Holocaust, with both Berlin and Vienna addressed in separate contributions. Ingrid Loschek's "Contributions of Jewish Fashion Designers in Berlin" provides a well-documented overview, while Christian Schramm would have been remiss not to have included in "Architecture in the German Department Store" the Wertheim, Tietz, and Erich Mendelsohn-designed Schocken department stores in Berlin.

Figure 2.3: Stairwell memorial at the Hausvogteiplatz U-Bahn: "From the Address Book of the Berlin Ready-To-Wear Firms". (Photo: K. Sark)

Irene Guenther's monumental 2004 monograph, *Nazi Chic? Fashioning Women in the Third Reich*, retraces and expands on this ground for an English-speaking readership. Like Westphal, Guenther's motivation is to dispel a myth: not that Jews accounted for 90% of German fashion but rather that Nazi fashion was an oxymoron. Her starting point is that German women, "especially in cities like Berlin and Hamburg, ranked among the most elegantly dressed in all of inter-war Europe" (18). How then, Guenther wonders, did the few with money and connections maintain this elegance in the 1930s? How did the majority experience the decreasing clothing options so characteristic of the Nazi years, and how did women deal with these transformations, especially as the consequences of a lengthy war led to severe shortages? (18) Drawing on the evidence in "surviving fashion magazines, society pages, fashion school archives, and advertisements" (275) as well as personal interviews, Guenther substantiates and expands on the conclusion of Angelika Klose's "Frauenmode im Dritten Reich" (Women's Fashion in the Third Reich): "many German women, whether in the upper echelons of society or in the middle or lower social rungs, tried to fashion themselves in their clothing and makeup according to the latest international trends. Using patterns, buying ready-to-wear from department stores, or ordering their fashions from exclusive salons, they preferred and generally wore the same styles that their sisters did in Britain, France and the United States, both before and during the World War" (Klose 265–6). Fashion, in other words, was able to withstand the war's destructiveness far better than other sectors of society. The failures of the Berlin-based German Fashion Institute, "which was established less than five months after Hitler came to power" (Guenther 167), are convincingly shown by Guenther to have been of its own making and not therefore to be attributed solely to the war (201). The institute was established as a response to an announcement by Hitler in early June 1933 that he wanted Berlin women to become the best-dressed women in Europe. The pronounced national slant of Hitler's interest is evident in both the name and mandate of the institute. Originally called the *Deutsches Modeamt* but soon renamed the *Deutsches Mode-Institut*, it was to come up with designs that would "reflect the nature and character of the German woman" (170). While Guenther's interest is similarly in the national, the capital Berlin and its fashion do figure in her work. In order to properly historically contextualize the Nazi period, Guenther provides preparatory chapters on the fashion debate in WWI and the "new" woman, both of which feature Berlin fashion, and she helpfully makes us aware of the founding not only of the Association of Women's Fashion and its Industry (45–8) but also the earlier founding, in December 1915, of the Fashion Museum Society, its "200 Years of Clothing Art 1700–1900" exhibit, discussed in the previous chapter, and the Berlin Fashion Week, which "was resurrected after only a short end-of-war hiatus" (59) and continued on a semiannual basis under increasingly difficult conditions until, in 1925, it was replaced by a *Bekleidungsmesse* or clothing fair (Fn 59, 312). Guenther finds Berlin's interwar golden years, 1924–1929, aptly summed up by Carl Zuckmayer's statement that then "[t]o conquer Berlin was to conquer the world" (Guenther 67), and one can't but agree with either that or her choice and elaboration of masculinization, Americanization, anti-French sentiment and anti-Semitism as the four cornerstones of Berlin's golden years.[5] In establishing just how personally the German nation as a whole took fashion both before and during WWII, Guenther makes clear that the propagandizing efforts of the Nazis to turn German women into unmodern, "Gretchen-like" plait- and dirndl-wearers, which she documents in great detail, were doomed to failure.

While Berlin is as little the intended focus of Judd Stitziel's 2005 *Fashioning Socialism: Clothing, Politics and Consumer Culture in East Germany* as it is of Guenther's study, the city played as large a role as a place of fashion in the German Democratic Republic as it did before and during the Third Reich. Both Guenther and Stitziel concentrate on explaining the seemingly contradictory existence of fashion under regimes which aimed to keep their societies under tight control. They show that both regimes understood themselves to be in fierce competition with cross-border opponents whose international fashion ranking was far superior (France and West Germany), both regimes found fashion an unavoidable and integral part of the larger struggles they waged, and both populations rejected their regimes' attempts to impose so-called folk costumes (*Trachtenkleider* like the dirndl) on them (Stitziel 52–4; Guenther 2004, chapter 5). Just as Hitler was keen on a German fashion institute that would make Berlin women the best-dressed in Europe, so too was one of the goals of the East German state's New Course in 1953 "to develop Berlin as a fashion center (*Modezentrum*)…and restore the city to its former glory as a 'center of German fashion'" (Stitziel 24). Officials in the ruling Socialist Unity Party (*Sozialistische Einheitspartei Deutschlands* or SED) "lamented that after 1948, West Berlin had built up virtually from scratch a formidable garment industry equipped with 'the most modern technology,' an industry that not only was leaving East Berlin's outdated factories behind on international markets [In 1956, the average machine in the GDR's textile industry was, according to Stitziel, thirty-three years old (40)], but also was stealing the GDR's best skilled garment workers. Berlin officials noted that the ready-to-wear industry was the only industrial branch in West Berlin 'that developed faster than the corresponding industrial branch' in East Berlin" (25). However, their ambitious plans to turn the pre-WWII area associated with the ready-to-wear industry – from Hausvogteiplatz to Dönhoffplatz to Spittelmarkt, which now lay in the East – into a "full-fledged 'ready-to-wear quarter'" (*Konfektionsviertel*) (Stitziel 24) were not able to get off the ground for reasons Stitziel elaborates in a chapter on the logic and contingencies of planning, producing, and distributing. One better appreciates the successes of the pre-WWII ready-to-wear industrialists when one reads of the difficulties the East German textile and garment industries ran into at every turn. The main state institution responsible for "designing, propagating, and facilitating the production and distribution of the official 'Fashion Line of the GDR' (*Modelinie der DDR*)" was founded in 1952 and called the Institute for Clothing Culture (*Institut für Bekleidungskultur*) but rebaptized five years later with the same name as the Nazi German Fashion Institute (*Deutsches Modeinstitut*), and Stitziel is quick to note the "many interesting points of comparison between the two organizations' missions, operations, and ultimate failures" (Fn 26, 179–80), both notably being charged with "promoting a clothing culture connected to our national cultural heritage" (54).

Equally interesting for comparative purposes are the Berlin Fashion Weeks held after WWI and those held between 1958 and 1962. Designed as an "achievement show" that would demonstrate the GDR's commitment to revitalizing the state-owned garment industry and to making Berlin a fashion center, the post-WWII fashion weeks had a much more overtly pedagogical mission, accompanied as they were by educational lectures and booths staffed by "fashion designers from the state-owned women's garment factories, from the fashion magazine *Sibylle*, and from the German Fashion Institute" on hand to explain the process of fashion production (Stitziel 74). Moreover, the reach of the East German fashion weeks seems to have at least tried to be larger as a number of smaller fashion shows were organized "in various districts throughout East Berlin and in factories during lunch breaks" (75). Stitziel shows that officials responded to complaints about the disparity between the fashion on display and the actual goods available for purchase in stores by ensuring that stock included "not only accessories, jewelry, and cosmetics, but also shoes, dresses, suits, and children's clothing" (77); the extent of that demand can be gauged by the increased sales figures Stitziel notes (from 1.2 million Deutsch Marks [DM] in the spring of 1960 to 3 million DM in the fall of 1961) (77). The East German variant of Berlin Fashion Week came to as quiet and abrupt a halt as its predecessor. Somehow a fall 1961 Fashion Week was still possible, with visitors viewing the event, unsurprisingly given the erection of the Wall in August of that year, as "solely a good shopping opportunity, especially for scare assortments" (77). However, Stitziel provides no further details or commentary, and much more remains to be brought forth from the archives to elucidate this pivotal period comprehensively.

The shortcomings of state planning, on the other hand, receive ample substantiation. Matching the supply of ready-to-wear goods in the stories to consumer demand was a trick that eluded East German officials for the duration of the country's existence. In 1973, for example, retail personnel "estimated that approximately half of the ready-to-wear articles currently in stores were 'difficult to market.' Low-quality goods continued to pile up while high-quality goods made of certain materials – especially synthetics – continued to be snapped up" (Stitziel 117). This gap was exacerbated by the one between price and the quality of East German apparel and the fact that it was much more expensive than its West German equivalent and of perceptibly inferior quality (81). Despite opening a special type of stores for cheap surplus goods (BIWA, a shortening of *Billige Waren*, or cheap goods) (104)[6] and *Luxusläden* (luxury shops) for higher quality goods, such as the Sibylle boutique, which opened on the corner of Unter den Linden and Friedrichstraße in 1957 (124–6), as well as the founding in 1954 of the VEB Maßatelier, a studio in Berlin for custom clothing, a workable balance proved elusive and was managed by exporting surpluses both to fellow Warsaw Pact countries on credit and to the West "'under special conditions,' a euphemism for large discounts" (117). Selling unpopular garments by the kilogram did nothing to improve the image of East German fashion. However, Berlin's own image remained relatively untarnished. Rather, it figured as a place of seductive success, no doubt in part because of the presence there of stores like the Sibylle boutique, "representative" stores that sold the creations of the German Fashion Institute and other "predominantly highly fashionable products" and came to be called Exquisit stores (127). In the DEFA production *Modell Bianka* (1951, dir. Richard Groschopp), for example, the Berlin garment factory and its female managers outsmart, and thereby hold their own in competition with, a male-managed garment factory in Saxony (Stitziel 68–9; cf. Feinstein 31). While East German fashion functionaries may have admonished their population that "We must not ogle the Kurfürstendamm (the famous shopping avenue in West Berlin) so much. That is decidedly unhealthy" (Stitziel 67), they were unable to prevent that population, like those in Guenther's and Purdy's studies, from pursuing fashion to the extent circumstances allowed, from shopping at Exquisit stores to visiting stores every week or two and trying to determine "when shipments arrived to be among the first to peruse the new goods" (146) to making or refashioning one's own clothes.

A very different image of fashion in East Berlin is to be found in Marco Wilms' documentary *Ein Traum in Erdbeerfolie: Comrade Couture* (*A Dream in Plastic for Strawberries: Comrade Couture*), whose debut at the 2008 Berlinale was followed by a fashion show.[7] Wilms worked as a model for the GDR's Fashion Institute in East Berlin, and the documentary self-consciously reflects on his encounter with the East Berlin underground fashion scene in the 1980s from the historical distance of the twenty years that have passed since the GDR's demise. Like the "Free within Limits/Borders: Fashion, Photography, Underground, GDR 1979–89" exhibition at the *Kunstgewerbemuseum* in the summer of 2009, discussed in the previous chapter, Wilms' project is a stereotype-bashing one.[8] He sets out to dispel the mistaken impression that official East German culture, that is, the one Stitziel found evidence of in the archives, was all there was. Rather, a lively alternative subculture existed that was heavily influenced by punk, Goth and New Wave aesthetics. The plastic for strawberries in Wilms' title pays homage to the ability of those in the East Berlin fashion underground to turn shortages to their creative advantage. Clothes were sewn out of every available material, including shower curtains and the plastic farmers used to wrap strawberries. In addition to these clothes, outrageous hair and make-up styles, and highly sexualized behavior served to provoke, outrage and challenge everything the GDR stood for and failed to deliver.

The East Berlin underground fashion subculture was made up of creative artists such as designer Sabine von Oettingen, hair-stylist Frank Schäfer, and photographer and model Robert Paris, who staged fashion shows and photo shoots that mocked and provoked the restrictions of the repressive GDR regime. Like the "Free within Limits/Borders" exhibition, Wilms' documentary features clips recorded of fashion performances by two groups: *Chic, Charmant und Dauerhaft* (Stylish, Charming and Durable), known as CCD, and *Allerleirauh* (All Kinds of Fur). These shows "grew increasingly elaborate, eventually featuring original music scores and over a hundred designs created purely for a handful of packed performances attended by a small network of fashionistas and rebels" (Winter). Wilms comments in the documentary that the inclusion of authentic footage was important as it made clear the stark contrast between the fashion rebels and their state: "the dismal performances celebrated the downfall… Because amidst the GDR decay they were young and full of life. Like me."[9] On the other hand, he recognizes the Janus-faced nature of the changes brought about by the end of that decay; while celebrating the GDR's end, he also admitted in an interview that it "destroyed my career as a top model" (Thönnissen).

In his quest to work through the ambivalence of having the revolutionary spirit of the underground fashion scene now associated with a regime that it was, at the time, at odds with, Wilms brings together some of its protagonists: Sabine von Oettingen still designs clothes from unusual fabrics but now buys those fabrics in Paris and sells the results from her studio in the small town of Polleben in Saxony-Anhalt; Frank Schäfer has a salon in Prenzlauer-Berg; and Robert Paris has become an orthodox Muslim. Together they recreate the experience of one of their fashion shows. Staged in an apartment in Neue Schönhauser Strasse (amidst the new fashion and designer scene in reunited Berlin that we discuss in Chapter Six), the show celebrates the craft that gave meaning to their youth and asserts the urbanity of their identity. Never do they refer to themselves as "Ossies." Rather it is their allegiance to East Berlin, and not East Germany, which motivates the show. The opening sequence before the credits, for example, features a row of Trabants pulling up in front of the Brandenburg Gate and models wearing outfits that hearken back to the socialist '70s twirling in front of them. It is followed by a scene involving musicians dressed in a mishmash of khaki clothing driving around in a military truck past socialist relics of significance to East Berlin's past. To a tune that for an international festival-attending film audience evokes an atmosphere similar to that of ex-Yugoslav films like Kusturica's 1995 *Underground*, they sing: "Vom Alex bis zum Tauntzien, überall ist nur Berlin. Du bist das Tor zur freien Welt, alles was mir fehlt ist Geld" (From Alex to Tauntzien, everywhere is only Berlin. You are the gate to the free world, all I lack is money). Wilms' band is on personal "Du" terms with the city. It is not an authoritative "Sie" for them but an equal, a friend. By repeatedly chanting "West Berlin, Ost Berlin, West Berlin, Ost Berlin, Nord Berlin, Süd Berlin, Rand Berlin, ganz Berlin" (west, east, west, east, north, south, edge, whole), they try to heal the city's divisions. At Alexanderplatz, they stop, and the lead singer announces through his megaphone: "Long live East Berlin and fashion from East Berlin!" While Berlin has been doing its best to attract workers in the creative industries, those for whom the designation "workers" implies solidarity, that is, those from the former East, feel just as dispossessed and at odds with their surroundings as they did in the GDR. Wilms' documentary is a poignant expression of this discomfort with the city's new capitalist underpinnings.

Another historical approach to Berlin fashion appears in the informative brochure Manuela Goos and Brigitte Heyde assembled for the "Kleider Machen Frauen" (Clothes Makes the Woman/Women Makes Clothes) exhibition, which was held from 7 November 1990 to 13 January 1991 in the Heimatmuseum Charlottenburg and focused on women in the post-WWII fashion industry in Charlottenburg, the borough in Berlin which radiates from the Kurfürstendamm west of Mitte and was the commercial center of West Berlin. Based on oral history-informed interviews with a wide range of workers formerly involved in the fashion industry ("berufsbiographische Interviews"), their study was written to provide a "realistic counterweight" to Cordula Moritz's 1971 romanticizing anecdotal account of the industry (Goos and Heyde 4). Because previous accounts of the women's outerwear industry in post-WWII Charlottenburg had been either in the service of the industry or the city's public relations, it was deemed important to provide an academic account, which "connects local history, oral history, the history of everyday life and gender studies" (8). This "history from below" takes its cues from, and is based on, the careers of representative women who were active in the industry between 1945 and 1985: Ursula Schewe, one of the few female fashion designers in Berlin to achieve success and international renown in the 1950s (14–17); a woman who worked as an independent "Zwischenmeisterin" and for fifteen years ran a small company that filled orders for Staebe-Seger, a prestigious Berlin couturier that closed in 1971; a Eurasian model, who worked for Gehringer & Glupp collections from 1956 to 1965 and showed items in the recent collections first in-house and then for out-of-town visitors and at the Düsseldorf fashion fairs; and finally three women who trained to be tailors and whose later careers in Berlin women's wear companies prove that measures designed to improve efficiency based on American industrial standards did not necessarily lead women to career dead ends (22). The first went on to work as a sewing machinist (*Maschinennäherin*) for a coat and dress factory that, in the 1960s, had a reputation as Germany's model company (23).

Another went on to work happily first as a cutter and then, after having a child and getting divorced, a further career training "especially young foreign women for the exam to become a seamstress (*Bekleidungsnäher-bzw. Fertiger*) (25). The third was encouraged by the Employment Office not to pursue her dreams of being an interior decorator but rather to train as a tailor and ended up finding more satisfactory employment as the Secretary for the Textile and Clothing Union.

The anecdotal approach Cordula Moritz adopted for her two books on Berlin fashion, which Goos and Heyde took as their object lesson for how not to write a history of Berlin fashion, reflects Moritz's long career (1946–1980) as fashion editor of Berlin's *Tagesspiegel* (*Daily Mirror*). Moritz's style is certainly among the breeziest and most personal of accountings of Berlin fashion. Unlike Westphal, who begins his story of Berlin fashion with Berlin's beginnings in the thirteenth century, and unlike Gretel Wagner, who begins the contribution she was asked to make to the *Berlin en vogue* catalogue by contrasting the beginning of haute couture in Paris and the slightly earlier beginnings of ready-to-wear in Berlin, Moritz uses the opportunity of reunification as an "elegant alibi" (1991, 8) in her memoir-like 1991 *Linienspiele: 70 Jahre Mode in Berlin* (*Games with Lines: 70 Years of Fashion in Berlin*) to remember back to the period she wishes she could have experienced personally had she only been twenty years older (10). The popular "golden '20s" is an era Moritz sees as having all but disappeared from Berliners' memories, and she calls it to mind as an incentive to regain the legendary status the city then enjoyed. Citing Karl Lagerfeld, that "When Berlin is again capital, it has the chance to again be the centre of fashion in Germany. Until now it hasn't been possible for there to be such a centre, no other city in Germany could create such a fashion centre" (8), Moritz underscores the lessons to be learned from this magical decade after the "first great caesura of the century," in which the "storm of history swept away bustles, whalebone corsets, long skirts and button-up boots" (10) and women were freed to pursue their own interests. Not everywhere, "[b]ut in the large cities, and especially here in Berlin, the capital, fashion and women took a courageous leap into a new age of self-confidence" (10), precisely the confidence she then follows as it is eradicated by Nazism, rebuilt after WWII around the Kurfürstendamm, and then, in the face of the Cold War division, forced to either relocate or regroup, such as in the Klub der Avantgarde Berlin (KAB) and Offline, a group of 17 small fashion firms that banded together in 1983 to offer a kind of anti-chic that proved popular during the 1980s.

The most recent and in many ways most impressive historical monograph to include Berlin fashion, Mila Ganeva's 2008 *Women in Weimar Fashion,* again returns to the glamorous interwar period. Pursuing a "cultural-historical investigation" that "focuses primarily on the years 1918–33 and limits its scope to Berlin and its sartorial practices because…it was there and then, in the German metropolis of the 1920s, that the most dazzling spectacles and spirited debates about women's fashion took place" (2008, 7, 1) Ganeva demonstrates that, despite the wealth of existing scholarship on Weimar and its modernity and modernism, the fashion of the period, whose technologically mediated depictions we locate in the following chapters, has received inordinately little attention. Taking her cues in the first instance from Patrice Petro's *Joyless Streets*, Janet Ward's *Weimar Surfaces* and Andreas Huyssen's *After the Great Divide*, Ganeva looks at both discourses on and displays of Berlin fashion.[10] In describing female fashion journalists as a cross between flâneurs and new women, she impressively condenses the scholarship on both before turning to the fashion journals and magazines they published in, which are presented as a type of "Frauenöffentlichkeit" (women's public sphere): "a sphere in which women openly began to participate as agents and in which specifically female attitudes toward modernity were intensively negotiated" (51). The scope of this sphere – "over 90 periodicals, including the fashion supplements to the daily newspapers" (51) – necessitates a selective approach, and Ganeva wisely settles on Ullstein House, the largest publishing empire in the Weimar Republic, and two of its periodicals: *Das Blatt der Hausfrau* (*The Housewife's Magazine*), which specialized in sewing patterns, and the "more high-brow and sumptuously illustrated *Die Dame*" (54), both of which in different ways "facilitated the rise of woman as an 'individualized personality' with autonomous aesthetic choices" (76). In further chapters she looks at the fashion writing of Berlin-born Helen (Hessel) Grund (1886–1982), "perhaps best known as the inspiration for the Jeanne Moreau character, Kathe, in François Truffant's film *Jules et Jim* (1962)" (85; cf. Stam); the fashion in *Gilgi*, the debut novel of Berlin-born Irmgard Keun (1905–1982); Weimar cinema as a continuation of the fashion show and fashion contest, most notably the *Konfektionskomödien* (fashion farces) but also Brigitte Helm vehicles such as the iconic *Metropolis*; and finally the ambiguous presence of both display window and live mannequins.

Fashion has been an influential factor in the larger historical transformations that have marked Berlin's growth, and historical accounts prove as invaluable a source of material on Berlin fashion as the collections and exhibitions documented in the previous chapter. These narratives have been shaped by the exigencies of modern historiography and tend to take the larger nation as the focus, detailing forces that have gone into its making (as in the studies of the eighteenth and nineteenth centuries) and examining decisive periods (primarily Weimar, the Third Reich and East Germany). While fashion as a subject has benefited from, and indeed exists thanks to, the expansion of historiographical methodologies to include social considerations such as gender and approaches such as oral and microhistory, as we will see in the rest of the study, there is still much that does not fit into such narratives. Ganeva's study points the way in this regard, expanding her scope to include popular cultural products, such as magazines and films. Rather than trying to figure out what really happened and to prove "how it really was" (*wie es eigentlich gewesen ist*), we need to recognize that how we read the accounts of what happened has been influenced by the style of the images and sounds we associate with the city, and so we need to include them in our considerations as well. In order to flesh out the specific qualities of Berlin fashion, the urban imaginary designated by the term "Berliner Chic," we turn next to technologically mediated modern cultural practices, beginning with photography.

Notes

1. For analyses of the *Historikerstreit*, see Maier and Eley.
2. For more on the *Mode Journal*, see the volume edited by Angela Borchert and Ralf Dressel of papers given at a June 2000 meeting to share results of the "DFG-Sonderforschungsbereich 482, Ereignis Weimar-Jena. Kultur um 1800." For a useful English-language review of this volume, see Anne Wanner's "Textiles in History" website: http://www.annatextiles.ch/book_rev/rev2005/r2306mode/r2306mod.htm.
3. There is a significant gap in the mid-nineteenth century in both Bertschik's and Zika's studies. Bertschik's moves from clothing symbolism in literature between 1770 and 1830 to the autonomy of clothing fashion in literature between 1880 and 1914, while Zika's jumps from looking at the development of German fashion magazines in the first half of the nineteenth century directly to the twentieth century, so that the Lipperheides and their influential *Modenwelt* are reduced to a passing reference (Zika 131).
4. *Herrenschlafröcke* – according to Gretel Wagner (1993, 114). She offers a further nuance in pointing out that Valentin left his brothers' business in 1839 to open his own shop at Oberwallstraße 6.
5. No scholar interested in German-language fashion can afford to ignore the compendium of sources Guenther lists in footnote 180 (324–5) or footnote 90 of the Introduction (289–91).
6. There were over 800 BIWA stores in the GDR in 1957 (105). *Die Bekleidung* (Clothing), "a magazine intended for both employees of the textile industry and regular consumers, noted 'the crass difference' between 'an unpleasant-looking' BIWA store in Berlin's recently renovated Schönhauser Allee and the streets' 'many modern stores'" (106).
7. A clip of the fashion show is available on YouTube under the title: "Comrade Couture – Ein Traum in Erdbeerfolie" (http://www.youtube.com/watch?v=Cb4SQ_p9c4o).
8. According to Waidenschlager, the curators of the exhibition developed their idea parallel to the documentary but purposefully maintained their own approach and focus (personal correspondence of 12 March 2010).
9. These are the English subtitles on the documentary. The original is: "Die düsteren Shows zelebrierten den Untergang. Vielleicht faszinierte mich der Gegensatz? Denn inmitten des DDR Verfalls, waren sie jung und voller Leben. Wie ich."
10. Like Guenther's, Ganeva's footnotes are enormously rich and an indispensable source of material in German and English for scholars interested in Berlin fashion.

Chapter 3

Berliner Chic and Photography

"Photography as such has no identity…[because i]t is a flickering across a field of institutional spaces…. [I]t is this field we must study, not photography as such…. What alone unites the diversity of sites in which photography operates is the social formation itself: the specific historical spaces for representation and practice which it constitutes."

(Tagg 246)

Fashion and photography have much in common, as Elizabeth Wilson notes at the beginning of the Foreword to the second edition of *Adorned in Dreams*:

Both are liminal forms, on the threshold between art and not-art. Both are industrially produced, yet deeply individual. Both are poised ambiguously between present and past: The photograph congeals the essence of the now, while fashion freezes the moment in an eternal gesture of the-only-right-way-to-be. Yet nothing more poignantly testifies to transience than the embalmed moments preserved in those old snapshots where we pose in yesterday's clothes. Far from stopping time, they locate us in history. "Now is past," wrote the eighteenth century poet, John Clare, and the "now" of fashion is nostalgia in the making. (Wilson vii)

Wilson owes much of this analysis to the work of two Berliners: Georg Simmel (1858–1918) and Walter Benjamin (1892–1940). In locating Simmel's and Benjamin's work on fashion and photography, we find that Berlin photographers of fashion approached their metier not as an avant-garde art practice but rather primarily as a welcome opportunity for securing a livelihood, which is not to deny or decry the artistic merit of their work but rather to point to the liminal position of its production vis-à-vis the art world and to the inherently split nature of that world, which is, as we know from Marshall Berman and Max Weber, one of the key characteristics of modernity. The main difference between the male photographers from Simmel's and Benjamin's Berlin – like Heinrich Zille, Helmut Newton, and Rico Puhlmann – and female ones – like Yva and Ringl & Pit – all of whose work we will be discussing in this chapter, is that the latter felt the need to adopt professional pseudonyms (only East German Sybille Bergemann did not). The city's industrial history made itself felt in the trade orientation and emphasis on socio-economics over aesthetics that is characteristic of all of their work. Newton may be the only one explicitly known as a "gun for hire" (Fig. 3.1),[1] but he was hardly the only one to understand himself in those terms.

Figure 3.1: "A Gun for Hire" exhibit at the Museum for Photography, 2005. (Photo: K. Sark)

The fleeting, ruptured, industrially modern qualities of Berlin, the city famously condemned by Karl Scheffler in 1910 to always become and never to be, ensured that both fashion and photography would flourish there in a way they couldn't elsewhere. Italian cities, for example, have had to deal with an aesthetic legacy that still prevents fashion photographers from receiving the recognition they deserve (a tendency the 2005 *Italian Eyes* project was developed to overcome). In mid-nineteenth-century France and Britain, there were also fierce debates about whether photography should be considered an art and admitted to exhibitions of, for example, the *Académie des beaux-arts*. In 1862, photography was classified as machinery at the International Exhibition in London (Gernsheim 1988, 35).

That Berlin has provided a fertile field for fashion, photography and the field in which they intersect, fashion photography, to be both theorized and practiced, is related to the city's uniquely parvenu nature and the fact that the city came of age with the new technology. The daguerreotype was immediately popular in the growing city. While invented in France, six daguerreotypes were ordered in advance of their publication by Louis Sachse, "an art-dealer and proprietor of a lithographic establishment in Berlin…who was in Paris on business in April 1839 [and] had arranged with Daguerre personally that he should be the first person in Germany to receive the apparatus" (Gernsheim 1982, 151). They arrived in Berlin on 6 September severely damaged, which impeded Sachse's advantage. On 15 September, "Sachse had the mortification of seeing a locally made apparatus exhibited at the premises of the optician Theodor Dörffel in Unter den Linden" (151). While by 1842–43 "all European capitals and large towns had one or more portrait studios, or at least were visited by itinerant photographers" (166), the Germans took a particularly keen interest in the daguerreotype, something "evinced by the surprisingly large number of ten publications which appeared within the first two months in Berlin, Stuttgart, Karlsruhe, Hamburg, Halle and Leipzig. In fact more brochures appeared in Germany than in any other country, though some of the earlier ones were mere compilations or translations of Donné's report in the *Journal des Débats*" (152). This interest in the new medium spilled over into improved techniques, such as the wet collodion process, a chemical process of affixing images to glass, which was invented by Frederick Scott Archer in 1851, the year of Daguerre's death and the first Great Exhibition (Gernsheim 1988, 11–17), and also into an interest in fashion and fashion publications.

A mere twenty years later, Berlin was the capital of the German Empire, a development that, as Eberhard Roters has noted, led to "an evolution that was so at odds with its subsequent growth into a metropolis that it could hardly be called harmonious" (10). Roters connects this history with the stylistic method of montage – the technique of assembling fragments into a new composite whole in a manner that draws attention to the fragmented nature of the work, often to generate a political reading. Roters has shown how urban art in Berlin took forms that directly reflected an engagement with chaotic social and economic circumstances and offers as one of his examples the Dada movement in Berlin, which coined the term "photomontage" around the end of WWI and, understanding itself as above and beyond fashion, was instrumental in making montage into a modern art-form. As we will see in the readings that follow, adding the two industrial cultural practices of fashion and photography into the mix of more canonical work (the fine arts, theatre, film, and literature) upon which Roters bases his conclusion shows the extent to which economic prosperity, and not only economic chaos, encouraged those from Berlin to engage with the industrial trade aspects of these cultural practices.

How Simmel Pictured Fashion

In his essay "On Fashion," Simmel stresses fashion's dual functionality. A product of social demands and class distinction (Simmel 105), fashion, as a social form like money and aesthetic judgment, mediates and structures the relations between individuals and their surroundings, relations which Patrizia McBride describes as ideally involving mirroring and protection: "Simmel's individual is endowed with a metaphysical space of introspection, whose integrity culture should both mirror and protect, and whose harmonious development it should foster" (McBride 754).[2] However, the superficial qualities of modern existence can overtax culture, and there is often a lack of fit between the inner unity of the individual and the unity or totality of modern existence, which results in alienation, "like the alienation the individual experiences in the metropolis" (754).[3] As Lehmann reminds us, it was a sartorial example that Simmel drew on in his 1900 *Philosophy of Money* "to exemplify modernity's fragmented reality, which his philosophy of life would subsequently seek to explain":

> The difference, for instance, between the modern clothing store, geared towards the utmost specialisation, and the work of the tailor whom one used to invite into one's home, sharply emphasises the growing objectivity of the economic cosmos, its supra-individual independence in relation to the consuming subject with whom it was originally closely identified... It is obvious how much this objectifies the whole character of transaction and how subjectivity is destroyed and transformed into cool reserve and anonymous objectivity once so many intermediate stages are introduced between the producer and the one who accepts his product that they lose sight of each other. (cited in Lehmann 135)

The realm of fashion is thus for Simmel an exemplary site to explain the onset of modernity.

The analogy that Simmel draws on in the fashion essay to emphasize the dual function of fashion as "union and segregation" is also of interest. He sees fashion as operating:

> like a number of other forms, honour especially, the double function of which consists in revolving within a given circle and at the same time emphasizing it as separate from others. Just as the frame of a picture characterizes the work of art inwardly as a coherent, homogeneous, independent entity and at the same time outwardly severs all direct relations with the surrounding space, just as the uniform energy of such forms cannot be

expressed unless we determine the double effect, both inward and outward, so honour owes its character, and above all its moral rights, to the fact that the individual in his personal honour at the same time represents and maintains that of his social circle and his class. (Simmel 105)

In likening apparel to a picture frame, Simmel nicely turns the individual into a Nietzschean work of art. However, in doing so he at the same time complicates the status of that work of art, something which Alexander Nehamas has shown in *Life as Literature* to be fundamentally literary. That the relation between Simmel's subjective and objective culture, "that is, between an individual's inner experience and the outer circumstances of everyday life" (McBride 754), is of a linguistic nature is a point also foregrounded by Alan Blum: "We would treat words then, always alive and magical, as making reference to the intrinsic courses of action they affirm, for even inanimate things such as jug and bridge, as words, imply for us ways of being with and towards such things (see Simmel, 1959)" (Blum 2003, 38–9). Both pictures and words, then, fulfill the mediating function of fashion for Simmel, but both, while modern, remain in the realm of the auratic.

The tiger's leap that Simmel did not make – the one that gave visuality an advantage in its fin-de-siècle struggle with textuality in Berlin and caused, or made possible (depending on one's point of view), fragmentation on a scale hitherto not possible – was into the world of technology. The nature of Simmel's strong aesthetic interest in modernity (cf. Frisby 39) can be discerned by his work on Rembrandt: what did individuality mean in the Renaissance? What was the experience of old age? Of piety? Of having one's portrait done? Why did the depiction of subjective experience come to the fore? In short, Simmel wrote nothing comparable to Benjamin's "Little History of Photography" or Kracauer's "On Photography," and if he had, it would likely have focused on the individual experience of having one's photograph taken rather than tracing the shifts in the development of the apparatus from its early studio existence to its growing fairground popularity and later appropriations by the avant-garde.

Benjamin's Tiger Leap into Technological Reproducibility

For his part, Benjamin's interest in fashion a few eventful and brutal decades later, while involving its subjective psychological effects, concentrated rather on the political implications of the technological form of its mediation.[4] Chéret's posters, Vernier's engravings, Grandville's lithographs, Gutzkow's handkerchief map of Paris – all captured his attention because of what he came to call their technological reproducibility and their relevance for understanding the historicity of technologically mediated modes of perception. We can only surmise what Benjamin's "Little History of Fashion" would have looked like, but from Susan Buck-Morss' and Ester Leslie's insightful readings, we know that it is highly unlikely not to have dealt with the fetishism of reified commodities.[5] As Buck-Morss draws attention to, fashion in Benjamin's project is conceptually close to the hell that he understands modernity to resemble:

Reified in commodities, the utopian promise of fashion's transitoriness undergoes a dialectical reversal: The living, human capacity for change and infinite variation becomes alienated, and is affirmed only as a quality of the inorganic object. In contrast, the ideal for human subjects (urged into rigorous conformity to fashion's dictates) becomes the biological rigor mortis of eternal youth. It is for this that the commodity is worshiped – in a ritual that is, of course, destined to fail. Valéry speaks of the "absurd superstition of the new." Benjamin makes us *see* it, in revealing the logic of modernity as "the time of Hell." (Buck-Morss 99, italics in original)

Like the river Lethe in Hades, fashion promotes oblivion, easing the transit of alienated modern souls. What Leslie adds to this analysis of our hellish commodified contemporary condition is the link between technology and fashion. Technology, in her reading of Benjamin, is what regulates the relationship between humanity and nature (Leslie 6). However, "[t]he overriding political factor of structures of ownership, relations of production, promotes a subversion of the 'natural' elective alliance between proletariat and technology, to which technology responds by revolting.... [W]hen the proletariat, under capital's command, wields technology in order to abuse nature, technology turns with unmatched ferocity on the cosmos" (6–7). *Technik*, as Benjamin tells us, "is not the mastery of nature but of the relation between nature and humanity," and fashion is its midwife, serving to ceaselessly dispense "novel ways of presentation, new looks, new images, and new purposes" (8) and to create a world "in which things rapidly petrify, turn alien and obsolete" (10), including people.[6] Leslie underscores how centrally fashion has been involved in this process:

The fashion industry provides, for Benjamin, a 'dialectical image' of the deadly social relations of production, illustrating both the reifying effects of the exchange mechanism and the brutal physical conditions that attend work. In Marx's account, the textile industry is central to the formation of the factory system of exploitation. It was in the cotton mills that women and children were employed en masse, cheaply, and mechanically spinning materials harvested by growing numbers of slaves, born to work and worked to death, in the U.S. slave states. *Das Kapital* supplies a materialist core for Benjamin's idea of the fashionable body as, symbolically and concretely, intimate with death. Marx details how 'the murderous, meaningless caprices of fashion' are linked to the anarchy of production, where demand cannot be predicted and where gluts lead to starvation. The connections between products and death alert Benjamin to the fact that everything consumed has been produced under conditions that occasioned suffering. Capital's rule – exercised through its technologies and techniques – fractures and fragments bodies, and these bodies that have been remade as prostituted, dehumanized commodities. Through the reifying operation of commodity fetishism, capital's organization murderously consumes life. (10)

Dialectical images (*Wortbilder*), such as of the nineteenth-century roots of the fashion industry, are caught up in *Jetztzeit*: "[T]he 'now-time,' the point at which objects, activities, and actions from the past may be cognized in a unique and heretofore unrecognizable constellation, as an image, a figure. For Benjamin, this dialectical image manifests a knowledge uniquely available to a specific present moment that will then pass. It is precious because it is generated by and includes the desires, needs, and contexts of the present and so can be lost if not formulated now" (Rosen 2). For Benjamin, then, we only gain access to events of the past at particular moments, which are important to attend to because of their rarity and the fact they "come to legibility only at a specific time" (Fioretos 551).

Benjamin recognized that photography bore a special relationship to history because of its ability to enact *Jetztzeit*, bringing historically situated viewers into contact with the specific moment a photograph was taken. Unlike the drawn-out process of a painting, but also unlike Chéret's posters, Vernier's engravings, Grandville's lithographs, and Gutzkow's handkerchief map of Paris, a reproduction of a photograph offers a particular historical connection to a viewer. The two epigraphs to Benjamin's convolute B on fashion – Leopardi's "Fashion: Madam Death! Madam Death!" and Balzac's "Nothing dies; all is transformed" – thus reveal more than his fascination with fashion's ephemerality, which Baudelaire identified as the hallmark of *modernité* (by which he meant, of course: "the ephemeral, the fugitive, the contingent, the half of art whose other half is the eternal and the immutable"). These epigraphs also do more than implicate fashion as one of capital's key service-providers. The transformative power of fashion *historicises*, as noted by Wilson in comparing it with photography. It allows for the enactment of "now-time" by consigning a style to a particular period, from which it can then be ripped into the present. Hence Benjamin sensually describes fashion with an almost Kiplingesque sensibility as having "the scent of the modern wherever it stirs in the thicket of what has been. It is the tiger's leap (*Tigersprung*) into the past," evoking the smells, feel and movement of garments that fulfill intense bodily desires and are therefore hunted out with a single-minded animal passion.[7]

The Questions of Place that Zille's Photography Poses

Thinking photography and history together locationally in the context of Berlin fashion, one can't help but notice that Benjamin preferred to consider August Sander's portraits and Eugène Atget's and Germaine Krull's empty Parisian street-scenes over the ones Heinrich Zille took of Berlin, such as the Berliner Chic storefront that motivated this study. Despite the fact that he associated Berlin with Sodom and Acheron in the same dream, which he published under the pseudonym Detlef Holz in *Die Literarische Welt* in November 1933 (Benjamin "Thought Figures," 725), Benjamin was not prejudiced against Berliners per se – his fondness for Gisèle Freund and her portraits is well known, as are the ones she did of him.[8] However, it must be admitted that the milieu Benjamin associated with her was not a Berlin one but rather the one he himself gravitated towards after, like Freund, finding it impossible to live an intellectually rich, self-sustaining existence in Berlin: namely, cultured Parisian society like the one of Freund's close friend and noted bookshop-owner, Adrienne Monnier.[9] Zille, on the other hand, had no French connections but was able to carve out a reasonable living for himself and his family with his trade work in, first, photography and then sketching and film. Zille did not fit into the narrative of decline and betrayal that Benjamin wanted to tell about the evolving social function of photography.[10] It is the "alienation of the Wilhelmine epoch" (Leslie 53) that Benjamin saw documented in the photographs of the period, such as those of himself and his brother in kiddy *Tracht* (folk costumes) against an Alpine backdrop and of a similarly tortured historicist Kafka.[11] In the "Mummerehlen" section of "Berlin Childhood around 1900," Benjamin offers a Simmelian description of the experience of being photographed, of finding himself in a photographer's studio, and "[w]herever I looked, I saw myself surrounded by folding screens, cushion, and pedestals which craved my image much as the shades of Hades craved the blood of the sacrificial animal" (391). The connections between photography, fashion and the hell of bourgeois modernity become more explicit later in the passage when he describes the rest of the photograph, which sadly seems to have gone missing: "Over to the side, near the curtained doorway, my mother stands motionless in her tight bodice. As though attending to a tailor's dummy, she scrutinizes my velvet suit, which for its part is laden with braid and other trimming and looks like something out of a fashion magazine. I, however, am distorted by similarity to all that surrounds me here" (392). The form that distortion takes contrasts with the "immensely sad eyes" of the six-year-old Kafka in "The Little History of Photography," who is described as surely lost in the greenhouse landscape background without those eyes (515).[12] Rather, Benjamin evokes in his description of the photo with his mother one of the senses that photographs cannot convey: "Thus, like a mollusk in its shell, I had my abode in the nineteenth century, which now lies hollow before me like an empty shell. I hold it to my ear" ("Berlin Childhood around 1900" 392). The murmurings of the past thus link him sonically with his mother ("mère" – in French a homonym of sea – "mer"), who died in 1930, two years before Benjamin began writing "Berlin Childhood" (his father had passed away in 1926). These murmurings also echo Benjamin's reflections on the acoustic nature of déjà vu in "Berlin Chronicle": "One ought to speak of events that reach us like an echo awakened by a call, a sound that seems to have been heard somewhere in the darkness of past life" ("Berlin Chronicle" 634) and underscore the remoteness of the past and what all he perceived as having gone lost in the taking of bourgeois portraits in the Wilhelmine period.

Zille was anything but bourgeois, but his success, while belated, would not have endeared him to Benjamin. In 1924, Zille was named to the Prussian Academy of Arts, and his death in 1929 was marked with a state funeral. When August Sander's portrait collection *Face of Time: Sixty Takes of Germans in the 20th Century* (*Das Antlitz der Zeit: Sechzig Aufnahmen deutscher Menschen des 20. Jahrhunderts*) was published in 1929, on the other hand, Benjamin could recognize it to be of as yet unheralded artistic significance. Similarly, much of Atget's appeal to Benjamin was in his being an unrecognized genius, something Benjamin clearly related to:

Atget was an actor who, disgusted with the profession, wiped off the mask and then set about removing the makeup from reality too. He lived in Paris poor and unknown, selling his pictures for a trifle to photographic enthusiasts scarcely less eccentric than himself; he died recently [in 1927], leaving behind an oeuvre of more than 4,000 pictures.... The contemporary journals 'knew nothing of the man, who for the most part hawked his photographs around the studios and sold them for next to nothing, often for the price of one of those picture postcards which, around 1900, showed such pretty town views, bathed in midnight blue, complete with touched-up moon. He reached the Pole of utmost mastery; but with the bitter modesty of a great craftsman who always lives in the shadows, he neglected to plant his flag there. Therefore many are able to flatter themselves that they have discovered the Pole, even though Atget was there before them.' (Benjamin "Little History" 518)

Atget and Sander were not, in Benjamin's day, fashionable (although they, like Benjamin, have since become so). They did not, in Benjamin's view, capitulate to fashion (526). Their photographs did not translate experience into "objects of distraction, amusement, consumption" (Leslie 60). Zille's didn't either, but his photographs were not what he was known for in 1929. It was only in the 1960s that the 400+ glass negatives and 100+ photographs in Zille's estate became known, and only in 1999 that the Heinrich Zille Society (Berlin e. V.) was founded with the mission to create a Zille museum, which it did in 2002 in the heart of the Nikolaiviertel (Fig. 3.2). Rather, it was Zille's very knowing, very cutesy sketches of Berlin's toiling classes that vaulted him into the ranks of the Berlin Secession in 1903 and provided him with a way to earn a living after he was fired from his position as a lithographer.

Given that Benjamin thought the task of the photographer was "to point out the guilty in his pictures" ("Little History" 527) and given that his history of photography favored those who "use photography according to the proper potential of the technology and, in doing so, create a critical and socially apt body of work" (Leslie 60), it is not unimaginable that Benjamin would have appreciated the socio-realistic qualities of Zille's photographs, had he been in a position to know them. While Zille did not consider himself an artist, he did have thirty years of artisanal photographic training from working at the Berlin Photographical Society (*Photographische Gesellschaft Berlin*) on Dönhoffplatz from 1877 to 1907 with a short interruption for military service. Zille had indeed learned "the lessons inherent in the authenticity of the photograph" ("Little History" 527), to the extent that he is assumed to have used his photographs to impart authenticity into his sketches.[13] Zille's photographs break down into two basic types: proletarian portraits, some faceless with their subjects' backs to the camera, and outdoor scenes, either peopled or empty, often of storefronts. Photos such as "An der Friedrichsgracht, nach 1901" ("On the Friedrichsgracht, after 1901") and "Krögelgasse nach Norden" ("Krögelgasse to the North") are as haunting as Atget's desolate Paris streetscapes, while the shadowy figures in "Durchgang zum Krügelhof" ("Passage to the Krügelhof") demonstrate that a scene can sometimes seem more deserted

Figure 3.2: Statue of Heinrich Zille in the Zille Museum. (Photo: S. Ingram)

when the space's effect on those who temporarily occupy it is shown.[14] Zille was not the kind of amateur "who returns home with great piles of artistic shots," whom Benjamin derided as "no more appealing a figure than the hunter who comes back with quantities of game that is useless to anyone but the merchant" ("Little History" 521-3). Zille was not "creative" in Benjamin's sense of photography that "frees itself from physiognomic, political, and scientific interest" (526). Rather, the purpose of Zille's photographs is indicated by the precise, often chronotopic titles with which he inscribed them. "This is where inscription must come into play," writes Benjamin, "which includes the photography of the literarization of the conditions of life, and without which all photographic construction must remain arrested in the approximate" (527). Zille documented with a socio-critical eye the working-class parts of the city he loved: the children in the streets, who were also the subject of the first book of sketches he published in 1908; the farmers' wives hauling produce to market; the workers on their way home from the factories. These were the characters who made up his "Milljöh" (Fig. 3.3). Two decades later, when Kracauer bemoaned "the loss of streets, buildings, and a city that seemed to vanish before his eyes…[and wrote] nostalgic descriptions of the old Berlin [that] portrayed corner stores that disappeared, vistas that no longer existed, and his unease about the new Berlin (and Germany) to come" (Till 2005, 31), we can understand that it was Zille's Berlin whose loss Kracauer was mourning in the face of the concomitant onslaught of fashion-driven office work and leisure.

Fashion does not figure as such in Zille's photographs, as clothing with a notably changing nature, any more than it does in his sketches. For him models are proletarians, women at work, and fashionable goods are wares. There is, for example, no glamour surrounding the furs in the photograph "Pelze und Rauchwaren" ("Furs and Smokes"). Stoles hang draped around the necks of torsos of mannequins with metal stands that huddle together along a foggy pavement. One cannot but notice how they resemble the bare trees and light standards and how, like the tiny figures in the background, all are abandoned to their fate in the barren, cold streets. However, Zille's working milieu differs from the one that caught Kracauer's attention. One does not find the very gendered working body parts of the Tiller Girls in Zille's photographs or any shop girls clandestinely dabbing their eyes before leaving a cinema. The link Kracauer makes between fashion and the economy (Kracauer 39) did not obtain, or was not as operative, for Zille as much as the one in Benjamin's convolute B between fashion and death. Hence Zille's photographs of the "Beerdigungsinstitut Gustav Aßmann, Berlin, Bergstraße 69, um 1910" ("Undertaker Gustav Aßmann, Berlin, Bergstraße 69, around 1910") and "Sargmagazin 'Thanatos', Berlin, Holzmarktstraße 45" ("Coffin Storage 'Thanatos', Berlin, Holzmarktstraße 45"). Our cover image, "Linienstrasse 34," with its unpeopled street scene focusing on the white Berliner Chic sign, distills this atmosphere of embryonic fashion-related industrial urbanity (Fig. 3.4). It is the visual equivalent of the anecdotes a distant relation tells during a visit that help one parse previously unimagined family secrets.

Figure 3.3: Statue of Heinrich Zille, next to the Nikolaikirche in the Nikolaiviertel. (Photo: K. Sark)

Figure 3.4: Zille Destille restaurant, Propststrasse 10. (Photo: K. Sark)

The Female Weimar Fashion Photographers

While there are some affinities between Benjamin's sensibilities and Zille's photographical project, the same cannot be said about the work of the Berlin fashion photographers he did have occasion to know, primarily because so many of them were women. Interestingly, professional photographers and freelance photojournalists in Weimar Berlin typically shared all of Benjamin's demographical traits except sex: "Most belonged to the generation born in the period around 1890 and many came from conventional, bourgeois Jewish families" (Ganeva 2003a, 3). Photography provided women such as Else Neuländer Simon, Grete Stern and Ellen Auerbach, known professionally as Yva and Ringl & Pit respectively, with the possibility of becoming something both personally satisfying and socially acceptable. Both Yva and Pit apprenticed in Berlin in the 1920s with well-placed male photographers: Yva with the experimental avant-garde photographer Heinz Hajek-Halke[15] and Pit with Walter Peterhans, who taught at the Bauhaus in Dessau. Both established very successful businesses in Berlin specializing in fashion and advertising photography, and both were forced by National Socialism to leave Berlin. Pit (who in 1933 was still Ellen Rosenberg, having not yet married Walter Auerbach) left for Palestine soon after the National Socialists assumed power, while Yva continued to work in Berlin until her 1942 deportation to Majdanek, where she is presumed to have perished.[16]

What did Benjamin begrudge the fashion photography that provided these women, and many like them, with the "economic freedom, artistic challenge, mobility, and public exposure of the profession" (Ganeva 2003a, 3)? In a word, its beauty, which he understood as implicated in politically objectionable social relations. As he insisted in the "Author as Producer" address he gave at the Institute for the Study of Fascism in Paris on 27 April 1934, photography that supplied a productive apparatus without changing it, that "succeeded in transforming even abject poverty – by apprehending it in a fashionably perfected manner – into an object of enjoyment" (Benjamin "Author as Producer" 775), was part of the reason he and so many others had had to leave Germany. In her review of the landmark 1979 exhibition on German avant-garde photography at the San Francisco Museum of Modern Art, Rosalind Krauss wonders whether "the left-wing intellectuals' phobic response to the sudden explosion of photo-culture [was] not simply the other side of the coin of The New Vision's enthusiastic advocacy of it – with neither side referring to anything more specific than photography-in-general" (105). Benjamin's condemnation has indeed since been tempered by the championing of the New Objectivity by Van Deren Coke, who organized the San Francisco exhibition soon after his arrival in there from the University of New Mexico Art Museum in Albuquerque, where he had served as founding director and to which he donated more than 1,200 items of his own collection. Coke intended the 1979 exhibition to heighten the profile of German photographers in the face of the popularity of Surrealists like Man Ray and to make their work more readily available for the debates about postmodernism in American art circles that were kicking into gear.[17] His was a proselytizing rather than a political project, and not an unsuccessful one.

The Influence of Berlin's History on Contrasting Views of Helmut Newton, Gun for Hire

Like Coke, the controversial fashion photographer Helmut Newton (1920–2004), was able to stretch the boundaries of the fashion photography canon.[18] Born in Berlin, Helmut Neustädter apprenticed in his teenage years with Yva (from 1936–1938). After fleeing Nazi Europe via Singapore and setting himself up in the fashion photography business in Australia, Newton, as he then called himself, approached his work much as Zille had, despite growing up in a milieu that resembled Benjamin's more than Zille's (Newton's father owned a button-making factory, Emil Benjamin was an art dealer, while Johann Traugott Zille was a blacksmith and mechanic). Never pretending to be an artist, Newton turned to fashion photography because he wanted to be a *Vogue* photographer. His success allowed him to build up a reserve of what he once called, in an interview with Charlie Rose, his "fuck you" money so he could turn down assignments that were not interesting to him.[19] By the 1970s he had become one of the most sought after, and most expensive, fashion photographers in the fashion world, in no small part by revolutionizing and sexifying the medium. In 1980 he moved to Monaco and continued to winter in Los Angeles.[20]

While Yva managed to find "her own unique and attractive visual language somewhere between the commercial clichés and the modernist idioms of her time," her real accomplishment was, as Ganeva further points out, being able to find "an image of the woman in fashion and advertisement photography of the 1920s and 1930s that was not degrading for the woman" (2003a, 20–1). Degrading women is precisely what Alice Schwarzer accused Newton of half a century later. In 1978, *EMMA*, the "political magazine about women" Schwarzer had founded the previous year, launched a highly public lawsuit against the German newsmagazine *Der Stern* for publishing cover illustrations that were humiliating to women.[21] She specifically singled out Newton's photograph of Grace Jones, in which the Jamaican-American singer-actress is shown bound in chains. As far as Schwarzer was concerned, such a depiction led incontrovertibly to pornography, something she continued to fight against in the highly visible "Por-NO" campaigns in 1988 and 2007.

For an opposite view of Newton, we can look to Francette Pacteau, who does not see Newton as the "high priest of pornography" Schwarzer figured him as, but rather an artist interested in showing off the staging involved in the making of this particular kind of art. In the "Dark Continent" chapter of her 1994 *The Symptom of Beauty*, Pacteau compares Newton's image to a more menacing one of Jones taken by Jean-Paul Goude, in which Jones is depicted as a snarling wild animal. She draws attention to the fact that in Newton's image "the instruments of enslavement do not tear the flesh; they are worn like fashion accessories. The chains, loosely draped around her ankles, do not seriously restrain her; she wraps the lash around her neck in the same way that she might a scarf or a tie" (140). Most importantly, Jones' "hands are free." Newton's image leaves Pacteau with the impression "of a performer who has not yet quite entered her role, who is perhaps unconvinced by the act she is required to play out for the camera: 'You mean like this...?'" (140). In her reading, Pacteau is taking her cues from Victor Burgin, who, in his "Newton's Gravity" essay, looked to Newton's photography in order to "travel further… toward a psychoanalytic consideration of unconscious investments in looking" (Burgin 1996a, 58).[22]

To appreciate the difference between Pacteau's and Burgin's view of Newton and Schwarzer's, one must take into consideration the texts of Newton's to which they were responding. Burgin and Pacteau analyze images that went into the 1987 *Helmut Newton Portraits*. Burgin begins his essay with a collage that highlights the autobiographical nature of the collection:

> Plates 1–22: Helmut; June;[23] doctors; models…1934–1986: June on the métro in 1957, alongside a much older woman; June in Paris twenty-five years later, looking down at a fresh postoperative scar that starts well above her navel and ends just above her pubis. June in Melbourne in 1947. June in Monte Carlo thirty-five years later. Helmut adolescent, sprawled on a Berlin beach, a girl in each arm and one between his knees. Helmut fifty-two years later, on his back for the doctors – Paris, San Francisco. (Burgin 1996a, 79)

The photograph Burgin chooses for detailed analysis is Newton's "Self-Portrait with Wife June and Models," taken in a Vogue studio in Paris in 1981, because it allows him to expound Newton's sophisticated understanding of the fetishistic aspect of his chosen craft and the nature of what photography can never reveal. By showing his wife watching him dressed as a flasher in an overcoat photographing a naked woman admiring herself in a mirror, Newton, in Burgin's view, captures a basic truth:

> Most men appreciate the existential fact of feminine sexuality as a fact, albeit one that is not to be grasped quite as simply as their own. The surrealists could not see what was "hidden in the forest" until they closed their eyes in order to imagine it; even then they could not be sure, for there are other forests to negotiate, not least amongst these the "forest of signs" which is the unconscious. Sooner or later, as in Newton's image, we open our eyes, come back to a tangible reality: here, that of the woman's body…. But what the man behind the camera will never know is what her sexuality means to her, although a lifetime may be devoted to the inquiry. Perhaps that is why, finally, Newton chooses to stage his perverse display under the gaze of his wife. (76)

This passage radiates Burgin's respect for his fellow-photographer and his ability to capture the vulnerability of the human form, most pronounced when it is at work.[24] Seen properly, it is the trench coat-wearing photographer, and not the stiletto-wearing model, who is naked in Newton's photograph.

Alice Schwarzer, on the other hand, was incensed by that fact that Newton's work for magazines had translated into an artistically respectable photographic collection. *White Women* appeared in 1976, two years after the publication of an American edition of Leni Riefenstahl's *The Last of the Nuba*, and the year after Susan Sontag's rejoinder to that volume,

"Fascinating Fascism," which first appeared in the 6 February 1975 issue of *The New York Review of Books*. That *The People of Kau*, an English version of the second volume of beautiful images Riefenstahl took of a neighboring tribe of Nuba in central Sudan, appeared in the same year as Newton's *White Women* only strengthened Schwarzer's resolve to stem what seemed to be a resurgence of artistic production in the spirit of the ideology that in the 1970s was only beginning to be worked through in her country.[25] In the later essay "Newton: Kunst oder Pornografie?" (Newton: Art or Pornography?), she expresses her ongoing concern with the violence wreaked by male imaginaries in recent German history and emphasizes Newton's Jewish-German background. Having had "a Jewish father," Newton should know better than to engage in the denigration of fellow human beings. Schwarzer invites her readers to imagine the public uproar there would be if, instead of women, Newton's images were of Jews or foreigners. Just as Ganeva argues for the importance of considering the likely viewers of Yva's fashion advertisements – and one cannot deny that the interest of middle-class women in Weimar Germany in shiny, run-free stockings would be different from either Walter Benjamin's or Helmut Newton's – , we must also be cognizant of how differently any image of Grace Jones, whether nude and in chains or not, would register against the very different backdrops of a Federal Republic of Germany just beginning to process a racialized genocide, and an America, in which Oprah is one of the most powerful popular cultural figures.[26]

It is not that Burgin is unaware of the significance of Newton's background, but what matters for his analyses of Newton's work is Newton as an artist capable of taking fascinating, captivating fashion photographs. When Burgin does turn his lens to Newton's hometown, as he does in *Some Cities*, the city comes in for the same kind of criticism that Schwarzer had for Newton. The Berlin that appears in the 1996 *Some Cities* is fashionably nostalgic; it is very much a pre-Wende Berlin, one that emphasizes the city's iconic modern status through the looking glass of the *Dialectic of Enlightenment*. The opening two photographs juxtapose, in one, an empty street with glistening puddles next to the Wall, and in the other, what is presumably an outdoor departure board at a train station. The ten destinations are all death camps, beginning with Auschwitz and ending with Bergen-Belsen, and the board seems to be connected to the "Wüstenrot Bank" building in the right half of the frame, evoking the behind-the-scenes financiering and profiteering of the Final Solution. This impression is furthered by the caption accompanying the photo, which reads "Berlin at that time was the showcase of capitalism" (Burgin 1996b, 82). However, "that time" remains as blurry as the figure striding across the book's front and back covers. If one looks into the history of the Wüstenrot Bank, one finds that it was first founded in 1968 in Ludwigsburg, far removed from any kind of dubious Holocaust-related doings. The rest of the chapter depicts and discusses posters of terrorists, the principle of panopticism, Victor Shklovsky's *Zoo, or Letters Not About Love* and the tendency Shklovsky noted of Russians to live around zoos. The photo of the grey-haired woman in sensible shoes wearing a leopard-patterned fur coat has a Zillean sensibility in that her back is towards the camera, while the presence of a sea lion at the edge of an artificial concrete pond facing the woman (and the camera and therefore the viewer), but separated from her by a wall, infuses the photo with a critique of the fashion industry.

Victor Burgin's 1996 photo-essay aims to be the pinnacle of Benjamin's approach to photography. Inscribing images with Benjaminian-inflected reflections, he aims "less to record traces I have left in some cities than it is to recall some traces some cities have left in me" (Burgin 1996b, 7). The collection is thus a postmodernly plural version of "Berlin Chronicle" with photographs. Beginning with his childhood speaking "Yorkshire dialect" (14), Burgin echoes Benjamin's mollusk murmurings. The photo of a smoking Sheffield steel factory with which Burgin opens *Some Cities* (it is by Bill Brandt) is comparable to Zille's drab, deserted and minimally titled "Fabrikanlage" (Factory). Both evoke a desolate bleakness, but Brandt's high-contrast photo includes tiny figures in the foreground, who are walking away from active smokestacks along a brick walkway beside railway tracks that glisten in the wake of rain. Zille's angle is much lower. He adopts the workers' perspective and aligns the viewer with the first worker arriving at work on an autumnal morning, while at the same time eliding that worker with the work of the camera. That Burgin chose this photo of his hometown for the purposes of contrast is clear from the rest of the text, which reads "Sheffield no longer has a steel industry. Bankers have accomplished what bombers failed to achieve. The street remains, but where the furnaces were is nothing but waste ground. The community of steelworkers is gone. Making nothing of steel, Sheffield makes no sense" (10). Only in the photo does Sheffield work, a frozen memory of industrial romance. Burgin means to touch his reader-viewer with this irony, as he does by juxtaposing a photo of a visibly South Asian female garment worker in Coventry, which he took "for a trade union publication" (18), with a snippet from the *Daily Telegraph* women's page about Yves Saint Laurent. He is emulating the same level of knowingness he appreciates in Newton's work.

Rico Puhlmann vs. Peter Lindbergh and F.C. Gundlach

While neither as controversial nor as well known as Helmut Newton (something true of the majority of fashion photographers), Rico Puhlmann had more in common with Newton than most.[27] Born Richard Georg Willi Puhlmann in Berlin in 1934, Puhlmann experienced the destruction of the war that Helmut Newton had been able to flee. After an early career as a child film star, Puhlmann studied fashion graphic design and art history at the Academy for Fine Arts in Berlin and became a fashion illustrator and very successful at placing his drawings and then his photographs in, first, the German fashion magazines in the 1950s, most notably *Constanze*, and then in the French *Vogue*, which first published his work in 1958. By the time he left for New York in 1970 at the age of 35, Puhlmann had a reputation as one of the most efficient, skillful and prolific fashion photographers in Europe. That reputation only grew in New York, where he worked freelance for such publications as *Glamour*, American *Vogue*, *Gentlemen's Quarterly*, *The New York Times* and the supplement *Fashions of the Times*, and where from 1973 to 1992 he was the chief photographer at *Harper's Bazaar*, the same upscale fashion magazine that featured the work of Richard Avedon during the two decades following WWII when Diana Vreeland reigned as fashion editor (she moved on to *Vogue* in 1963). Despite working and living in New York, Puhlmann remained a Berliner at heart. He maintained his apartment in the Nassauische Strasse in Wilmersdorf and confessed in an interview in *Die Welt* in 1986 to having "a great longing for Europe" and being unhappy if he couldn't manage to go back once or twice a year, something his work enabled (Fig. 3.5).[28] Much of Puhlmann's cachet in New York lay in his European cultivation, fine manners, gentlemanly behavior and the superior craftsmanship of his work. Like Newton, he worked with the supermodels and celebrities of the day, as well as working on advertising campaigns for such designers and cosmetic companies as Ungaro, Fendi, Donna Karan, Calvin Klein, Estée Lauder, L'Oréal, Clinique and Revlon. Also like Newton, he died tragically in a crash – not of an automobile but of an airplane: TWA flight 800, in 1996.

Figure 3.5: Cover of *Amica*, 14 November 1995. (Photo: Rico Puhlmann, Archive Rico Puhlmann)

The harmony between Puhlmann's, Newton's and Zille's approach to their craft becomes evident when one compares them with the other German photographers to have "made it" in the star-studded world of late twentieth-century fashion photography: Peter Lindbergh and F.C. Gundlach. Lindbergh was born on the Polish border to Germany in 1944, grew up in what was at the time a flourishing center of heavy industry in the Ruhr Valley, namely Duisburg, and, desiring to be a concept artist, pursued studies in painting and then an apprenticeship with the advertising photographer Hans Lux. Hired on by *Harper's Bazaar* in 1992, the year editor-in-chief Anthony Mazzola and Puhlmann left the magazine, Lindbergh was offered a ten-year contract, something unheard of in the industry. His subsequent work with supermodels such as Christy Turlington, Naomi Campbell, Linda Evangelista und Tatjana Patitz and designers such as Hugo Boss, Giorgio Armani, Calvin Klein and Jil Sander garnered him enormous success. In 1997 Lindbergh was awarded the International Fashion Awards best fashion photographer prize in Paris. (There was an exhibition devoted to Lindbergh's fashion photography at the Art Library in Berlin in the fall of 1997 to mark this accomplishment.) Lindbergh enjoys being known as a "poet of glamour," and sees his black-and-white cinematic images in particular as having "redefined the world of fashion photography with their compelling realism, lack of pretension and ineffable depth of emotion."[29] Lindbergh's artistic sensibilities are evident in his original intention to become a painter as well as on his website, where in an essay on "Creativity" (1996), he underscores the artistic expressivity that he clearly sees as the motivation and purpose of his work: "When someone creates something: a painting, a poem, a photograph, the creativity comes from an idea, from a feeling, from emotion, or from a combination of ideas, feelings and emotions that are somehow 'reborn' from all our experiences and perspectives."[30] The contrast with Puhlmann's training in graphic design and focus on craftsmanship could not be more pronounced. Indeed the two are usually only mentioned together with Newton in terms of their nationality. Otherwise one finds references to Lindbergh's interest in the avant-garde, such as the dancing of Pina Bausch, as well as ones that situate him in those circles, such as "any number of contemporary artist-photographers, including Peter Lindbergh, Jeff Wall, Anna Gaskell, and Jessica Craig-Martin" (Smith). Lindbergh's choosing to live in Paris, which he has since 1978, and his feeling rather antipathetic towards the fashion industry,[31] also underscore Puhlmann's respect for his craft and connection to Berlin.

The work of F.C. Gundlach, one of the most renowned fashion photographers of the 1950s and 1960s, may appear at first glance to have a similar aesthetic sensibility to Lindbergh's, but the philosophy guiding that work is more akin to Puhlmann's and Newton's, with an emphasis on, and respect for, work- and craftsmanship. When describing his training in an interview, Gundlach couldn't have put this view more plainly: "Fotographie war einfach Handwerk. Aus. Schluss" ("Photography was simply a craft, that's it, end of discussion").[32] Later in the interview, he reiterates this view: "Im Prinzip sind wir Dienstleister, wir verbringen eine Dienstleistung, und möglichst optimal" ("In principle we provide a service, as optimally as possible"). This attitude, he admits, has come under attack by those who ascribe to the more hegemonic approach to photography as art, but it is also one very much in line with Berliner Chic, and Berlin has, indeed, a key place in his biography. Born in 1926, six years after Newton, eight years before Puhlmann and eighteen before Lindbergh, in the little town of Heinebach, somewhat southeast of Kassel, Gundlach got his first camera, an Agfa-Box, when he was ten. After receiving a so-called "Kriegsabitur" in 1943 and surviving the end of the war, he completed an apprenticeship in photography in Kassel between 1947 and 1949 with Rolf W. Nehrdich. His first freelance publications were theatre and film reports for newsmagazines like *Stern*, *Quick* and *Revue*. This work attracted the attention of film studios, which began engaging him to shoot publicity stills of their stars. In 1953 he began to work for *Film und Frau*, a Hamburg-based magazine that found a bourgeois female readership in the economic miracle years and sought, through film and fashion, "to restore the war-damaged façade of 'bürgerliche Sittlichkeit' (bourgeois ethics) in its copper font and generous layout" (Honnef 38). Documenting the fashion of Berlin designers and Paris haute couture, as well as portraits and fashion shots of international film stars, Gundlach gained recognition for his sophisticated style (Fig. 3.6). A decade later, he added the magazine that was becoming Germany's leading women's publication, *Brigitte*, to his portfolio, eventually creating more than 5,500 pages as well as about 180 magazine covers for it, from 1966 with an exclusive contract.[33]

Gundlach's contributions to the profession are unprecedented. He went on to found companies that provided professional laboratory services to photographers; he opened one

Figure 3.6: Flirting in the Stadium, Candy and Michael Cramer in Berlin's Olympic Stadium, Clothing Lindenstaedt und Brettschneiter, F.C. Gundlach, Berlin 1954. (Stiftung F. C. Gundlach)

of the first photo galleries in Germany dedicated to photography (PPS Galerie in 1975); he taught at Berlin's *Hochschule der Künste* (University of the Arts), accepting a position as Professor in 1988; and he formed a foundation, the Stiftung F.C. Gundlach, for his extensive collection of fashion photography, which included but was by no means limited to his own work. In 2003, he was appointed founding director of the House of Photography in the Deichtorhallen by the Senate of Hamburg, and he has since dedicated his personal collection "The Human Image in Photography" to the Deichtorhallen as a permanent loan. He has also curated a number of influential exhibitions of fashion photography,[34] including the results of the research project on fashion photography he ran with designer Uli Richter at the *Hochschule der Künste. Berlin en vogue: Berliner Mode in der Photographie* documents the history of Berlin fashion "in its fashionable, societal and social aspects" (Gundlach 1993, 10). The comprehensive accompanying catalogue includes three major essays: Enno Kaufhold's on photography, Katja Aschke's on film and Gretel Wagner's on fashion in Berlin. Gundlach's stature as one of the most important German fashion photographers, and the one who has done the most to promote and preserve fashion photography, was confirmed by a retrospective of his work exhibited at the Martin-Gropius-Bau from 20 November 2009 to 14 March 2010.

Sybille Bergemann

A final telling comparison is with another fashion photographer whose work is increasingly exhibited in Berlin: Sybille Bergemann. Born in 1941 in Berlin, Bergemann worked in sales before beginning to study photography in 1966 with Arno Fischer, whom she married in 1985. A sense of the range and sensitivity of her work can be gleaned from noting some of the high-profile work she has done: a) for the East German fashion magazine *Sibylle*, b) her documentation of the building of the statues of Marx and Engels (known colloquially as the "old pensioners") that now grace the Marx-Engels Forum, c) the accompanying photographs she provided for two of East German playwright Heiner Müller's plays performed at the Deutsches Theater in Berlin during the transitional period of 1987–1990 (*Lohndrücker* [*The Scab*] and *Hamletmaschine* [*Hamlet Machine*]), and d) since 1990, her work for such magazines as *GEO, Die Zeit, Spiegel, Stern,* and the *New York Times Magazine*. Recognized as the grande dame of East German photography, and one of the most important contemporary German photographers, Bergemann's work has been featured in an increasing number of exhibitions and has contributed to the increasing presence of photography from the former East Germany in Berlin museums.[35] One of the most insightful commentators of it, Mattias Flügge, notes that: "It is as though Sibylle Bergemann's intention was to refuse to have anything to do with all the clichés relating to the way this city is generally perceived…. In this city that has been photographed ad nauseum, practically no one else has succeeded in taking pictures that are so obviously free from stylization. They have only one single subject: how people live in a transitory place, between the past and a future that is an uncertain promise" (1992, 13). It cannot be coincidental that the other photographer whose images of Berlin are equally free from stylization and for whom Berlin mediated a similar "Milljöh" relation for its inhabitants is one for whom Flügge also provided an introduction: Heinrich Zille.

We began this chapter with Elizabeth Wilson's likening of fashion and photography. In concluding it, we return to the distinctive quality of Berlin photography related to fashion – that it is neither "high" sophisticated fashion, aesthetically oriented beautiful art, nor a cousin of performance art (Smith 2009). Rather, it is characterized by a recognition and respect for its industrial and trade-like qualities.[36] Could that be one of the reasons that the impact of fashion photography has not been that large, not only pertaining to Berlin but to the country as a whole? In discussing contemporary young German fashion photographers, Paris-based Markus Ebner, the Editor in Chief of the German fashion magazine *Achtung*, points to this larger, nation-wide trend:[37]

> [I]n the eyes of the international art world, photography from Germany is regarded as unrivalled, and photographers such as Andreas Gursky, Thomas Ruff, Thomas Demand, Thomas Struth, Wolfgang Tillmans or Candida Höfer are recognised stars who command top fees, fill up museums and influence other media.... But if one starts to discuss German fashion photography as such, things become very quiet. After F.C. Gundlach, there was no photographer of distinction who was both working in Germany [let alone Berlin] and also internationally recognized. Well-known individuals such as Peter Lindbergh, Ellen von Unwerth, Jürgen Teller and many others have settled abroad, and publish their works there, too. (Ebner)

However, this situation is beginning to change. Ebner notes that Berlin's emergence as Germany's "unofficial fashion capital" has had consequences in the area of fashion photography as well: "many young photographers have returned to their homeland after training abroad, to cultivate the fallow field of fashion photography here" (Ebner). One would imagine that revisiting the conjunction of Berlin, fashion and photography in a decade would reveal a greatly expanded field, but it is nevertheless likely to still be one very much in the trade-oriented, professional, modern spirit we have identified in this chapter.

Notes

1. The phrase stems from a remark Newton made in an interview: "Some people's photography is an art. Mine is not. If they happen to be exhibited in a gallery or a museum, that's fine. But that's not why I do them. I'm a gun for hire" (Thomas 2004). It was chosen for the memorial exhibition of Newton's work at the Museum for Photography, the catalogue for which also bears the phrase (Newton).
2. Both McBride and Janet Stewart note the similarities between Simmel's and Adolf Loos's views of fashion as protecting individual subjectivity. See Stewart 128.

3. Ganeva foreshadows our argument about the gendered nature of the differing perceptions of modern fashion in noting that fashion is nevertheless "in general well suited to the needs of the modern subject, especially in the metropolis, as a means of effecting social adaptation and social mobility, as well as individual differentiation within a dynamic, rapidly changing urban environment." While for Simmel and Lehmann the glass is not only nowhere near half-full but rather shattered, for Gavena it is nevertheless still serviceable (Ganeva 2008, 9).

4. See Leslie, Chapter 2 on "Benjamin's Objectives" for a stellar account of Benjamin's interest in and engagement with new, particularly visual, technologies. While one of the first convolutes of Benjamin's Arcades Project is devoted entirely to fashion (B), remarks about fashion are scattered throughout; as Peter Wollen notes: "it would be quite wrong to assume that all of Benjamin's citations and observations on the subject of fashion – more specifically, on fashion with respect to clothes – are to be found only there. Remarks devoted to fashion are scattered throughout the rest of the volume, hidden away in various other batches of material" (131). However, as there is nothing substantively different elsewhere, we rely mostly on the convolute for our analysis here and thank Lee Kuhnle for thinking of us while he was doing research in the Benjamin archives in Berlin and for bringing us back a much cherished copy of the original hand-written convolute B.

5. Peter McIsaac would likely concur with this assessment, given his noting the ideological lines along which Benjamin critiqued Bode: "Bode's success in revealing these possibilities – and particularly because he integrated them into a conservative political agenda – is likely one reason why Walter Benjamin targeted Bode's museums in his essay on the contemporary German collector Eduard Fuchs. Although it goes beyond the scope of this essay to demonstrate this claim, in Benjamin's essay Fuchs emerges, point for point, as the revolutionary, dialectical Marxist answer to Bode and his private collectors" (McIsaac 388, Fn 22).

6. Identifying fashion as the midwife of technology plays with Werner Sombart's much-cited phrase that fashion is capitalism's favorite child (*des Capitalismus liebstes Kind*), cited in Wagner 1993, 116.

7. Cited in Wollen 132–3, Lehmann xvi ff. This passage is Lehmann's leitmotif for his study of fashion in modernity.

8. Photos of Benjamin by Freund grace the frontispieces of *Walter Benjamin: Selected Writings*, volumes 3 and 4.

9. Like Helen Grund-Hessel and Irmgard Keun, Freund's professional success was predicated on leaving Berlin, cf. Ganeva 2003b. Benjamin's penchant for Paris is made clear in the following passage: "[I]t had to be Paris, where the walls and quays, the asphalt surfaces, the collections and the rubbish, the railings and the squares, the arcades and the kiosks, teach a language so singular that our relations to people attain, in the solitude encompassing us in our immersion in that world of things, the depths of a sleep in which the dream image waits to show the people their true faces" (Benjamin "Berlin Chronicle" 614).

10. "'In our age there is no work of art that is looked at so closely as a photograph of oneself, one's closest relatives and friends, one's sweetheart,' wrote Lichtwark back in 1907, thereby moving the inquiry out of the realm of aesthetic distinctions into that of social functions. Only from this vantage point can it be carried further" (Benjamin "Little History" 520).

11. See Witte 11–12 and Rugg 168–9 for the illustrations.

12. One cannot help but wonder at the influence these eyes may have had on anime design.

13. Flügge notes that Winfried Ranke's 1975 monograph *Heinrich Zille. Photographien Berlin 1890–1910* was the first one to appear on Zille's photographs. Ranke locates Zille's photos in the divided city of his day, most of which is hardly recognizable in Zille's photos, and notes connections between them and Zille's sketches (Flügge 1993, 8–9).

14. Kemp and Rheuban make this point from a different perspective: "The people who appear in the photographs seem to have so thoroughly adapted themselves to the drab monotony of their daily environment that often one does not notice them at first glance" (125).

15. For a synopsis of Yva's career achievements and an accounting of their parting of ways, see Ganeva 2003a. There is also information on Yva, including a C.V., on "Die Geschichte Berlins" website, run by the Verein für die Geschichte Berlins: http://www.diegeschichteberlins.de/geschichteberlins/persoenlichkeiten/persoenlichkeitenuz/368-yva.html.

16. As Ganeva notes, it is only recently that Yva's highly challenging opus has begun to receive the scholarly attention it deserves, and this despite Yva having been respected "by her contemporaries no less than other contemporary female photographers such as Marianne Breslauer, Lucia Moholy, Florence Henri, Anneliese Kretschmer, Lotte Jacobi, Grete Stern, and Ellen Auerbach," despite her work having been included "in almost every exhibition of German photography from the mid-1920s on," and despite her photographs having been "widely published in the trade press and in mainstream fashion, women's, and illustrated magazines" of her day (Ganeva 2003a, 4). The first Yva exhibition took place in the Galerie Bodo Niemann in Berlin in 1995: "YVA – Eine Berliner Photographin der dreißiger Jahre." It was followed in 2001 by "YVA-Photographien 1925–1938," a comprehensive exhibition on her work organized by Marion Beckers and Elisabeth Moortgat, which toured Berlin, Munich, Aachen, and Bremen (Ganeva 2003a, 22).

17. The 1983 publication of Hal Foster's *Anti-Aesthetic* was a pivotal moment in this regard. See also Part Three "Toward the Postmodern" in Huyssen's *After the Great Divide*, especially ch. 9 "The Search for Tradition: Avantgarde and Postmodernism in the 1970s."

18. The mistaken attribution of an Australian background to Newton in the following quote is an indication of the cosmopolitan nature of his identity: "The exhibiting careers of those fashion/style photographers who did produce numerous exhibitions during the 1980s and 1990s were either those who were seen to cross the boundaries between fashion and art, or those whose work challenged notions of public taste. Two such examples are the French partnership of Pierre et Gilles (whose wildly innovative work was seen frequently in museums and public galleries from the mid-1980s to the mid-1990s, including at venues such as the Museum of Modern Art in Oxford, UK, the Centre Georges Pompidou in Paris, and the Cartier Foundation, Paris) and *the Australian-born fashion photographer Helmut Newton* (whose work was much in demand by venues including the Photographers Gallery, London, the Biennale d'Lyon, and the Royal Academy of Arts, London throughout the 1970s, 1980s, and 1990s)" (Williams 211, italics added).

19. The interview took place on 29 November 1999 and is available on the Charlie Rose website: http://www.charlierose.com/view/interview/3971. This direct quote is not intended to be offensive but rather to convey Newton's own register, something very much in line with his declaration of being a "gun for hire."

20. Thanks to Newton's British agents at Maconochie Photography for their help with the details in this section.

21. *Emma*'s justification for the lawsuit is in their August 1978 edition, available online (http://www.emma.de/hefte/ausgaben-1978/august-1978/die-stern-klage/). An inventory of all of the *EMMA* articles dealing with the issue of pornography, including the Stern trial and Schwarzer's later feud with Newton, can be found on its website at: http://www.emma.de/kampagnen/grosse-themen-pornografie/. See also Schwarzer.

22. The compatibility of Pacteau's and Burgin's psychoanalytically informed approaches to art is evident in their collaborations: the "Victor Burgin/Francette Pacteau: The Embrace" exhibition, held at the Fotohof gallery in Salzburg from 11 August 1998 to 19 September 1998, and the audio installation "The Little House" at the MAK Center, Los Angeles, in 2008.

23. June is his wife, also a photographer, whose adopted professional name, Alice Springs, reveals both her Australian origins and whimsical nature.
24. Cf. Maynard 63–5 for a reading of Newton's "Beautiful Beast Looks" from 1961, which features two suited male photographers taking pictures of a caged woman wearing a leopard-skinned hat and jacket. Newton's thematization of his profession was not only an integral part of his practice in his later years.
25. Klaus Theweleit's magisterial study *Männerphantasien* (*Male Fantasies*), which offered a psychoanalytic analysis on the body imagery, uniform fetishes, etc. of the Freikorps, appeared in two volumes in 1977 and 1978.
26. After having taught in England from 1967 to 1988, Burgin moved to California, where he taught in the History of Consciousness program at the University of California, Santa Cruz until 2001.
27. The following section has been parsed from information available in the ifa Künstler-Datenbank (http://kuenstlerdatenbank.ifa.de/datenblatt.php3?ID=634&NAME=puhlmann&ACTION=kue nstler&SUB_ACTION=1|8); on the Rico Puhlmann website (http://www.ricopuhlmann.com); and in the catalogue for the "Rico Puhlmann: A Fashion Legacy: Photographs and Illustrations 1955–1996" exhibition.
28. A copy of the article "Ein Star mit der Kamera für Stars vor der Kamera" is available at: http://www.ricopuhlmann.com/deutsch/puhlmann_05_01.html. Besides Berlin, Puhlmann also indicates in the article that he enjoys visiting London but not Paris, which never spoke to him.
29. From the "Biographical Overview" section of Peter Lindbergh's website (http://www.peterlindbergh.net/biography.html).
30. From the "Essay" section of Peter Lindbergh's website (http://peterlindbergh.net/essay.html),
31. For example, in an interview with Heinz-Norbert Jocks, Lindbergh declared: "A few years ago I resolved to withdraw as far as possible from the fashion world, as I was really irritated by the fact that the work produced among the photographers who went to all the fashion shows was pretty much all of the same. They all follow the same stimuli. My dream, and I would like to get a little closer to realizing it, is to be a fashion photographer who is independent of what happens in the world of fashion.... Once you turn your back on the fashion-world diary, you at long last find time for your own visions. And producing something of your own, an independent vision, can lead to images that inspire the designers.... Only if a person's soul appears in the photo do I as the photographer feel I have achieved what I wanted." See Jocks. The interview is available on Lindbergh's website in the "Press" section (http://www.peterlindbergh.net/#PRESSPRINT/24).
32. The interview is part of *F.C. Gundlach: Fotograph* (2008, dir. Reiner Holzemer and Hans-Michael Koetzle), the documentary that was made to accompany the "F.C. Gundlach – das fotografische Werk" exhibition.
33. *Brigitte* readers were different from those of *Film und Frau*, and Gundlach's shift in photographic language and composition reflected both their differences and larger trends in the industry. In the 1950s, he presented in staged and arranged interior shots the "dream of matter-of-fact luxury;" in the late 1950s travel fashion photography shot on location in Egypt, Kenya or Morocco captured the yearning for far-away places; in the 1960s confidently mannered poses mirrored a new corporeality and emancipation; and in the 1970s fashion photography became liberated from the dictates of staging. Women were no longer portrayed as society ladies, strongly rooted in their urban environment and rather limited by staged gracefulness in their poses, but increasingly began to resemble today's young, dynamic globe-trotters, perhaps best iconicized by the *Drei-Wetter-Taft* hairspray commercial of the 1980s and '90s, in which a woman steps out of a jet plane in a different city three times a day, while her hair remains perfectly styled (Lux 162).

34. The exhibits of fashion photography Gundlach has curated include: "From New Look to Petticoat: German Fashion Photography of the 1950s" (*Vom New Look zum Petticoat. Deutsche Modephotographie der fünfziger Jahre*, Berlin 1984) and the well-received and subsequently well-traveled "Fashion Worlds" (*ModeWelten*) exhibition at the Hochschule der Künste in 1986. After "*Berlin en vogue*," he followed up with "Fashion Images, Images of Fashion: German Fashion Photography 1945–1995" (*Modebilder, Bildermode Deutsche Modephotographie 1945–1995*) for the IFA (*Institut für Auslandsbeziehungen*/Institute for Foreign Affairs), which showed at the Art Library from 25 August 1994 to 1 October 1995 before going on an international tour. "The Pose as Body Language" (*Die Pose als Körpersprache*, 1999) and "Images Make Fashion" (*Bilder machen Mode*, 2004) were followed by the 2007 "Heartbeat of Fashion" exhibition, which featured almost 100 photos selected from this collection, covering the years 1843 to 2006, in order to prove his thesis that "fashion photography is much more than the reproduction of clothes" (10).

35. In the summer of 2009 there were two such exhibitions: one at the *Kunstgewerbemuseum* ("Free of Limits/Borders – Fashion, Photography, Underground GDR 1979–89") and one at the *Haus der Kulturen der Welt* ("Ostzeit: Stories from a Vanished Country," Photography Exhibition with photographs by Sibylle Bergemann, Ute Mahler, Werner Mahler, Harald Hauswald, Maurice Weiss).

36. The non-Berlin qualities are the ones Smith identifies in reviewing the following exhibitions: "Weird Beauty: Fashion Photography Now;" "Edward Steichen: In High Fashion: The Condé Nast Years, 1923–1937;" "This Is Not a Fashion Photograph;" and "Munkacsi's Lost Archive."

37. For more biographical material on Ebner, see the "Who is ACHTUNG ZEITGEIST?" section of the *ACHTUNG: Zeitschrift für Mode* website (http://www.achtung-mode.com/en/who+is+achtung+zeitgeist).

Chapter 4

Berliner Chic on the Silver Screen

"To look is to desire, to want to touch and caress, to slip a hand into a seam or fold. Whatever the price of pain, we want Joan Crawford's shoes. But is it the shoes we want, or the fantasy of a fashionable existence – the secret dream of Mildred Pierce?"

(Benstock and Ferriss 3)

Film, the technologically mediated cultural practice that followed photography and is the topic of this chapter, arrived in photography's wake. As with photography, historiography and museums, Berlin fashion also figures prominently in the institutions that provided challenges to existing film hegemonies. In the first part of the chapter we identify three historical caesuras that were crucial in establishing Berlin as central to global cinema and explore fashion's position and circumstances in relation to them. The first came about in a shift resulting from WWI. Tom Saunders sets the scene for us in *Hollywood in Berlin*: "Before World War I European audiences saw, apart from the preponderant French films, English, Italian, American and Scandinavian pictures. Different countries gained genre-specific identities – Italy in costume spectacle, the United States in slapstick and westerns, Denmark in chamber drama – but the market was not characterized by chauvinism" (Saunders 9). By 1918, however, "French dominance had given way to an unprecedented degree of international market control by American film. The United States produced several times the number of feature films annually as its nearest competitor, Germany, and had almost as many cinema seats as all other countries combined" (51). As we will see, the vertical control that was exercised from the outskirts of Berlin by UFA (the *Universum Film Aktien Gesellschaft*) was strong enough to, if not successfully challenge Hollywood, imprint itself on film history, in no small part insofar as fashion is concerned, due to one of the key stars to desert it for Hollywood: Marlene Dietrich. A second caesura occurred mid-century with radical shifts in cinema and fashion aesthetics that came with the swinging, prêt-à-porter 1960s and the new German cinema. Finally, towards the end of the century, the opportunity provided by another caesura – reunification – lit a slow fuse, which in a series of unexpectedly successful local and international films has added another facet to Berlin's image. Like the duality of Dietrich's hardworking approach and glitzy nightclub numbers, recent Berlin film fashion is also marked by a split between street-style and the glamour of festival culture.

Beginnings

Most accounts of German film point out that almost two months before the Lumière brothers' famous screenings on 28 December 1895, Max and Emil Skladanowsky held a public film screening as part of a variety show in front of an audience of 1,500 viewers at the Wintergarten in Berlin to demonstrate the Bioskop film projector they had invented. Most also note that both it and a screening of the Skladonowskys' shorts the following year were aesthetically and technically inferior to the Lumières' productions and that "the Cinématographe Lumière soon dominated European markets, whereas the German competition remained small and underfinanced" (Hake 2008, 10). At least initially. After a "pioneering" phase led by Oskar Messter, "the Wilhelmine cinema's first universal film genius [who] alone, for a brief period, combined all the functions which were eventually separated under a rigid division of labour: inventor of an improved projector, manufacturer of photographic and cinematic equipment, head of a film production company, director of 'Tonbilder' (sound-on-disk filmed opera-scenes)," there was a phase "centred on the constitution of a 'market' (national and international) as well as a standard product, which in turn defines not a use, but an experience, itself differentiated by genres, stars, audiences and exhibition spaces."[1] In this first phase, all costumes except historical ones were the responsibility of the actors, who were expected to provide them themselves from their rather meager earnings. According to Aschke, the yearly salary of a German actress in 1896 averaged 600 to 1,000 marks, which left little for any private luxuries after purchasing the requisite professional wardrobe (239), and the celebrated Viennese soprano Fritzi Massary was the first star of stage and screen to set a fashion agenda: "not only the highest paid stage star in Berlin, she was also the top model of the latest 'Paris fashions' from the house of Clara Schultz, which after its move from Postdamer Straße 132 to Tiergartenstraße 7 named its most beautiful showroom, designed by the architect Alfred Caspari, after its famous customer" (241). In the phase of restructuring and consolidation that followed, companies specializing in the manufacture of clothing for the stage and the screen such as Hugo Baruch & Cie, Verch and Flotow, and Theaterkunst (which remains Germany's largest costumer) were increasingly relied on for costumes and built up an international clientele. Hermann J. Kaufmann assumed control of Theaterkunst in 1918 after having owned a shop specializing in leather goods. Through work on Ernst Lubitsch's historical films *Carmen* (1918), *Madame Dubarry* (1919), and *Anna Boleyn* (1920), he earned the company international recognition and a contract to provide the 1925 MGM version of *Ben Hur* with 8,000 costumes (Aschke 240).

Fashion figures prominently in Lubitsch films, and "[c]ritics and biographers repeatedly point to Lubitsch's own family origins in the clothing industry and his training as an apprentice in that industry" (Weinstein 120–1). While early critics like Lotte Eisner dismissed Lubitsch's early *Konfektionskomödien* (ready-to-wear comedies) as "crude, clumsy and embarrassing,"[2] more recently Sabine Hake has cautioned against allowing the biographical to substitute for critical reflection. Another perspective is provided by Thomas Elsaesser, who sees in Lubitsch a clear example of a key characteristic of the consolidating phase of German cinema:

[T]he connection of the cinema to the world of commerce and marketing, of consumer goods, fashion, lifestyle, travel – what used to be called, dismissively "Die Konfektion" (the rag trade).… Featuring locations and intrigues that effectively mirrored or parodied the cinema itself, [Lubitsch's] films not only exposed how clever young men were making their fortune by trading on the vanities and anxieties of a new breed of (often female) consumers. Lubitsch also understood – and demonstrated in action – how in this world of make-believe, imposture can become itself a higher form of sincerity, and flattery the subtle pact film stars conclude with their public. (Elsaesser 1996, 25)

The first two such female stars were Asta Nielsen and Henny Porten. That only Nielsen is included in Aschke's accounting of film and fashion in Berlin speaks to the great differences in their images. "With her long blonde hair, plain features, and buxom figure, Porten personified traditional Germanic womanhood even when she appeared in rustic comedies that showed off her considerable comic talents" (Hake 2008, 16). Danish-born Nielsen, on the other hand, became a scintillating international film star, arguably the first, after accepting a contract from German producer Paul Davidson reputedly worth 85,000 marks for 1914 alone. She was also the first actress to set international fashion trends. Singled out in the 1913 *Zur Soziologie des Kinos* for her "unrivalled fame" (cited in Ganeva 2008, 142, Fn 4), she influenced hairstyles, hats, postures and attitudes around the world; according to Pablo Diaz's 1920 biography, that influence stretched from Paris and San Francisco to Brazil and Melbourne (Aschke 244).

While Nielsen's popularity and influence remained unaffected, WWI brought many changes to the film world, including a shift of power to Berlin not unrelated to Nielsen. Her 1910 star vehicle *Afgrunden* (*The Abyss*), her first film directed by Urban Gad, whom she soon married, introduced a new style of vertical integration into the process of film distribution based on Paul Davidson's recognition of her star qualities: "I had not been thinking about film production. But then I saw the first Asta Nielsen film. I realised that the age of the short film was past. And above all I realised that this woman was the first artist in the medium of film. Asta Nielsen, I instantly felt, could be a global success. It was 'International Film Sales' that provided 'Union' with eight Nielsen films per year. I built her a studio in Tempelhof, and set up a big production staff around her" (cited in Lähn, 85).

Davidson's company, PAGU (*Projektions-Aktiengesellschaft "Union"*), relocated its head office from Frankfurt to Berlin in 1912, but the onset of war two years later cut off his supply of Pathé films, causing him to suffer tremendous losses (Elsaesser 2000b, 112). In August 1915, he sold his movie theatres to the Danish Nordisk Film, the company Nielsen had begun with in 1910, and then, "under considerable secrecy," on 18 December 1917 both companies, together with a number of others, became part of the UFA conglomerate (Elsaesser 2000b, 112–13; cf. Hake 2008, 24).

There has been considerable debate surrounding UFA, the motivations for its wartime founding and ideologically inflected cartel-like corporate and corporatist dealings. Unquestionable is its status as "the" leading German concern of the interwar period and its role in providing a counter-hegemonic challenge to the dominance of Hollywood. As Elsaesser has shown, it was able to at least partly achieve this dominance until it was forced into a disastrous partnership in 1925 with Paramount and MGM, after which it needed to be bailed out in 1927 by the industrialist and newspaper magnate Alfred Hugenberg. Basing its "financing, management structure and economic performance" on both "other large industrial conglomerates emerging in Germany from the First World War (say, the press and publishing industries)" as well as international film industry competitors and predecessors, specifically pre-war French and post-war American film industries (Elsaesser 2000b, 109–10), UFA operated via the two principles of vertical integration and product differentiation thanks to Erich Pommer, who assumed control over production at UFA in 1923, two years after UFA took over its main rival DECLA-Bioscop, which Pommer headed. Saunders helpfully summarizes UFA's accomplishments:

> Thanks to the studies of Siegfried Kracauer and Lotte Eisner the inflationary period is usually seen as Weimar cinema's commercial and artistic golden age. In the cinema, as in other sectors of the German economy, inflation, though ultimately catastrophic in proportions and impact, massively aided the cause of postwar recovery. By sheltering the domestic market from foreign interference and encouraging industrial concentration, it fostered experimentation and growth. UFA's absorption in 1921 of Decla-Bioscop, a company which under the direction of Erich Pommer championed national cinema art, marked the confluence of industrial and creative trends which characterized this period. From the flowering of Expressionism in Robert Wiene's *Das Cabinet des Dr. Caligari*, through the chamber dramas of Lupu Pick and F. W. Murnau, the early thrillers of Fritz Lang, the comic and epic classics scripted by Hans Kraely and directed by Ernst Lubitsch, to the historical and mythical works of Richard Oswald and Paul Wegener, Weimar cinema expanded rapidly and won international prominence. (52)

The inflation of the early 1920s thus underwrote a remarkable boom that, as we saw in Chapter One on collections and exhibitions, also propelled the fashion world, which was by that time already well-established, into the limelight.

One could, as Katja Aschke has, begin documenting the "shimmering visions" of Berlin's fashion houses to appear on screen in the interwar period. Certainly Aschke draws welcome attention to an on-screen presence usually neglected in film studies.[3] What is striking in comparing Aschke's survey of the conjoining of film and fashion during the "golden age" of Weimar with the accountings by film scholars of the predominance of Hollywood and its interactions with its Berlin-led German counterpart is that the American trendsetting did not occur at the expense of the local fashion industry but rather helped make it arguably the strongest and most present in the global cultural imaginary that it has ever been. While "[t]he influence of American culture on modern mass culture was visible in all areas of everyday life, from fashion styles and consumption patterns to the dramatic changes in social and sexual roles…[and] the pervasiveness of these new designs for living remained strongest in the cinema" (Hake 2008, 245), that influence did not translate into material production. The studios at Tempelhof and Neubabelsberg continued to source from local costumers like Theaterkunst as well as increasingly from the Berlin fashion houses directly. For example (and these are Aschke's examples), S. Adam made the outfits in Murnau's 1921 *Haunted Castle* (*Schloß Vogelöd*), Flatow & Schädler did his 1922 *Phantom* and Fritz Lang's 1922 *Dr. Mabuse, the Gambler* (*Dr. Mabuse, der Spieler*). For Richard Eichberg's 1923 *Miss Raffka* (*Fräulein Raffke*), the Berlin fashion house Paula Behmer was contracted, while for his 1925 *Trophy Wife* (*Luxusweibchen*) it was Michaelis & Co, and for the 1927 *Der Fürst von Pappenheim* Gerson, Berlin's best-known design house, was chosen (Ganeva 2009, 132). Often, these connections were established by the stars themselves. For example, Aud Eged Nissen, who featured in *Phantom* and *Dr Mabuse*, also modeled for Flatow & Schädler and so would not have considered another house for her film costumes (Aschke 248). Similarly, the Javanese-born Lil Dagover – the female protagonist in *Phantom*, but notably before that in Robert Wiene's 1920 *Cabinet of Dr Caligari* and Fritz Lang's exotic 1919 *Harakiri* (her breakthrough role), *Spiders* (*Die Spinnen*, 1919), and *Destiny* (*Der müde Tod*, 1921) – was known for her elegant appearance and featured in both fashion magazines like the *Elegante Welt* as well as film ones such as *Der Kinofreund* (*Cinema Friend*), *Bühne und Film* (*Stage and Film*), and *Illustrierte Filmwoche* (*Illustrated Film Weekly*). All of these magazines devoted an increasing amount of space during the 1920s to their coverage of fashion and further compounded the spinoff effects for the local fashion industry (Aschke 251).

It was, however, neither Dagover nor Nissen nor even Asta Nielsen who ended up embodying the quintessence of Weimar cinematic fashion. After almost a decade of grunt-work in film, theatre and advertising, Marlene Dietrich catapulted herself with *The Blue Angel* (*Der blaue Engel*) at the same time both out of Berlin and into the global cinematic imaginary as *the* most fashionable Berlin film star ever. The night of *Blue Angel*'s première, 1 April 1930, "in a floor-length white fur coat with 25 suitcases filled with clothes from the Max Becker fashion house, she boarded the night train for Bremerhaven" and a ship bound for America (Aschke 252). The renowned UFA costume designer Tihamer Varady was supposed to have provided Dietrich's costumes for *Blue Angel*, but, as Dietrich recounts in her 1976 memoir *Ich bin, Gott sei Gank, Berlinerin*,[4] thanks to director Joseph von Sternberg, things went better than intended: "When I made *The Blue Angel*, it wasn't usual for a young actress to design or create her own costumes. One didn't have enough trust in her. But under von Sternberg's sharp eye, I managed just fine. The costumes that I wear in *Blue Angel* became a symbol of my personality and for the decade that this film influenced" (Cited in Aschke 251). In Hollywood, Dietrich and Sternberg took advantage of being associated with the raunchy, raucous Weimar Berlin of *The Blue Angel* to carve out for themselves libinally laden "European" identities. Dietrich has been described as the "most famous product of Sternbergian flummery...[having] played Galatea to his Pygmalion in seven films that straddle the boundary between collaboration and obsession."[5] The pair collaborated on *Morocco* (1930), in which Dietrich debuted her soon-to-be-famous trousers and kissed a female co-star; *Dishonored* (1931), in which she plays a prostitute turned Austrian spy;

Shanghai Express (1932), in which she plays the notorious courtesan Shanghai Lily; *Blonde Venus* (1932), in which she plays a club singer willing to do anything, including dress up in a gorilla costume, to earn money to restore her American chemist-husband to health; *The Scarlet Empress* (1934), in which she plays a young Catherine the Great; and *The Devil is a Woman* (1935), in which she plays a Spanish temptress. The seventh of their collaborations was the 1935 documentary *The Fashion Side of Hollywood*, von Sternberg's last production for Paramount, about which he stated: "Miss Dietrich and I have progressed as far as possible together. My being with her will not help her or me. If we continued, we would get into a pattern that would be harmful to both of us."[6] Von Sternberg seemed to be trying to avoid the inevitable. After making *The King Steps Out*, a 1936 operetta about the Austrian Empress Sisi, for Columbia, a series of disastrous directorial engagements followed. Dietrich, on the other hand, continued to thrive, becoming an American citizen in 1939 and, at the same time, ever more a Berliner. Her wartime engagement on the frontlines in Europe and Africa entertaining Allied troops earned her the appreciation of her adopted country as well as a Presidential Medal of Freedom and the title of Chevalier de la Legion d'Honneur. Her post-war cinematic work showed increasing respect for the specificity of her Berlin, and not simply "old world," background. Austrian Billy Wilder, who had had to leave his promising Berlin carrier as a screenwriter in 1933 and who lost family members at Auschwitz, played up Dietrich's Berlin roots in the 1948 rubble film *A Foreign Affair* and in the 1957 Agatha Christie mystery *Witness for the Prosecution*. For the former, set in occupied Berlin, he cast Dietrich as a local nightclub singer whose American boyfriend tries to help her conceal her former relationship with a wanted Nazi; the latter centers on the testimony of the untrustworthy German wife of a man accused of murder. Dietrich's identification with Berlin was further strengthened by her performance in the 1961 *Judgement at Nuremberg* as the widow of a Nazi officer and by her final appearance in film, the 1978 German-language *Schöner Gigolo, Armer Gigolo (Just a Gigolo)*, with a cameo as an aristocratic madame who runs a post-WWI brothel in Berlin at which David Bowie works as the eponymous gigolo. The fate of Dietrich and her belongings after her death in 1992 cemented her association with Berlin fashion. After a public funeral in Paris, where she had been living in seclusion during the final decade of her life, her remains were returned to and buried in Berlin's Friedenau cemetery in the Stubenrauchstraße, not far from her mother's. Helmut Newton's ashes were buried nearby in an honorary grave in 2004, and like Newton's estate, Dietrich's has also found its way into the Berlin museum scene. The majority of it was sold to the Stiftung Deutsche Kinemathek in 1993, and it has since become the core of the exhibition at the Filmmuseum Berlin. The Marlene Dietrich Collection is comprised of "over 3,000 textile items from the twenties to the nineties, including 50 film and 70 show costumes, by among others Jean Louis, Travis Banton, Edith Head, Eddie Schmidt," as well as "1,000 individual items from her private wardrobe including 50 handbags, 150 pairs of gloves (by among others Elizabeth Arden, Balenciaga, Balmain, Chanel, Courreges, Dior, Givenchy, Guerlain, Irene, Knize, Lee, Levis, Schiaparelli, Ungaro), 400 hats, 440 pairs of shoes (by, among others Agnes, Aprile, Cavanagh, Lilly Dache, Delman, Edouard, John Frederics, Massaro)…[and]

80 pieces of luggage (trunks, suitcases, hat boxes, vanity cases)."[7] From this listing it is not hard to understand why for many, whether they have visited the fabulous displays in the Filmmuseum at Potsdamerplatz or not, Dietrich is synonymous with Berlin fashion.

Meanwhile, back in the Berlin some felt she had deserted and turned her back on in the years leading up to WWII, the film industry was reeling on account of the introduction of sound, the world economic crisis, and the rise of National Socialism (Hake 2008, 49). The combined effect of these events on fashion was to shift the image of women and the source of their inspiration. After 1933 it became rare for actresses to appear in society tabloids as "multipliers of elegant fashion" (Aschke 255). Rather, films featured more mature and sensible, if still slim and attractive, mentor-figures, like the German female athletes who march into Berlin's Olympic Stadium in *Fest der Völker* (*The Festival of Nations*), part one of Leni Riefenstahl's *Olympia*, looking very trim in their bright white suits and starting a trend that lasted for years for short-waisted jackets, long narrow skirts and white caps worn at a rakish slant (Aschke 255). Moreover, the introduction of sound proved to be an opportunity for new talent, "with female stars such as Renate Müller, Lilian Harvey and Marika Rökk beginning to catch up in the popularity stakes with their male colleagues (Willy Fritsch, Heinz Rühmann and Hans Albers) and ensuring not only that the German film industry was by far the strongest in Europe (with over 500 sound films produces between 1930 and 1933), but was also able to lure talents from France and Italy to Berlin throughout the 1930s" (Elsaesser 2000, 387). Foreign markets remained important for UFA, with "Scandinavia, Central and Eastern Europe, Turkey and the Balkans form[ing] the most lucrative international audience for German films" (404). This helps to explain the in many ways cosmopolitan choice of subjects, as well as the stars that were promoted: the English Lilian Harvey, Hungarian Marika Rökk and Käthe von Nagy, Swedish Zarah Leander and Kristina Söderbaum, and Czech Lida Baarova (404).[8]

These foreign actresses were increasingly clothed according to the standards of international (meaning Hollywood) cinema. Gertrud Steckler, who was responsible for advising on costumes at UFA during the period, confessed to Katja Aschke in an interview that: "Each time before we discussed the costumes for a new film, we'd go to the cinema, to see an American film. We only watched American films – as long as it was possible. All the good ideas for my clothes came from American films" (cited in Aschke 256). The ideological incoherence that Dieter Schäfer describes in *The Divided Consciousness: German Culture and the Reality of Life 1933–1945* and Thomas Elsaesser draws on in his chapter on early 1930s film as "lifestyle propaganda" is particularly prominent in the realm of pre-WWII film fashion. Hollywood costume design reached an apex in the 1930s: "Paquin, Redfern, Lanvin, Alix, Agnés, Coco Chanel, and Worth all worked on American films in the 1930s. Especially successful were Elsa Schiaparelli and Madeleine Vionnet, who served as inspiration for all of the sophisticated evening dresses Edith Head, the most highly decorated costume designer in the history of film, made for Jean Harlow, Carole Lombard and Marlene Dietrich" (Aschke 256). This glamour and elegance were greatly coveted (the stuff that dreams and commodity fetishism are made of). Yet at the same time, as Elsaesser notes, these individual desires were set in dialectical contradiction with the sacrifices demanded by collectives: "It is as if, once part of the collective, one is lost, already sacrificed" (2000, 414). Yet spontaneous collectivities, and fashion, were not only possible but for a time, as we saw in Irene Guenther's work in Chapter Two, even encouraged in Nazi Germany. How to understand this? Elsaesser helpfully encourages his readers to consider their own subject-positions by pointing out the difficulty German audiences still have in responding to Nazi cinema:

> The common denominator would be consumption and "lifestyle" aspirations, rather than totalitarian ideology: if this is the recognition-effect that today's German audiences respond to, when wanting to know what it meant to be alive in the period, it makes the protective screen doubly necessary, for how could it share a *Lebensgefühl* that also colluded with such unimaginable physical horrors and permitted itself unspeakable moral depravities, with thinking itself sharing also that lifestyle's hideous underside? What one can be grateful for, perhaps, is that present social realities and political values seem so different. Even television seems to "protect" us from those "others" who look upon our lifestyle cynicisms, self-ironies and post-modern media-events rather less charitably than we do ourselves. (2000, 415)

After the War is Before the War?

Two of the main tendencies of Nazi Berlin fashion – its valorization of American film and the increasing necessity for creative cost-saving measures – made the war's end after the decisive Battle of Berlin and the surrender by German troops to the Soviets on 2 May 1945 seem less of a caesura than it is usually treated as by historians. That both the film and fashion industries were able to so quickly raise themselves up from the ashes (the relevant section of Aschke's text bears the heading "Phoenix") still tends to astonish those who have not experienced a war and its hardships and are not thinking of what Aschke poignantly describes as "the human need for alternate realities (*Gegenwirklickeiten*), which veil the visible or offer visions of marvellous transformations" (260). Twenty-two of the city's sixty UFA cinemas remained intact enough for screenings, at first of only foreign films in the original and then with makeshift subtitles (260). The first film studio to begin production again was DEFA (Deutsche Film AG), which was founded on 17 May 1946 after the Soviets licensed its first project, *The Murderers Are Among Us* (*Die Mörder Sind Unter Uns*, directed by Wolfgang Staudte). The Western Allies were keen to prevent the kind of vertical integration that had allowed UFA its monopolistic success and so bound their licenses to involvement in only one sector of the industry (production, distribution or exhibition) (Hickethier 195). By the late 1940s distribution companies were able to establish market dominance by "showing old Hollywood films, including many B pictures, as well as a large number of UFA films reclassified as harmless entertainment" (Hake 2008, 89). Film production started up in the new Federal Republic in an equally decentralized and localized manner with close to two hundred film production companies founded in the early postwar years (Hickethier 195). While many of the most important and productive companies were in Hamburg, such as Helmut Käutner's Camera-Film Produktion, Rolf Meyer's Junge Film-Union and Gyula Trebitsche and Walter Koppel's Real-Film (Hickethier 195), production resumed in the American sector in the Bavaria studios in Munich-Geiselgasteig and the Neue Deutsche Filmgesellschaft (NDF) (also in Munich), while "in the British zone, Rolf Thiele and Hans Abich established a small centre of film-making in Göttingen with Filmaufbau AG, a studio that became known for its controversial subject matter" (Hake 2008, 90). In Berlin, there were also a number of startups in the western sectors. Taking advantage of the concentration of talent in the former capital, among the most prominent were "Kurt Ulrich's Berolina-Film, which launched the successful Heimatfilm wave of the 1950s, and Horst Wendtland's Rialto-Film, which started the popular Edgar Wallace and Karl May series in the early 1960s. The most successful Berlin-based company was Artur Brauner's CCC (Central Cinema Company) studio, whose mixture of literary adaptions, social dramas, and lifestyle comedies embodied best the postwar compromise between cultural ambition and economic growth" (Hake 2008, 89–90; cf. Dillmann-Kühn 1990).

That the kind of compromises taking place in the making of film also occurred in contemporary fashion is revealed in the following remembrance: "In the beginning the material consisted of bedsheets, which André fashioned in such an opulent (*üppig*) manner with sequins that no one noticed" (cited in Aschke 261). André is the pseudonym of Walter Endres, as well as the name of the costume company and salon he started up to service Berlin's post-war acting profession. He was joined in July 1947 by the Rudow-Brosda salon, which also provided luxurious clothing in the spirit of an American cinema in the throes of Dior's sumptuous New Look.

The two Berlin fashion designers who became the costuming doyens of the postwar period chose not to merely imitate the foreign styles but to chart their own path. They are the ones, as we learned in Chapter One, whose work has been celebrated in exhibitions since reunification: Heinz Oestergaard and Uli Richter. Oestergaard's democratizing of fashion in the early post-war years was aimed at making Parisian style available to a larger swath of the German population, beginning with prominent film stars like Romy Schneider and Hildegard Knef. Oestergaard's costumes appear in the 1950 *Piquancy* (*Pikanterie*, directed by Artur Braun) on Irene von Meyendorff and Marina Ried, in the 1953 *Ave Maria* on Zarah Leander (Fig. 4.1), as well as in the 1955 *Master over Life and Death* (*Herr über Leben und Tod*, directed by Victor Vicas), the 1957 *Yes, Women Are Dangerous* (*Ja, die Frauen sind gefährlich*, directed by Peter Alexander) and the 1958 *Love Can Be Like Poison* (*Liebe kann wie Gift sein*, directed by Veit Harlen).[9]

Uli Richter was an equally youthful, sporty type when he entered the Berlin fashion world by way of an apprenticeship with the same renowned firm, Schröder-Eggeringhaus, that Heinz Oestergaard had started with (Fig. 4.2). When Oestergaard left the firm to become independent in 1952, moving his atelier to the villa at Ahornstraße 4, where he worked with around 300 employees until leaving Berlin for Munich in 1967 (Oestergaard 40), Richter

Figure 4.1: Zarah Leander at a fitting with Heinz Oestergaard, April 1954. (Deutsches Historisches Museum)

took his place as designer. When Hermann Eggeringhaus died in May 1959, Richter and his partner Dorothea Köhlich established "Uli Richter Modelle GmbH" (Richter 16). While Richter was the first German designer to offer a strictly ready-to-wear line, following in the influential footsteps of Yves Saint Laurent, his sporty elegance found no place on a screen whose silver was increasingly tarnished by interfering distributors who, because they financed most films, found it their right "to interfere in the making of a film, to demand changes in the screenplay, to interfere in casting decisions, and to call for reedited versions of already completed films" (Hickethier 202). Richter preferred to design wedding dresses for the likes of Princess Kyra of Prussia, Margaretha Ley (the founder, together with her husband Wolfgang, of the Escada label) and singer-actress Hildegard Knef. He counted the most elegant of celebrity wives among his best customers, such as Rut Brandt, whose husband Willy was mayor of West Berlin from 1957 to 1966 and Chancellor of West Germany from 1969 to 1974; Ebelin Bucerius, wife of the Hamburg publishing giant Gerd Bucerius; and the pianist Ignes Ponto, whose husband Jürgen was one of Germany's leading bankers and who was assassinated in 1977 in his summer villa by members of the *Rote Armee Fraktion* (Red Army Faction) in the lead-up to the so-called German Autumn (Aschke 268; Richter collection, ff. 186).

From the examples of Oestergaard and Richter, it is clear that, while there was a certain amount of continuity in the postwar period, not all remained as it had been. Just as the Weimar period had been marked by changing modes of femininity – "in particular the poles of androgyny and motherliness" – so too did the postwar period mark a departure from the previous styles "associated either with the New Woman of Weimar or with the feminine ideal of Nazism" (Baer 154). These modes found their visual representation, as they had before the war, both in film and in the fashion press, and these media coalesced in *Film und Frau*,

Figure 4.2: Uli Richter. (Münchner Stadtmuseum, Sammlung Fotographie)

founded in 1948 in Hamburg and soon the second most popular German film magazine in the postwar period after *Film Revue* and the second most popular women's magazine after *Constanze* (Baer 154, Fn 1). Film and fashion comprised the two largest parts of each issue, although it is often difficult to tell where the one ends and the other starts, as actresses sporting the latest fashions were one of the magazine's staples. As Hester Baer convincingly establishes, the magazine portrays both film and fashion "both as high art that should be viewed for its own sake, and as a functional artform that could have an effect on the everyday lives of female consumers" (162). These effects lasted until the decline of German popular cinema and changes in the cinema audiences of the 1960s forced its amalgamation into *Moderne Frau* (*The Modern Woman*) in 1966, but that they were different in East and West Berlin is acknowledged by the special section that ran in the Hamburg-based magazine from 1959 to 1962, on "From Berlin Fashion Houses" (Wagner 1993, 139).

If there is a real caesura in the postwar period, it happened sometime after the East Germans closed the border to West Berlin on 13 August 1961 and erected their "anti-fascist protective barrier." The local fashion and film industries were decimated. The number of those employed in Berlin's textile industry dropped from around 60,000 in 1956 to 17,500 in 1982, while the percentage of German films made in Berlin dropped from 90% before 1945 to 12% in 1974 (Aschke 269). A more subtle and extensive cultural shift accompanied this transition, something evident in the transition from *Film und Frau* to filmmaker Helke Sander's founding in 1974 of *Frauen und Film*, "the first and only European feminist film journal and…the oldest existing feminist film journal in the world" (Eigler and Kord 182). In a fiery opening editorial, Sander made clear that the purpose of the new journal was to provide a forum for feminist film work like her own: "We want to address women as spectators constantly confronted with filmic images and themes. The dominant culture may not have produced these images and themes, but it reproduces and reinforces them. *frauen und film* should give women the courage to withdraw from this brainwashing and to acknowledge their own experiences. This is also true for women who work directly in the media" (Lennsen 49). In other words, the "elegant Berlinerin" of the 1950s had become a bourgeois terrorist target à la Ignes Ponto, and while the New German Cinema's best-known directors were male (Fassbinder, Herzog, Wenders, Kluge, Syberberg, Schlöndorff, etc.), one also sees in their female counterparts the backlash against "the fathers" that motivated the movement.

That backlash constituted one of the most important paradigm shifts in the world of fashion, one we have already seen in the realm of fashion photography. The move from haute couture to ready-to-wear opened the door for the kind of street-style "anti-fashion" that is still a hallmark of film fashion (cf. Vinken). We will discuss two examples that are emblematic of this trend in greater detail in the next chapter on the alternative music scene: *Christiane F.* (*Christiane F. – Wir Kinder vom Bahnhof Zoo*, 1981) and *Run Lola Run* (*Lola rennt*, 1998). However, this chapter fortunately does not have to end on the downbeat "anti-fashion" note on which Aschke's 1993 article does. Aschke decries the lot of costume designers like Monika Jacobs, whose excellent work on everything from Fassbinder's epic

Berlin Alexanderplatz and *Veronika Voss* to *Wings of Desire* and, more recently, Tykwer's *Run Lola Run* and *The Princess and the Warrior* has largely gone unnoted. While Jacobs was able to provide Liv Ullmann with a wardrobe by Jil Sander for the 1989 *The Rosegarden*, largely because it was the follow-up film to director Fons Rademakers' Academy Award-winning *The Assault*, she reports that the costume budgets of most films were usually not enough to purchase even one such outfit and that designers were often reduced to asking actors, "Don't you have anything at home in your closet?" (Aschke 271). The situation in East Germany was only slightly rosier, with DEFA maintaining a well-trained costume department of at least 50 tailors. But it was not without its own problems either, particularly in terms of access to affordable materials and international patterns (271–2).

Reunification's G-local Effects

Reunification brought yet another set of challenges. DEFA was sold in 1992 to a French conglomerate, Compagnie Générale des Eaux (CGE), and Volker Schlöndorff was called on to serve as studio head from 1992 to 1997. Schlöndorff is, as Randall Halle points out, not only a veteran German director but one of the few with substantial transnational connections, having studied and worked as a director's assistant in France with Louis Malle, Ludwig Berger, Jean-Pierre Melville and Alain Resnais, and then moving to the U.S. in 1985 to direct films there (Halle 2008, 64–5). Schlöndorff is best known for his literary adaptations – of Musil's *Young Torless* (*Der junge Törless*, 1966), Kleist's *Michael Kohlhaas – Der Rebell* (in English known as *Man on Horseback*, 1969), Böll's *The Lost Honour of Katharina Blum* (*Die verlorene Ehre der Katharina Blum*, 1975), Grass's *The Tin Drum* (*Die Blechtrommel*, 1979, which won an Oscar for best foreign film), Tolstoy's *War and Peace* (*Krieg und Frieden*, 1982), Proust's *Un amour de Swann* (*Swann in Love*, 1984), Miller's *Death of a Salesman* (1985), Hadley Chase's *Palmetto* (1998), Atwood's *The Handmaid's Tale* (1990), and Frisch's *Homo Faber* (in English known as *Voyager*, 1991) – films which "evidence a precision in their camerawork, but as adaptations...often leave critics uninspired" (Halle 2008, 65). In other words, Schlöndorff approaches his craft in the same way the fashion photographers detailed in the previous chapter approached theirs, as a *Handwerker* or craftsman (65).

Schlöndorff set about turning the DEFA facilities at Babelsberg into "a centre of European film and television production" (Hake 2008, 180), but this did not mean rejecting Hollywood as much as it meant attempting to match it: Schlöndorff "sought for all of Europe what the United States has in Hollywood" (Halle 69). The end of Schlöndorff's tenure as studio head in 1997 corresponded with changes in CGE. After buying up DEFA in 1992, it continued to expand through the 1990s, something Jean-Marie Messier accelerated when he took control of the company and turned it into Vivendi Universal, one of the world's largest conglomerates with interests "in such diverse sectors as transportation, communications, healthcare, construction, property management, entertainment, software, desalination plants, and media" (Halle 2008, 60).[10] By 2004 Messier had been removed as CEO and charged with mismanagement, and the Babelsberg studios sent reeling with the rest of the Vivendi empire as the stock market boom of the 1990s ended (83). In 2004 it was sold to new owners, Carl Woebcken and Christoph Fisser, who went public and put the company Studio Babelsberg AG on the stock market the following year. After having produced only one film in 2006, the studio made twelve major feature films in 2007 and eight in 2008.[11] The international orientation of those films has increased notably as well. Since the 2002 *The Pianist* (directed by Roman Polanski) starring Adrien Brody, who went on to be the face of Zegna's 2003 collections, Babelsberg can now boast such international hits as the last two Bourne films with Matt Damon (*Supremacy*, 2004, and *Ultimatum*, 2007, directed by Paul Greengrass), *Around the World in Eighty Days* starring Jackie Chan (2004, directed by Frank Coraci), *The Constant Gardener* starring Ralph Fiennes and Rachel Weisz (2005, directed by Fernando Meirelles), *V for Vendetta* starring Natalie Portman and Hugo Weaving (2005, directed by James McTeigue), *The Reader*, for which Kate Winslet won an Academy Award as Best Actress (2008, directed by Stephen Daldry), Tom Cruise's *Valkyrie* (2008, directed by Bryan Singer) and Quentin Tarantino's *Inglourious Basterds* (2009). Ending this list of cinematic glitterati with Tom Tykwer's *The International* (2009, starring Clive Owens and Naomi Watts) nicely captures the heightened standing the Berlin studio has been able to establish for itself as a publicly traded company, in no small part due to one of its key champions, Hollywood producer Joel Silver, with whom the Studio Babelsberg entered into a strategic alliance at the end of 2008. It is becoming increasingly common to see actors associated with Berlin in international productions; for example, Franka Potente, star of *Run Lola Run*, is the female love interest in *The Bourne Supremacy*, while Daniel Brühl of *Goodbye Lenin!* and *The Edukators* fame features in *Inglourious Basterds* and has a cameo in *The Bourne Ultimatum*. Berlin sites are also appearing more often on international screens, a tendency we address in greater detail in the excursus that follows this chapter.

This international tendency has been matched by, and has in part helped to engender parallel and also counter-movements among local talent. In addition to X-Filme, which producer Stefan Arndt and directors Wolfgang Becker, Dani Levy and Tom Tykwer founded in 1994 in Berlin on the model of Harvey Weinstein's Miramax (Baute), a number of other Germanophone directors, such as Andreas Dresen, Oskar Roehler, Leander Haußmann and Hans Weingartner have made films featuring Berlin that have enjoyed critical and commercial success. More closely associated with the city is the school of filmmakers known as the *Berliner Schule* (Berlin School), so-called because the directors first associated with it got to know each other in the late 1980s and early 1990s at the German Film and Television Academy Berlin (DFFB) – in the first instance, Christian Petzold, Thomas Arslan und Angela Schanelec, but also a host of others.[12] While their films are set in a range of locales, often far beyond the city's borders, there is a common aesthetic characterizing the school's work: "in describing the realism of the 'Berliner Schule,' one speaks of slowness, of exactitude, of everyday life. These films are set in the here and now and deal with people and stories which one would not be surprised to encounter in everyday life" (Baute). In other words, this is not action cinema, or any other entertainment genre but rather form-oriented attempts to portray reality in a way which, because it is intended to seem as natural as possible, ends up appearing highly, if roughly stylized just as much European intellectual everyday life can appear to be to those (usually from the new world) used to clothing that can be divided into office formal and weekend casual. In our final chapter on fashion retail, we mention the example of a recent book which satirizes the shops in which clothing for this look is bought, and the aesthetic will be one not unfamiliar to viewers of *Berliner Schule* films: rather pricy jeans and t-shirts deliberately made to look unremarkable but still chic. The author of this satire, Ralph Martin, describes the style as offending his white-scarf Manhattan sensibilities, something at which many Manhattanites would surely wonder.

Finally, mention of scarves reminds us that any account of fashion in relation to Berlin film would be remiss not to include the Berlinale (Fig. 4.3), whose director since 2001, the

Figure 4.3: Berlinale statue in the Sony Centre. (Photo: K. Sark)

year after it moved into its current home in the Theater am Potsdamer Platz, has been Dieter Kosslick. Known for his dapper appearance (his scarves often come in for comment)[13] as much as for his energy, good humor, and business acumen, Kosslick is responsible for making key changes to the festival that have supported the recent surge in German film, such as introducing the *Perspektive Deutsches Kino* and Talent Campus series. Under his leadership, the Berlin film festival, which was started up in 1951 as part of postwar American efforts to rejuvenate the country's cultural scene and get a foot up in the Cold War, has regained some of its original glamour.[14] While the first decade was mostly influenced by Hollywood (for example, the film that opened the festival was Hitchcock's *Rebecca*, and its stars Laurence Olivier and Joan Fontaine came to Berlin for the screening), political events and concerns increasingly exerted their influence. A high point was reached in 1970, the only year no prizes were awarded on account of Michael Verhoeven's controversial *O.K.*, about a Vietnamese girl who is gang-raped by soldiers wearing American uniforms (and speaking with broad Bavarian accents) and then murdered. Reunification, the move to Potsdamer Platz and the appointment of Kosslick have since helped the festival regain momentum, and of the thousands of film festivals that now take place each year, the Berlinale is recognized as one of the "big five," which are, in calendar order: "Sundance, January; Berlin, February; Cannes, May; Venice, August; Toronto, September. That's it" (Marshall 65). One could find no better summation than that of the status of Berlin's current film renaissance, which has added fuel to the city's surging popularity and helped to shape its new fashion-related image.

Excursus: Berlin as Backdrop in Early 21st-Century Dystopian Science Fiction Film

"One of the problems of Berlin today is that fascism is the 'environment' which it inherits as part of the problem it must negotiate under modern circumstances, the problem of renewing itself as a liberal city in the teeth of this inheritance. That is, the problem of Berlin is not just to 'think globally' but to work out a just relation between its form and its material conditions (material conditions that, as an environment, including its Nazi heritage)." (Blum 2003, 81)

If contemporary cinema is any indication, Berlin will long be imprisoned, and its visual imaginary influenced, by the horrible events that were directed from it leading up to, during and in the aftermath of WWII. Films like *Downfall* (*Der Untergang,* 2004, directed by Oliver Hirschbiegel), *Valkyrie* (2008, directed by Bryan Singer) and *Inglourious Basterds* (2009, directed by Quentin Tarantino), to name but a few, demonstrate the continued popularity of historical films about Hitler and Nazi Germany.[15] However, even in films not set in, or in any way involving, Nazi Berlin but rather only filmed on location in the city, one finds that the material memories of Berlin's buildings exert an influence whose gravitational field seems to be centered around the same totalitarian tensions that attracted the British punks to the city in the late 1970s and were displayed with great swagger during U2's Zoo TV tour. Cities, as we know, "are never the sum of their physical parts but are always saturated in the symbolic, increasingly couched in filmic images and filmic texts" (Law 522). As we see in the rest of this excursus, the historical resonances of Berlin's urban visual imaginary in two relatively obscure science fiction action films reflect a clear gendered dimension that translates into eerily similar geo-aesthetic styles with subtle yet important differences. Identifying these differences – between a modern, Euro-American and dominantly female approach and a postmodern, global and dominantly male one – helps in mapping key features in the tradition of city films, especially those prominently associated with Berlin.

Karen Kusama's *Aeon Flux* (2005) and Kurt Wimmer's *Equilibrium* (2002) seem to beg for comparison on account of their uncanny similarities. Both are set in dystopian city-states of the future (*Equilibrium* in Libria; *Aeon Flux* in Bregna). The populations of both of these totalitarian societies are held in check by means of biotechnology (the drug Prozium keeps Librians from feeling, while Bregnans are clone-like humans made of recycled DNA and the implanted memories of the dead). Both films feature protagonists who are trained killing machines set on assassinating an authoritarian leader to liberate their societies from the technologically controlled stasis they have fallen into. Both protagonists become involved with resistance movements to help bring about that end, and both work with double-crossing partners who are visible minorities. Both films were made by neophyte American directors, and neither enjoyed much critical or commercial success.[16] Of greatest pertinence to this study is the fact that both films were shot on location in Berlin after Brasilia, the planned city designed by architect Oscar Niemeyer that became Brazil's capital in 1960, proved too difficult and expensive to be feasible.[17] In addition to Berlin's impressive and relatively inexpensive studio facilities, one of the attractions of the city for both Kusama and Wimmer was that, while cinematic, much of the city was not (yet) recognizable for a global, and in the first instance American, audience. However, while both directors avoid or disguise Berlin's relatively few iconic landmarks – the Reichstag, the Victory Column, the Brandenburg Gate, the TV tower at Alexanderplatz, the Olympic Stadium, and what's left of the Wall[18] – Bregna and Libria still bear distinctive traces of Berlin and its traumatic history, though interestingly antithetical ones. Despite their overwhelming similarities, the two films approach the genre of dystopian science fiction in diametrically opposed ways: *Equilibrium* self-consciously places itself firmly in the footsteps of the Wachowski Brothers' *Matrix* franchise (something very evident in the poster for it), while *Aeon Flux* sets itself decidedly apart from this tradition while remaining within its skin-tight black-and-white leather fashion register.

To understand how trapped in its history Berlin seems destined to remain and how this has translated into a discernible film style, we outline Kusama's and Wimmer's Berlin imaginaries and find that the urban visual imaginary in Kusama's *Aeon Flux* reflects a female-inflected experience of enlightened European modernity, a world which is a sanctuary as well as a prison, in which nature and the feminine can turn deadly. Wimmer's, on the other hand, takes its cues from the Asian-inflected global turbo-capitalism already present in *Blade Runner*. Its totalitarian imaginary is a mythical male one in which undesirables are incinerated. So while Wimmer perpetuates a Valkyrie-esque fascination with the bloodthirsty destructiveness once housed on Berlin soil, Kusama can be seen to be creating an environment which enlivens the rootedness of a cultivated tradition and provides shelter from the onslaughts of global turbo-capitalism. Berlin's urban visual imaginary can thus be shown to reveal how the split nature of the *Dialectic of Enlightenment* experience of modernity is gendered.

Kusama's Berlin

When Karen Kusama decided that her second feature film after the award-winning indie hit *Girlfight* of 2000 would be based on the global TV cult hit *Aeon Flux*, she deliberately set out to make a filmic "companion piece," a "parallel separate entity" to, and not simply an adaptation of, the MTV animation series created by Korean-American Peter Chung.[19] What Kusama didn't want to take on board was Chung's relentlessly bleak vision, preferring the utopianism expressed in Aeon's culminating voice-over: "now we can move forward, to live once, *for real*, and then give way to people who might do it better" (italics added). Unlike the eponymous protagonist of the original TV series, who is a cruel, impossibly narrow-waisted dominatrix involved in a mutually sadomasochistic relationship with Trevor Goodchild, the technocratic leader of the walled city of Bregna, and who is violently killed off in each episode of the shorts (although not in the half-hour episodes, with one exception), Kusama's Aeon wouldn't hurt a fly, or would prefer not to. This point is made quite literally in the opening sequence. Each of Chung's episodes begins with the lashes of an animated eye snapping down and trapping a fly. Kusama's Aeon is equally quick, but she lets the fly her eyelashes have trapped go. She is not a black widow, Venus flytrap or any of the other castrating creatures that populate the mainstream (male) sci-fi imaginary,[20] but rather an all-too-human being of flesh and feelings, forced to respond to a dystopian set of circumstances not of her making but also not beyond her control. Played by a top-fit Charlize Theron fresh from her Oscar-winning performance in the 2003 *Monster* and sporting a skin-tight black bodysuit and an equally slick, pointy black haircut, Kusama's Aeon is not the rootless, nihilistic loner Chung's is. On the contrary. She has a kid sister, Una, who means the world to her, and there is a touching scene after the opening sequence of them shopping together at an outdoor market. Government thugs murdering Una motivates Kusama's Aeon to assassinate Goodchild. However, in the attempt she learns that he is in fact the love of her life and that this love stretches back seven generations. As is underscored repeatedly on the accompanying features on the DVD, Kusama's *Aeon Flux* is in the first instance a love story, and it needed a setting that would provide an appropriately authoritarian yet "organic" (another word that features prominently in the DVD interviews) environment in which love could take root and literally blossom, like the cherry trees in the climactic shootout, to which we will return shortly.

Baudrillard advises us in *America* to move outward from the screen towards the city: "The American city seems to have stepped right out of the movies. To grasp its secret, you should not, then, begin with the city and move inwards to the screen; you should begin with the screen and move outwards to the city" (cited in Law 522). Doing so, we find that the Berlin sites Kusama chose for her film provide a balance of organicism and authoritarianism while at the same time drawing on various layers in the city's troubled history to create a vision that is convincingly futuristic. For example, to evoke the everyday life of Bregna's citizens, the luscious eighteenth-century terracing of Sanssouci, absolutist monarch Friedrich the Great's summer palace in Potsdam, which made its film debut in *Aeon Flux* (a fact the filmmakers repeat with evident pride in the DVD interviews), is used in the opening sequence of the film. The state-provided apartment complex Una and her husband live in is the Bauhaus museum Walter Gropius designed. Una's husband, one of the good-guy scientists, is shown in a tropical greenhouse setting with a panoply of bright orange bird-of-paradise flowers. The ethereal "handler space" in which the assassins get their instructions from an angelic-looking red-haired being is the Langhans building, which dates back to 1790 when it was built to house a veterinarian school (*Tierarzneischule*) founded by Friedrich the Great in order to provide better care for his horses. Trevor Goodchild's governmental inner circle, on the other hand, does not meet in a garden but rather among the towering columns of the interior of the Crematorium Baumschulenweg. Aeon infiltrates these governmental quarters via the equally imposing *Trudelwindkanal*, which was used as an aerodynamic testing facility for Nazi aircraft (*Deutsche Versuchsanstalt für Luftfahrt*). The place she and Trevor reconnect is the underground historicist brick waterworks in Friedrichshagen, which, upon its completion in 1893, provided the city with state-of-the-art technology using sand to filter and purify the Berlin water supply – the purity of his undying feelings for her, which motivated his scientific attempts to transfer DNA and thus prolong human life in its singularity, is thus reflected in their surroundings. The play of absolutist and organic "good guy" locations off against more modern and massively monumental concrete "bad guy" ones is integrated into the central site of the film: Trevor's private quarters, in reality Berlin's Tierheim animal shelter facility, which was designed by architect Dietrich Bangert and went into service in 2001. With its concrete rimmed courtyard, this remarkable structure was able to incorporate both governmental monumentality and domestic organicism. The grove of cherry trees in the facility's courtyard, which picks up on the vegetational, good-guy associations of Una's husband's birds of paradise, is one of the rare times in the film that the filmmakers added anything substantial to an existing location or used background CGI. However, the presence of a grove of blossoming cherry trees was deemed crucial enough for the climactic shootout that one was specially constructed.

From this account it should be clear that Kusama's *Aeon Flux* does not offer a typical dystopian sci-fi cinematic urban imaginary. While it might open with the usual conventions describing how the world in the film has gotten into the totalitarian mess it has ("2011. A virus kills 99% of the world's population. A scientist, Trevor Goodchild, develops a cure. The five million survivors live in Bregna, the last city on earth. The Goodchild dynasty rules for 400 years. Rebels emerge to challenge the Goodchild regime"), it goes on to rub the genre against the grain to expose a particular kind of rootedness. This did not endear it to the fans of Peter Chung's dystopian vision of Bregna, which is a relentlessly bleak, bunker-like environment. Part spaceship, part laboratory, part Barbican, and part *Blade Runner*, Chung's Bregna is as lacking in nurturing, tender qualities as its protagonist. While both Bregnas are highly advanced civilizations of great technological sophistication, only Kusama's contains spaces of comfort and contemplation: tropical gardens, markets, and cherry groves – spaces, in other words, that help humans buttress the alienation of modern life. In creating a world of the future, what Kusama in fact did was recreate a world of the past, and not just any past but one associated with an emancipatory culture noted for historically providing Jews, women and other minorities access to means of cultivating their own livelihoods. Her vision of Berlin is of a historically saturated cityscape shielded from the globalizing pressures that marked the latter parts of the twentieth century. In order to see what was shielded out of that vision and to appreciate how much this view contrasts with the dystopian male urban vision of global cyberpunk, we turn next to *Equilibrium*.

Wimmer's Berlin

Unlike the verdantly terraced, enlightened Bregna with which Kusama's film opens, Wimmer's Libria begins by evoking a war-ravaged cityscape with ruins reminiscent of those cleared by the *Trümmerfrauen* (rubble women) in the aftermath of WWII. This bunker-like, mostly CGI-generated city may look like *Metropolis* to the uninitiated, but Wimmer is quick on the DVD Director's Commentary to point out that, on the contrary, not Fritz Lang but Hugh Ferriss, an early twentieth-century conceptual artist, was the source of his inspiration for *Equilibrium*'s cityscapes – that is, the same Ferriss known for influencing the cityscapes in *Batman* and Kerry Conran's *Sky Captain and the World of Tomorrow*. Whatever its inspiration, Wimmer's world of tomorrow with its massive, imposing grey stone settings unmistakably hearkens back to the monumental architectural achievements of the fascist period. Wimmer seems to be deliberately conjuring up images that ensure that the city in his film is associated with the Berlin that Alexandra Ritchie has termed "Faust's Metropolis" – a Berlin notably absent in Kusama's *Aeon Flux*. Not only does the establishing shot of *Equilibrium*'s cityscape echo Lang, the creeping fascist undertones of that era are underscored by including a Zeppelin-type dirigible in the initial cityscape and then cutting, first, to a flag with an iron-cross-like symbol in the center that looks remarkably like a swastika and then, should any doubts still persist, to a clip of Hitler addressing troops who sit listening to him in the same type of drill formation as the Librians are shown listening to their leader in. That the scene itself was actually not shot in Berlin does not alter its imaginary fascist connections but rather strengthens them; it was filmed in Rome, specifically at the *Esposizione Universale Romana*, or EUR, the area where Mussolini had planned to host a world exhibition celebrating Fascist Italy. Scheduled for 1942, the plans were abandoned when the war broke out, with only a few of the monumental structures completed. As Wimmer relates in the commentary that accompanies the DVD, "I chose Rome because I kind of shot Berlin out, and Rome was the only other place that had a similar fascist, sort of neoclassical, uh, fascist take on neoclassical architecture that, you know, Hitler's production designers had sort of invented, and so we had to go there." Wimmer is also on record as identifying the stark, obsolete architecture of the Nazi period as something Berlin offered that no other city could: "'That spare architecture does convey a sense of power and a sense of the whole being more important than the individual,' he says. 'But it also is an architecture that pretty much disappeared after World War II. You don't see it in the rest of the world so it feels uniquely frozen in time, which is precisely the feeling I wanted for Libria.'"[21] Wimmer and one of his producers, Lucas Foster, who also offers a commentary on the DVD, make no bones about how much they "absolutely loved" Hitler's architecture and how perfect they found it for the film. As though a bit embarrassed by the effusiveness of his praise for the Olympic Stadium built for the infamous 1936 games – he exclaims: "We just loved it. We saw it, and we were like, my God, this is made of granite and stone and limestone, and it seems permanent, and we want to get this on film" – , Foster goes on to clarify: "We clearly don't admire the Nazis but some of the buildings that they built just, it's amazing the permanence that they have. You know, there's no building like them anywhere else." Wimmer agrees that Nazis were actually "fairly cultured" and "contributed a lot to design."

Given its setting, one is not surprised that Libria is, indeed, a fascist society ruled by a dictator called, with a bluntness rivaling that of the Hitler clip, the Father. Images of the Father are everywhere in Libria: on televisions in homes, on the walls of offices, outside on screens, and even on the Zeppelin overhead – a much more powerful cult of personality than Bregna's Trevor Goodchild, who appears only on a Japanese-style flag before transforming into the main love interest. Libria's Father "wields power through a group of Ninja-like 'clerics' who enforce his vision of peace through the chemical control of all emotion,"[22] and the plot revolves around the highest ranking of these clerics, John Preston – played by a top-fit Christian Bale en route from *American Psycho* to *Batman* with slicked-back dark hair and a high-collared black *Matrix* raincoat.[23] One day Preston accidentally knocks his morning dose of Prozium off the bathroom counter, and it shatters on the floor. When he cannot get a replacement because a terrorist attack closes the Equilibrium Center (a CG-enhanced version of the back of the Olympic Stadium known as the *Glockenturm* or bell tower), he begins to experience emotions. These emotions are set off in the brutal literalism of the film in terms of puppy love. Preston, who proves from the opening to the climactic fight scenes that he is as speedy and molecular as his name would suggest, is confronted with two creatures faced with extermination because their kind is capable of, in fact renowned for, generating feelings. While he is able to save the dog, who licks his face hopefully, the incineration of the woman, who did not respond with a kiss to his stroking of her face, fuels his determination to bring about the regime's end. The result of Preston's awakening is not, however, the enlightened bringing down of walls, the note on which *Aeon Flux* ends, but rather a storming-of-the-Bastille-style palace (actually EUR) revolt made possible by his taking down of the man who has been running things behind the screen of the Father, namely the Vice-Counsel, whose very title is intended to radiate the evil he represents. After making short shrift of the Father's black-helmeted security personnel in their black trench-coats in a scene straight out of the *Matrix*, Preston, now conspicuously clad all in white à la Bruce Lee in *The Chinese Connection*,[24] enters the inner chamber of power, which is decked out to appear Rococo with marble pillars, a dignified chandelier and vaguely Baroque paintings on the walls with white flailing figures against dark backgrounds.[25] After more protracted displays of Gun Kata, a fighting technique Wimmer invented for *Equilibrium*, and the climactic execution of the faux-father figure, there is a final denouement, in which Preston, clutching the ribbon he had found among the incinerated woman's effects, grimly smiles as he looks out over a Libria eerily similar to the Los Angeles in the film Kusama deliberately set her *Aeon Flux* against. Given how prototypical its dystopian sci-fi cinematic urban imaginary has become and that our two films position themselves against it in such diametrically opposed ways, we turn next to *Blade Runner*.

Future Noir vs Future Perfect

Blade Runner focuses on the efforts of a Blade Runner named Decker, played by Harrison Ford, who is assigned to hunt down a half-dozen replicants who have managed to come to Los Angeles to track down their maker, the head of the Tyrell Corporation. The film begins with what has become the iconic image of dystopian urbanity. A sea of orange-tinged lights stretching as far as the eye can see calls to mind flying into LAX, an impression encouraged by a text indicating that we are in the Los Angeles of 2019.[26] This opening, establishing shot of Ridley Scott's 1982 genre-refining cult film, echoed in *Equilibrium*'s concluding cityscape and countered by *Aeon Flux*'s sunny, verdantly terraced steps of Sanssouci, has served to entrench *Blade Runner* as "the definitive screen depiction of the nightmare future city. Its imagery has become the standard visual iconography for the science fiction metropolis: super-tall buildings; poorly-lit streets and alleys; smog; rain; heavy industry belching fire into the sky; neon advertisements; overcrowding; ethnically diverse (that is, non-white) crowds; eclectic punk-inspired costumes and hairstyles; retrofitted buildings of varying architectural styles; scavenged props, and so on" (Rowley 203). By locating her Bregna in Berlin and eschewing CGI, Kusama was able to provide her film with a setting that looks futuristic but was before neon and industrial pollution. The architecture in *Aeon Flux* is not of the postmodern glass-and-steel-skyscraper variety that dominates the cityscapes of Hong Kong and Tokyo and inspired *Blade Runner*. Rather, it is primarily concrete, wood and grass; this future looks softer and less regressive than the one in *Equilibrium* and *Blade Runner*.

The past that *Blade Runner* evokes has been described as down-beat and destructive (Redmond 174). Time in both *Blade Runner* and *Equilibrium* has "gone back to earlier, 'bloodier' periods of human existence" (175): *Equilibrium* to a past that is blatantly fascist; *Blade Runner* to one that is more varied: "In this mish-mash of historical reference points, the economic and existential crisis of 1940s America is co-joined with the 'lost civilisation' of the Mayans...and the tyrannical Ancient Egyptians whose lust for power provided the model for autocratic rule that *Blade Runner* aspires to" (175). In Kusama's *Aeon Flux,* as we have seen, the autocratic impulses hearkened back to are at the same time enlightened. Nor can one maintain of it, as Bruno does of *Blade Runner,* that:

> The explosive Orient dominates, the Orient of yesterday incorporating the Orient of today. Overlooking the city is the "Japanese simulacrum," the huge advertisement which alternates a seductive Japanese face and a Coca Cola sign. In the postindustrial city the explosion of urbanization, melting the futuristic high-tech look into an intercultural scenario, recreates the third world inside the first. One travels almost without moving, for the Orient occupies the next block. The Los Angeles of *Blade Runner* is China(in) town. (66)

Kusama's cityscape contains no noodle-shops, or any other kind of ethnic restaurants for that matter – only a market. Even the martial arts moves her characters specialize in are primarily Brazilian capoeira, gymnastics and street-fighting, rather than the kung fu, jujitsu and other styles notably adopted in the "Asian invasion" of Hollywood action films (such as in the *Matrix* and *Kill Bill* franchises), which motivated Wimmer to invent Gun Kata.

That is not to say there are no traces of Asian style in *Aeon Flux,* but the ones there differ in noteworthy ways from the Asian-inspired exteriors in *Blade Runner* and the Asian-inspired costumes, sunglasses, and fight sequences in *Equilibrium.* The interiors of Trevor Goodchild's and Aeon's kid-sister's apartments are minimalist Asian in their aesthetic; both radiate the wooded warmth of an elegant sushi bar. They are Asian as refracted through a tastefully modern European sensibility rather than through pan-Pacific popular culture. Perhaps most illustrative in this regard are the Asian billboards in *Blade Runner* and *Aeon Flux.* In the latter, it is a large white poster towering over the citizens of Bregna emblazoned with a portrait of a spiky-haired, autocratic-looking Trevor Goodchild gazing resolutely into the distance next to a red, flower-embossed circle evocative of the Japanese flag. This billboard first appears in the opening sequence in which Aeon's voiceover expands on the caption about Bregna's history. While she explains that "the Goodchilds built Bregna to ensure us a future," we see a scan of what appears to be the Goodchild dynasty in Andy Warhol-type portraits followed by the face-embossed flag, which cuts to the civilized gardens of Sanssouci. The image appears again a few scenes later in the background after Aeon gets her orders to infiltrate and disrupt the government's surveillance system (interestingly, the only time in the film she wears a white bodysuit). However, the image proves merely to have been an establishing shot so that we later recognize "the leader;" we never see it again.

The "Japanese simulacrum" in *Blade Runner,* on the other hand, offers a more prominent and more thematically significant leitmotif.[27] That the female Japanese face on the illuminated screen of a tall skyscraper with flowers in her hair signifies as motherly is indicated by her first appearance, which occurs immediately after Leon shoots the interrogator who asks about his mother. Unlike humans, replicants are incapable of emotional response and Blade Runners identify them by subjecting them to a test which measures how they respond to stimuli intended to generate emotional responses: "*Blade Runner* begins with such a test as it is being administered to Leon, a replicant who is trying to hide his identity. Leon succeeds up to a certain point, but there arises a question which he cannot handle. Asked to name all the good things that come to his mind thinking about his mother, Leon explodes, 'My mother, I'll tell you about my mother,' and kills the inquirer" (Bruno 71).

The second time we see the Japanese female screen mother is after Decker is taken from the Asian restaurant by the police. As they rise vertically in the police space-cruiser, Decker looks forlornly out the window into the rain, and we cut to her smiling at him; he is then shown in the cruiser eating the noodles he has brought with him from the restaurant as though encouraged to finish his supper. When Decker is flown to the Tyrrell building to interrogate Rachel, they pass the same screen both on the way there and on the way back, but both times it shows a bright-red Coca-Cola sign indicative of the corporate nature of the trip. The Japanese face then reappears to smile benevolently after Decker and Rachel's passionate embrace, and it is pictured twice more smiling down through the roof of the Bradbury Building, in which the genetic designer J.F. Sebastian lives: first when J.F. invites in Pris, the "basic pleasure model" replicant played by Daryl Hannah, whom he has found in a garbage heap, and again when Decker arrives at the building to track down her and Roy Batty, the leader of the group of replicants whose escape and search for Tyrell drives the film's plot. As Decker enters into the open central foyer of the great Los Angeles architectural landmark,[28] he looks up through the wrought-iron encased skylight to see the woman on the screen looking down and singing him something soothing. While being associated with a virtual mother further strengthens the possibility of Decker being a replicant, both she and the spider in Rachel's dream have also been interpreted as being references to the city.[29] The spider evokes the same trauma as mention of Leon's mother and prompts an equally violent and destructive response,[30] but the Japanese screen mother prevails (as do Decker and Rachel). She is the future noir.

Bruno attributes Rachel's survival, her success, to the possession of a photograph: "She has a document – as we know, the foundation of history. Her document is a photograph, a photograph of her mother, hugging her, a child, against her, wakening in her the rumpled softness of, most probably, a hamburger" (61). Decker also owns photographs, which are on display on his piano and capture Rachel's imagination. Leon, on the other hand, is unsuccessful at getting back what Roy Batty scornfully refers to as his "precious photos." Having possession of Leon's photos allows Decker to track down and kill Zhora, the snake-like female replicant, while Rachel shoots Leon to save Decker. Clearly, photographs are of a similar phallic significance to the replicants as Indiana Jones's hat in that franchise and Neo's sunglasses in *The Matrix*. The astute viewer quickly realizes that losing these magically powerful objects – when, for example, the wind blows off Indie's hat or Agent Smith knocks off Neo's sunglasses – renders the heroes vulnerable.

Bruno builds on the role of photographs in *Blade Runner* to establish a theoretical link between photography, history and maternity that is also of relevance to *Aeon Flux* and *Equilibrium* (71):

History is that time when my mother was alive before me. It is the trace of the dream of unity, of its impossibility. The all-nourishing mother is there, yet as that which has been given up. The Imaginary exists as a loss. Photographs are documents of existence in a history to be transformed into memories, monuments of the past. Such is the very challenge of history, as Michel Foucault has pointed out. 'History is that which transforms documents into monuments.' The document is for Foucault a central question of history; for *Blade Runner* it is the essential element for the establishment of a temporality, of perceiving past and future. (72)

Photographs, in other words, provide provenance. In *Blade Runner* they are the only guarantors of Decker's past, underscoring the unreliability of memory and the possibility that he is not the human viewers initially assume him to be. In *Equilibrium*, it is through a photograph that Preston learns what it means to live as a feeling human being. He finds a photograph among the personal effects of the partner he is forced to eliminate for feeling, in which his partner appears together with a woman. On the back of the photograph the partner had written "Freedom," which puzzles Preston until he has a chance to interrogate the woman and discover his own feelings for her. Photographs in *Aeon Flux* also provide provenance. They are the only surviving traces of the disappeared, their value indicated by an amber shell. We see one such photograph when an older man, driven to desperation and near madness, wanders through the market showing people a small yellow stone containing his daughter's likeness and asking if anyone has seen her. "She disappeared two months ago," he explains in a Latin-tinged accent suggestive of the Argentinean Mothers of the Plaza de Mayo, who took action to find the whereabouts of their children kidnapped by agents of the military government during the Dirty War years (1976–1983). The main photograph in *Aeon Flux* is the one Aeon finds in Trevor's lab of herself in her previous existence as his wife. It, and learning her previous name (Kathryn), provide her with an identity; through the history Trevor shares with her, the history he has kept alive through the photo when he believed her DNA to have gone lost, she comes to know who she is.

Bruno calls to mind Barthes' observation that "the photograph's immobility is the result of perverse confusion between two concepts: the Real and the Live. By attesting that the object has been real, the photograph surreptitiously induces belief that it is alive.... Photography, moreover, began historically as an art of the Person: of civil status, of what we might call, in all senses of the term, the body's formality. Replicants rely on photography for its perverse confusion, as it induces the surreptitious belief and hope of being alive" (72–3). Photographs become necessary for the continuation of replicant life and render them oddly human; the replicants' "assurance of a future relies on the possibility of acquiring a past...[on] the proof of having existed and therefore of having the right to exist" (70–1). Because photographs can reproduce what appear to have been humans, rather than the mechanically reproduced objects that they themselves are, they can create the possibility that those pictured once actually were humans, that they had a past, a future, and therefore a history and an identity.

Photographs are thus like mothers: "necessary to the claiming of a history, to the affirmation of an identity over time" (71).

Why the virtual Japanese screen mother prevails in *Blade Runner*, a film about the identification of human-looking beings produced to provide slave labor for the colonizing of "outer" worlds, has to do with the science-fiction Frankenstein tradition of monstrous creation it is part of, in which humans (usually male scientists) take it upon themselves to create artificial life, and their god-like ambitions eventually run off the rails and result in havoc.[31] Unlike *Aeon Flux*, whose characters all contain human DNA and both good and bad guys aspire, and compete, to control the motherhood function of reproducing a human population, in *Blade Runner* and *Equilibrium* the mother function is depicted as that which separates humans from non-humans. In *Equilibrium*, it is through the mother and her photograph that one can connect with the human and position oneself on her side in the monumental Manichean battle of good and evil, while in *Blade Runner*, because this is a tragic impossibility, mere mention of motherhood triggers violent destruction.[32] In Wimmer's film, the mother is lost and all that remains of her is a satin ribbon, which Preston fingers longingly as he stares out over the embattled cityscape in *Equilibrium*'s final sequence. In Kusama's film, on the other hand, it is not the mother who is necessary for this claiming, but rather the city itself – specifically Berlin, the quintessentially modern, authoritarian-organic city. The city takes over this identity-affirming role, rendering the symbolic mother – the dirigible containing the DNA, which in the end crashes into and brings down the wall that protects Bregna from the surrounding jungle (a form of mothership if ever there was one) – unnecessary.

We can account for the differences in these cinematic urban visions by the gendered critiques of Fredric Jameson's analysis of modernism and postmodernism. Camilla Griggers, for example:

> argues that 'postmodernism' must mean something very different for a female audience than for a male one, since the experience of twentieth-century modernity has been so different for women. Jameson's view of modernism as an artistic movement of progressive resistance to industrial society (1983) speaks little to women's experience of the repressive material discourse that addressed them as wives and mothers during the same period. Postmodernism…in representations of women for a female audience, demonstrates the anxiety of a break with motherhood experienced by the new generation of middle-class women in the post-war period…. For women it is not Jameson's loss of a sense of history that is the problem, but the lived history of a loss of sense. (Griggers 92, cited in Bradby 159)

It is precisely this anxiety we find in Kusama's *Aeon Flux*, the plot of which hinges on the discovery of the fact that every newborn child in Bregna is actually a clone created with recycled DNA so that instead of dying, individuals are reborn and newborns carry the traces of their antecedents' memories. Trevor's evil brother, Oren, confesses in the final confrontation that his real enemy is not his brother but mother nature: "Beat death, beat nature, we've gone beyond you.... Nature's the one who's obsolete, not us." Oren also sees this obsolescence in the inter-human bonds that Aeon's kid-sister's husband remains loyal to and, before ordering him killed, states that: "I don't understand people like you and Trevor. Your sentimentality, your devotion to the past. Two things that are gone."[33] Oren attempts to have all of the evidence pointing to the possibility of natural pregnancies, such as Una's, destroyed in order to stay in power and live forever, and it's up to Aeon to bring down both him and the dirigible which stores the DNA, which she does from the cherry grove. The film ends with the dirigible crashing through the wall to the tropical jungle that surrounds Bregna, opening up the city to a future in which its citizens can live "real" lives. We can thus understand how Berlin helps Kusama to overcome *Blade Runner*'s and *Equilibrium*'s postmodern approach to history. It replaces the mother in providing for "the affirmation of an identity over time." No other city evokes as successfully the same sense of time having been frozen into and then released from totalitarianism and therefore has the same sense, not of possibility, but of recovery, of starting up, as Berlin. To see how this was true even before the fall of the Wall, one has only to call to mind Wim Wender's classic Berlin film, the 1987 *Wings of Desire* (*Der Himmel über Berlin*).

Wender's Berlin

The parts of this film about an angel who decides to become human that are told from the perspective of the angels are shot in mournful black-and-white. As David Harvey recounts, for the two angels, "time and space just are, an infinite present in an infinite space which reduces the whole world to a monochromatic state. Everything seems to float in the same undifferentiated present" (315). This frozen world reflects the trauma induced by WWII, which, as Harvey points out, is repeatedly referred to "as if this was indeed when this time began and when the spaces of the city were shattered" (317). It thaws, so to speak, and shifts from black-and-white to color, when the angel Damiel falls in love with the circus-performer Marion and decides to abandon his otherworldly eternal life, to live, like Aeon, "once, for real, and then give way to people who might do it better."[34] Even without the Wall having fallen, *Wings of Desire* is still a partly colorful love story, one which, like those in *Blade Runner, Equilibrium* and *Aeon Flux*, hinges on photographs. Just as Trevor's love, symbolized in the photo he keeps of her, provides Aeon with a sense of identity and well-being and Preston's love for the woman in his partner's photograph provides him with purpose and a goal, Damiel's love for Marion provides answers to the questions that haunt them: "'Why am I me and not you?' 'Why am I here and not there?' and 'Where did time begin and where does space end?' What is born of their coming together, reflects Damiel as he helps her to practice her trapeze act after their first night together, is not a child but an immortal image that all can share and live by" (Harvey 320). Marion believes she can produce a new future for herself with the help of photos from a photo-booth, while Damiel's love for her is cemented by studying the photographs on the wall of her trailer.[35]

What saves Wenders's film from sliding irrevocably into banality, at least for Harvey, is the final shift back to "the monochrome of enduring time" (320), and the return of Homer, the old storyteller who cannot find Potsdamer Platz and is shown in the final scene heading directly for the Wall as though the embodiment of Benjamin's destructive character: "The destructive character sees nothing permanent. But for this very reason he sees ways everywhere. Where others encounter walls or mountains, there too he sees a way. But because he sees a way everywhere, he has to clear things from it everywhere. Not always by brute force; sometimes by the most refined. Because he sees ways everywhere, he always positions himself at crossroads. No moment can know what the next will bring" (Benjamin, "The Destructive Character" 542). What Harvey appreciates about Homer is that: "Becoming, according to him, has to be more than creating just another set of depthless images. It has to be situated and understood historically" (321). From this, however, Harvey draws an odd conclusion: "But that presupposes that history can be captured without the use of images" (321). Watching the final image of Homer heading toward the Wall twenty years after it came down would seem to invalidate this presupposition. Neither the image of Homer nor the one of the Cassiel, the angel who remained behind, leaning dejectedly against the Angel atop the Victory Column, are depthless. On the contrary, they demand to be situated and understood historically, something many of the thousands who gathered to catch a glimpse of Barack Obama, when he spoke against the backdrop of the Victory Column in the summer of 2008 as part of his successful presidential campaign, likely realized if the setting turned their thoughts to Wender's films and made them wonder whether Cassiel and Damiel would vote for Obama. Making the connection between Damiel's decision to become mortal and the campaign slogan that made Obama immortal draws attention to the historical distance, the 21 years, between these two moments.

The sense of recoverability that Berlin manages to exude has to do with the relentlessly dialectical nature of modernity and its incessant movement forward through time. Having been a divided outpost for the better part of three decades after having housed one of the most infamous regimes in modern history, Berlin still manages, as David Harvey notes in his reading of Wender's film, to provide spaces in which "some sense of identity [can] be forged and sustained" (317). Those spaces in Wender's film are the library and the circus, which marry the high and low aspects of culture in the seemingly effortless way Berlin makes possible. These humanizing spaces of contemplation, comfort and even cotton-candy, like the gardens and markets in *Aeon Flux*, are precisely the spaces the clerics in *Equilibrium* are trained to destroy. We can identify the importance of the modernity of these spaces and why they are in Berlin and not in *Blade Runner* by concluding our considerations with the spatial organization of Fritz Lang's 1927 *Metropolis*, a film whose influence on *Blade Runner* and urban imaginaries in general has been profound.

Metropolis Meets City of Angels

The garden in *Metropolis* is a fateful space of transgression. When Maria, whom Andreas Huyssen describes in his important reading of "The Vamp and the Machine" as "the woman of the depths who preaches peace and social harmony to the workers" (1986, 66), enters the pleasure gardens in which Freder, the son of Metropolis's master, is frolicking as Faust and Gretchen do in Murnau's 1926 classic, she is surrounded by the workers' children. Freder's love-at-first-sight moment is thus redolent with biblical imagery, just as Faust's of Margarete is. This Edenic site of transformative encounter contrasts with the terraces of Sanssouci with which *Aeon Flux* opens and the library in *Wings of Desire*, in that the latter two provide public spaces for citizens to take breaks from their busy lives and contemplate what it would take to transcend their frozen, controlled and controlling environments and become agents of their own destiny. The vertical organization of the cinematic worlds in *Blade Runner*, *Metropolis* and *Equilibrium* reflect their societies' rigid class divisions: the elites live in towers and the toiling masses below (in the case of *Metropolis* literally below ground). While the interpretation of this juxtaposition of opulent grandeur and grinding working-class poverty, which is given an ethnicized postcolonial twist in *Blade Runner*, has been fiercely debated,[36] their schematics have not. The Berlin of *Aeon Flux* and *Wings of Desire*, on the other hand, is horizontal, with walls separating those who are implicitly on the same level. While verticality is a feature of those films as well, it demarcates a divine realm from a universal human space. The angels falling and the DNA-dirigible being brought down are statements not about class-warfare but rather about the need to recognize a common humanity. Under the sky of Berlin, they tell us, we can all unfreeze and start anew, just as the city has had to on account of its horrific history, time and time again.

Notes

1. These are the phases Thomas Elsaesser has distinguished on the basis of Corinna Müller's *Frühe deutsche Kinematographie* (Elsaesser 1996, 14–24). Sabine Hake, on the other hand, divides Wilhelmine cinema into three phases: the early years of emergence and experimentation (1895–1906), the period of expansion and consolidation (1906–1910), and the process of standardization identified with the longer film (1910–18) (2008, 10).
2. *derb, schwerfällig und peinlich*, cited in Aschke 243.
3. Aschke 247–8. This work has since been complemented in the field of German cinema by Ganeva, Weinstein and Baer. For examples of work on fashion and popular cinema, see Bruzzi and Moseley.
4. This memoir was a complicated affair: "Apart from the letters and the press clippings the third big area of the estate are the writings. Here we find versions of her *ABC*, a book too many biographers have ignored…. Then there is the original manuscript of her autobiography, which was written in English but never published. The German edition is a translation from the English. The French edition is a translation from the German, and the American copy is a translation from the French. To make things even more complicated, two different versions of her memoirs were published in

Germany. *Nehmt nur mein Leben* (*Just Take My Life*) is a translation of the original manuscript; *Ich bin Gott sei Dank Berlinerin* (*I am, Thank God, a Berliner*) is a retranslation of one of the many foreign versions. No matter which edition one quotes, one never quotes the original. That, too, is typical of Marlene" (Sudendorf 382–3).

5. See the program notes on the University of California Berkeley Art Museum and Pacific Film Archive's website, from which this quote was taken, for the "Josef von Sternberg: Eros and Abstraction" series they ran between 15 January and 22 February 2009 (http://www.bampfa. berkeley.edu/filmseries/sternberg2009).

6. In the entry on *The Fashion Side of Hollywood* available on the IMDb website (http://www.imdb. com/title/tt0228292/).

7. This information is from the website run by the Marlene Dietrich Collection: http://www.marlene. com/berlin.html.

8. Many of these actresses have far more interesting backgrounds than Elsaesser credits them with. Rökk, for example, "was born in Cairo, Egypt, the daughter of the Hungarian architect Eduard Rökk and his wife Maria Karoly. She spent her childhood in Budapest, but in 1924 her family moved to Paris. Here she learned to dance and starred as a dancer in the Moulin Rouge. After a tour in the USA she came to England where she acted in her first film. In 1934 she was offered a contract with Universum Film AG (UFA) in Germany, where she became one of the most famous filmstars of the time" (http://en.wikipedia.org/wiki/Marika_Rökk). For more on Rökk, Leander and Soderbaum, see Bruns and for Harvey: Borgelt.

9. This list is compiled from the Oestergaard catalogue and www.imdb.de. For more on his other artistic and professional endeavors, see his personal website: http://heinz-oestergaard.de.

10. Halle notes that the title of a 2003 biography of Messier is *The Man Who Tried to Buy the World* (2008, 60).

11. See "Hollywood Helps Revive Berlin's Former Movie Glory," *Deutsche Welle* 09.08.2008 <http:// www.dw-world.de/dw/article/0,2144,3549403,00.html>.

12. A list of the early DFFB graduates would begin with Christoph Dreher, Bärbel Freund, Frank Behnke, Reinhold Vorschneider, Wolfgang Schmidt, Angelika Becker, Ludger Blanke, and Michel Freericks (Baute).

13. Tilmann's biographical article on Kosslick begins: "His trademarks: floppy hat, red (mostly) scarf and unshakeable good mood" (Tilmann). Mayor Klaus Wowereit opens his welcome in the 2006 Berlinale magazine on an uncannily similar note: "Entrance Kosslick: tuxedo, white scarf, bow-tie only occasionally, but always a beaming smile and an appropriate witty remark (Auftritt Kosslick: Smoking, weißer Schal, Fliege nur manchmal, dafür immer ein strahlendes Lächeln und ein passender launiger Spruch" (Aggio 169).

14. The arte.tv website has a succinct but informative account of the "Geschichte der Berlinale," on which we have drawn: http://www.arte.tv/de/film/berlinale/1097246,CmC=1097248.html.

15. For a comprehensive discussion of the ongoing appeal of fascism in cinema, see Strzelczyk 2001, 2008.

16. The relevant statistics are available on the films' English Wikipedia sites: "On February 9, 2006, [*Aeon Flux*] completed its theatrical run, grossing a domestic take of $25,874,337 and a worldwide box office total of $52,304,001. Critical reaction was mixed to negative. The film holds an 11% positive rating on Rotten Tomatoes and a score of 36 out of 100 on Metacritic." Similarly *Equilibrium* "received generally negative reviews from critics. The review aggregator Rotten Tomatoes reported that 35% of critics gave the film positive reviews, based on 79 reviews. Metacritic reported the film had an average score of 33 out of 100, based on 22 reviews."

17. We are grateful to Emilie Dionne for bringing *Equilibrium*'s Berlin connection to our attention.

18. To appreciate the global nature of the cinematic imaginary under discussion here and how much it has shifted over the past decade, one can note that the places the makers of the 1998 *Run Lola Run*, most of them residents of Berlin, avoided as "too popular" are now no longer considered iconic representations of the city: "the *Lola rennt* filmmakers...wanted to show the German capital from its less-familiar side. Producer Stefan Arndt: 'So for once, no Zoo Station, Memorial Church, and so on, but rather the fascinating places that are only discovered by a second look'" (http://german.about.com/library/bllolafotos.htm). Another point of interest is that this use of Berlin as "the" anonymous modern city has a tradition practically as long as the history of Berlin cinema. Thanks to Nora Gortcheva, June Hwang and Ina Murdock-Hinrichs for sharing their ideas on this in the context of their work on Wilhelmine and Weimar cinema.

19. Chung's TV series premiered in 1991 on MTV's Liquid Television in a six-part serial of short films that was followed in 1992 by five individual short episodes and then in 1995 with a season of ten half-hour episodes aired as a stand-alone series. The description of the relationship is by the film's screenwriters, Phil Hay and Matt Manfredi.

20. See the chapter on cyberpunk in Andrew Ross's *Strange Weather*.

21. This quote is from a Sean Bean fan website: http://www.compleatseanbean.com/equilibrium3.html, hereafter csb.com.

22. This section is based on information available on csb.com and the English Wikipedia entry on *Equilibrium*.

23. On the commentary, Wimmer reflects on this connection: "There are people who said that this film took the costumes from the *Matrix*. I don't see that at all.... Neo wasn't wearing Prada at all. But it's interesting when I see the costumes for *Reloaded*, the costumes were very similar to this. And I'm sure the motivation was the same, that Neo, you know, assuming theological, god-like proportions and so that's why he has a semi-religious tone to his outfits. But also there's the set in the teaser, where his fighting is actually quite similar to this [final take out of the bodyguards], 19th-century semi-classical."

24. Wimmer explains in the commentary, when reminded of the allusion by Foster, that Lee goes to a funeral in a white mourning suit, comments, that yes, "they look rocking on him, and I figured it would look rocking on Christian."

25. Wimmer comments in the commentary that: "The Palace that I wanted to shoot in, which we weren't allowed to shoot in, would have looked something like this. Wolf actually modeled this room after... 'one of Frederick's' [Lucas pipes in] – yeah, that's right. It's not as sumptuous as I would have liked but, you know I was actually pretty down on it at the time. I was pretty depressed about it, but at the end of the day it does its job."

26. The illusion is an impressive accomplishment given that the set was a miniature, 18 feet long and 13 feet deep (Bukatman 27). While Scott's initial idea for the scene was motivated by a flight into New York, the lighting for the scene came to chief modelmaker, Mark Stetson, when he was flying into Los Angeles at night and suddenly realized why the original plan for toplit fluorescent lamps hadn't worked (Sammon 234).

27. Scott's intentions with this imagery, as related by special effects supervisor, David Dryer, are revealing: "What happened...was that Ridley and I had a meeting where he told me, 'I want a bunch of phony oriental commercials where geisha girls are doing unhealthy things. Smoking, taking drugs or whatever. To kind of continue with the oppressive feeling throughout the landscape'" (Sammon 242–3). Dryer also reveals the idea he had for the type of pills the geisha is seen to be swallowing, namely, birth control pills: "This was strictly my idea – it seemed to make sense that birth control would be heavily advertised in such an overpopulated future" (Sammon 243). This is in keeping with the figure's virtuality; she cannot be a biological mother.

28. Another is Frank Lloyd Wright's Ennis-Brown House of 1923, on which Deckard's apartment is modeled (Bukatman 81). For more on the cinematic appearances of these buildings, see *Los Angeles Plays Itself* (2003, dir. Thom Andersen).

29. See, for example, http://scribble.com/uwi/br/br-misog.html: "Whenever we see the city, it is crowded by people, and every image seems to be an idol to consumerism, be they adverts for the Off World Colonies, or Coca-Cola. On the few occasions the city is barren, it is also burnt out and spent. Thus the mother figure of the spider, evidently a reference to the archaic mother, shows that this figure is also represented by the city."

30. Decker is able to convince Rachel, Tyrell's assistant, that she is a replicant with implanted memories by telling her about a dream she has had in which hundreds of baby spiders eat their mother: "You remember the spider that lived in a bush outside your window? Orange body. Green legs. Watched her build a web all summer. Then one day there was a big egg in it. The egg hatched… And a hundred baby spiders came out and ate her." That these eggs are indeed being imagined from the perspective of male castration anxiety becomes clear in a later breakfast scene in which J.F. Sebastian, one of the genetic designers responsible for the creation of the replicants, boils eggs for his replicant guests. When Pris, the "basic pleasure model" replicant played by Daryl Hannah, shows that she has what it takes to get at the polysemic eggs, one realizes that Sebastian's days are even more limited than the replicants'. Given that the slang word for testicles is "eggs" in German, one could view this scene as a multilingual juvenile pun.

31. Sharalyn Orbaugh explores this issue in "Frankenstein and the Cyborg Metropolis" in Steven T. Brown's collection on *Cinema Anime*.

32. Bruno identifies the mother as a "breaking point" in the text (71) and points to the opening scene, which is subsequently replayed on video and with a voice-over – the repetition indicative of the trauma it manifests and the evident need for working through it.

33. One recalls that Emma Bovary was described by the narrator in Flaubert's novel as "more sentimental than artistic." Huyssen uses this quote as a springboard in his essay "Mass Culture as Woman: Modernism's Other."

34. For more on the significance of the color shift in *Wings of Desire*, see Batchelor.

35. Interestingly, there is a motherly Asian connection to this relation parallel to the Asian billboard in *Blade Runner*. When Damien turns back to look at Marion again after studying the photos, there is a drawing of a Japanese woman over the bed behind her. When the scene shifts to color a few moments later and the walls become turquoise, the picture remains black-and-white.

36. See the section in Elsaesser (2000a) on "Interpreting 'Metropolis': Reading for the Plot" 42–56 and Peter Brooker's and Sean Redmond's contributions to *The Blade Runner Experience*.

Chapter 5

Berlin Calling: Sex and Drugs and Punk and Techno

"Tomorrow belongs to those who can hear it coming" (the phrase with which RCA trailed the release of *Heroes* in 1977)

(Seabrook 244)

Why is the world's first and only Ramones Museum, dedicated to the band from the suburban New York borough of Queens, a band that was among the first to put punk rock on the global map, located not in New York but in Berlin, specifically, around the corner from the fabulously renovated New Synagogue in Oranienburger Strasse in Mitte? As is the case when one examines the relation of fashion and museums, historiography, photography and film in Berlin, one finds here too that the city occupies a special position in the institutionalizing of alternative music scenes. In looking to account for what would at first appear to be the most unlikely presence of the Ramones Museum in Berlin, we find the traces of raves, of the ravaged (*Christiane F. – Wir Kinder vom Bahnhof Zoo*, 1981) and the ravishing (*Lola Rennt*, 1998), that catapulted spots like Zoo Station into the lyrics of global hits and turned Berlin into an international magnet for clubbers.

One problem with the conceptualization of space in studies of popular musical subcultures is that it is "usually theorised as that realm of musical activity which escapes global cultural influences" (Laughey 101). The music scenes in Berlin discussed in this chapter are nothing if not global, or perhaps better: transnational, insofar as participants are marked and often referred to by ethno-national markers such as language. One reads, for example, of encounters with, or of overhearing, Spanish, Swedish, and American and British English. These spaces encourage one to attend to their glocality as they are inhabited and constructed by a mix of those who call Berlin home and those who visit for shorter periods of time but also nonetheless feel attached to the city on account of those visits. The relative strength of Berlin and of particular localities within the city as music scenes confirms the perceptions of the young people Laughey interviewed about the importance of clearly defined localities for music scenes and how they differ from place to place (102). What it adds to these understandings is an appreciation of the struggles necessary as those who have participated in these scenes age and find themselves having to engage entrepreneurially with global market forces.

The Hansa Studios and SO36: The Global and Local Ground Zeroes of Berlin's Music Scene

"This ain't Rock'n'Roll. This is Genocide"

David Bowie, "Future Legend," *Diamond Dogs* (1974)

It does not seem too daring to suggest that without the Hansa Tonstudios (*Ton* means "sound" or "tone" in German), Berlin's music scene would not have developed with the same alternative flair that it has (Fig. 5.1).[1] Originally founded in 1964 by brothers Peter and Thomas Meisel, the studio moved in 1972 into the *Meistersaal*, a majestic building

Figure 5.1: Meistersaal building, list of occupants in entryway. (Photo: K. Sark)

Figure 5.2: Meistersaal building, Köthener Straße 38, exterior view. (Photo: K. Sark)

from the *Gründerzeit* in the Köthener Strasse, around the corner from Potsdamer Platz and, at that time, down the street from the Wall. One of the only buildings on the street to have survived WWII reasonably intact, its spatial qualities corresponded with the Meisels' dreams of multiple studio production (Fig. 5.2). They quickly built up a stable of hit-generating performers and a reputation as one of the leading music labels in West Germany. As in the expression "it takes money to make money," its reputation helped the Hansa Studios attract an increasingly international clientele, beginning with Iggy Pop and David Bowie.[2]

As Thomas Seabrook attests, "During the 1970s, David Bowie was British pop's most talismanic, chameleonic character" (22), one who distinguished himself from his contemporaries by "his ability to shock and awe in the same breath" (23). By the mid-1970s, however, Bowie was beginning to be consumed by his musical personas. He managed to retire Aladdin Sane and then, "at the close of a performance at London's Hammersmith Odeon on July 3, 1973," Ziggy Stardust: "His famous declaration – 'not only is this the last show of the tour, but it's the last show we'll ever do' – did not, as was originally thought, mean the end for David Bowie, just his crimson-haired alter ego" (24). The cocaine-addled, anorexic Thin White Duke who followed Ziggy was harder to shake, but moving to Berlin in 1976 was precisely what any doctor should have ordered. It took Bowie out of the destructive Los Angeles environment he had settled into in April 1975 after three years of heavy touring and relentless record-making and provided him with a stimulating musical trajectory to explore, namely the new German electronic music of Kraftwerk and their "less mechanical contemporaries, among them Can, Faust, and Neu!…later dubbed (to their dismay) krautrock or, to use their own term, kosmische musik" (85). However, as Seabrook points out, had Bowie wanted to merely "reproduce the sound that was coming out of Köln, he probably would have headed straight for Plank's studio – just as a number of other British acts would do later in the 1970s, including Ultravox, Eurythmics, and even Brian Eno" (85), the producer of Bowie's three Berlin albums.

Much more pulled Bowie to Berlin than its music, something evident in his meeting with Christopher Isherwood, who attended the concert he gave at the Englewood Forum in Los Angeles on 11 February 1976. They reportedly "spoke at some length…[with] Bowie probing the writer with questions about Berlin, principally in relation to its atmosphere of decadence and artistic liberty, which, by way of *Cabaret* [1972], had already informed the mood of the Station to Station tour" (85). Keith Negus situates Bowie's musical development in Berlin as a placing of rock "within a series of musical dialogues…. Rock was not ending and has not died; it was just going 'somewhere else'" (152). Tricia Henry and Jon Stratton have given that "somewhere else" cultural definition, establishing that "there is a trajectory in Bowie's work during the 1970s that shows an increasing fascination with apocalypse" (Stratton 2007, 136), which Henry situates as anticipating punk (36) and Stratton argues "serves as the metaphoric understanding for the culturally traumatic recognition and acknowledgment of the Judeocide" (2007, 136). Stratton establishes that Bowie's close friend, Iggy Pop, the so-called "godfather of punk," has "the emotional structure of a

Holocaust Jew" (2005, 89): engaging in on-stage self-mutilation in front of his Jewish soon-to-be wife, remembering the best man at his wedding as wearing an SS uniform rather than the *Luftwaffe* fighter pilot's jacket the best man records himself as having worn, and generally evidencing "internalised destruction and the retreat from a reality that is too awful to contemplate" (89). Iggy accompanied Bowie to Berlin, made two records with him there, and shared an apartment with him at Hauptstrasse 155 in Schöneberg, within walking distance of the Hansa Studios. In reading punk as an "affective expression of that cultural trauma [namely, the Holocaust] before it was acknowledged and named" (102), Stratton offers a well-documented explanation of Berlin's attractiveness for punk:

> By 1976/7 Berlin was to become a strong attractor for punk. In these years Iggy and David Bowie lived there and their albums *Lust for Life*, *The Idiot* and *Low* and *Heroes* were conceived there. In 1977 the Sex Pistols went to Berlin to escape the media frenzy in England. It was while there that they wrote 'Holidays in the Sun' which contains the line: 'I wanna go to a new Belsen'. In 1978 the English punk band the Vibrators wrote their second album, V2, in Berlin.... Berlin became an epicentre for, especially English, punk. The draw of Berlin for these artists is usually couched in terms of its freedom, its decadence, the youth of its population. However, what is not suggested is that Berlin had been the capital of Nazi Germany. At this time in the late 1970s, it was still a divided and occupied city. Here, then, we may be getting closer to its fascination, a fascination that seems to start with Reed's death-soaked album. (94)

Titled *Berlin*, that 1973 album was Lou Reed's third solo one, and followed *Transformer*, which Bowie had produced. Aptly described as "psychologically gruelling and unremittingly dark," it tells the story of "two junkies in love in Berlin. The songs variously concern domestic abuse ("Caroline Says I," "Caroline Says II"), drug addiction ("How Do You Think It Feels"), adultery and prostitution ("The Kids"), and suicide ("The Bed").[3]

While Stratton's account is a convincing one as far as the emergence of the Holocaust discourse in Anglo-American culture is concerned, it accounts neither for the continued popularity of punk well after the Holocaust had become an established part of contemporary discourse nor for the positive effects that Berlin had on its visitors. *Heroes* was released in the fall of 1977, and in his media appearances promoting the album, Bowie "introduced yet another new look...or rather a non-look. Bowie's new mode of dress seemed to take its cue from 'Heroes' and its suggestion that 'we can be us / Forever and ever,' the lavish costumes of old replaced by jeans and plain shirts, the shock of coloured hair brushed simply back and left in its natural shade of brown. For this new, everyman Bowie, even the pleated trousers of the Station to Station tour were too much" (Seabrook 195). While convinced of the need to steer clear of anything that might resemble a "normal" life, which he told an interviewer "would just ruin everything. I don't think I'd ever write again" (195), Bowie managed in Berlin to make significant and necessary changes to his lifestyle, which pundits expect would have otherwise done him in by the end of the decade (202).

It is ironic that while Bowie was cleaning up his act in Berlin, which mostly involved a shift away from drugs to alcohol, he became associated musically with the city's drug scene by providing the soundtrack for the 1981 film *Christiane F. – Wir Kinder vom Bahnhof Zoo* (known in English simply as *Christiane F*). The film was based on the story that emerged from interviews two journalists from the German news magazine *Stern* conducted with the real-life Christiane Felscherinow in 1978 while researching a story on the problematic teenage heroin and prostitution scene around the Bahnhof Zoologischer Garten, at the time the city's central train station.[4] Christiane was a witness in a trial against a man who paid underaged girls with heroin in return for sex and was only too happy to talk about her life experiences. The initial two-hour interview turned into two months, and the articles the journalists published turned into an enormously successful full-length ghost-written first-person account of the years 1975 to 1978, when she was aged 12 to 15. Bowie figures prominently in the story as Christiane's favorite singer, and the film includes a scene in which she attends a concert he gives at the Berlin *Deutschlandhalle*, after which she convinces her friends to let her take heroin for the first time. The soundtrack Bowie provided for the film was a compilation from the *Station to Station* and *Heroes* albums, as well as two tracks – "Look Back in Anger" and "Boys Keep Swinging" – from *Lodger*, the third of his Berlin trilogy, which was released in 1979 after he had left the city. From their titles, one could be forgiven for thinking that they, like the title-track "Heroes," had been written especially for the film. The ongoing popularity of Christiane's story (she continues to live off the royalties) and the later success of the *Trainspotting* phenomenon – the 1993 novel by Irving Welsh about a group of teenage heroin addicts in Edinburgh was turned into the 1996 film directed by Danny Boyle, with a soundtrack notably featuring Iggy Pop, Bowie and Brian Eno – speak to the voyeuristic attractiveness of teenage drug milieux as well as their being underpinned by music associated with the Hansa Studios.[5] While the former has been amply critiqued in fashion and advertising scholarship under the rubric of heroin chic and associated in the first instance with Kate Moss (see, for example, Kelly's review), much less has been made of the music and its Hansa-Berlin connection.

There also remains the question of the attractiveness of punk for Berliners. Just as *Heroes* hit the stores, a twenty-two year old described as "one of the most innovative artists to emerge from the punk scene" (McLeod 195) brought a band and a style into the Hansa Studios that further strengthened the city's alternative image. Born and schooled in Prenzlauer Berg, Nina Hagen had become dissident songster Wolf Biermann's step-daughter when he began a relationship with her mother in 1967, and then spent the year after her family's expatriation from East Germany in 1976 in England's punk scene (the Sex Pistols had formed in 1975 and enjoyed a two-year long heyday – from their first show on 6 November 1975 through the end of 1977). Hagen left England as the Sex Pistols were planning their first and only U.S. tour, which took place in January 1978 and resulted in their breaking up amidst "chaos and acrimony."[6] The Nina Hagen Band she formed upon her return to West Berlin did not do much better. After releasing their successful debut album entitled *The Nina Hagen Band*, they also suffered an acrimonious break-up, one signaled in the title of the second album they were contractually obligated to make: *Unbehagen* (*Discomfort*, recorded and mixed at the Hansa Studios in October and November 1979). Like Sid Vicious, who has been described as "an early poster-boy for heroin chic" (Miklitsch para. 64), Hagen decided to go solo in the U.S., but rather than self-destructing on the east coast as Vicious did, she headed west and cultivated a reputation as a flaky but fiery, UFO-spotting punk diva. She was outfitted for her performance at the 1985 Rock in Rio, for example, by Jean-Paul Gaultier and appeared similarly clad in a black leather bustier, black-and-white paisley tights and thigh-high black leather boots for a 1985 interview on *Late Night with David Letterman*.[7] A punkish cross between Marlene Dietrich and Madonna, like them both (she is three years older than Madonna and eight years younger than Bowie and Iggy), Hagen has continued to perform well into middle age, returning in 1998 to Berlin, where for Bertold Brecht's 100th anniversary, she and singer-actress Meret Becker put on a "Punk Brecht Evening" called "We Were Both Called Anna" ("*Wir hießen beide Anna*"). Hagen also took part in a CD recording of Brecht and Weill's *Three Penny Opera*. The biography she coauthored with Marcel Feige, *Nina Hagen. That's Why the Lady Is a Punk,* quickly sold out after its release in 2003 and has become a collector's item, ensuring that Hagen's reputation continues to provide Berlin's music scene with alternative associations.

Besides Hagen, other punk and experimental bands began forming in the late 1970s, which later came to be known as the *Neue Deutsche Welle* (NDW, new German wave). Often recording on a more do-it-yourself basis than Hagen, they centered around the Kreuzberg club SO36, which celebrated its opening in the Oranienstraße on 12–13 August 1978 with a two-day "Wall-building Festival" (*Mauerbaufestival*) (Schneider 73). Thanks to Martin Kippenberger, it was able to avoid bankruptcy and became a center for avant-garde artists as well as musicians, just as his Ratinger Hof in Düsseldorf had been. In Berlin, however, there was a backlash from the punks, who were put off by the pretensions and high prices of the art. During a concert of a visiting English band, Wire, in November 1979, the club's ticket office was robbed in an action called "Kommando gegen Konsumterror," the proceeds of which were rumored to have gone towards the founding of a punk center, KZ36 (75). Kippenberger left for Paris, and the club went on to become renowned as one of the premiere centers of the pre-unification new German wave scene, something occasional clashes with the authorities helped to sustain.

One of the main hallmarks of this scene, like its British counterpart, was a rejection of the liberal ideology of progress. "There is no future in England's dreaming," the Sex Pistols famously proclaimed, which translated into German, as Diedrich Diederichsen explains, not just as the end of utopias but rather as the end of the socialist utopia, at least in the case of those on the left. "[A]ll of us who were young then," as Diederichsen puts it, "could not understand those who claimed to suddenly abandon hope in socialism in 1989: neither its newness, nor the hectic panic with which so many '68ers insisted on crossing sides and thought that critique had to be abandoned together with the concrete utopia" (2008, 163).[8] Negation and rejection in general came to be the scene's guiding principle, as nicely captured in the contagiously catchy lyrics of the hit-song "Rebell" by Berlin's Die Ärzte (The Doctors): "I am against [the implication that this means against everything on principle is confirmed two lines later], because you are for / I am against, I am not like you / I am against, no matter what it is / I am against, because you don't understand" (*Ich bin dagegen, denn Ihr seid dafür / Ich bin dagegen, ich bin nicht so wie Ihr / Ich bin dagegen, egal worum es geht / Ich bin dagegen, weil Ihr nichts davon versteht*)."

The negativity of the local scene attracted and had a positive influence on the international musicians who came to Berlin to record at the Hansa Studios, which might seem paradoxical if it didn't correspond so well to the street-style trend in fashion. For example, Depeche Mode, the English electronic band from Essex who took their name from a French fashion magazine, went to Berlin to mix their third album, the 1983 *Construction Time Again*, at Hansa Studios, which is why the West Berlin cityscape features prominently in the video to "Everything Counts," the first in a long line of industrial-inspired singles by the band. So liking the new sound they were able to generate under the influence of such local groups as the Einstürzende Neubauten (Crashing Down New Buildings), Depeche Mode recorded their next two albums at Hansa: the 1984 *Some Great Reward* and the 1985 *Black Celebration*, the albums which first put the group on the U.S. charts.

In *Eigenblutdoping* (the performance-enhancing injection of one's own blood), Diederichsen characterizes the 1960s, '70s and '80s by, respectively, counterculture, glamour and punk, and discusses how the punk generation found its way to electronic music, namely via synthesizers: "Synthesizers were here desired not like in the hippie days as the ideal expanding means to produce 'unprecedented' and new sounds but as a nothing-media that was simple to use, ahistorical or history-forgetting. Thus it was precisely the cheap Casio keyboards, which were guaranteed to sound abrasive and functioned rather like a tempered metronome, that set the scene" (2008, 169). In comparing Depeche Mode with U2, another international band with an even more prominent, if briefer, Berlin and Hansa Studios connection, we become aware of this transition. Just as Depeche Mode, which was founded in 1980 (the same year, incidentally, as the Einstürzende Neubauten), discovered a new sound in its Berlin recordings that catapulted it to another level of stardom, so too did U2, but with far more spectacular results in terms of fashioning a Berlin connection for themselves in the global cultural imaginary. Starting out as "just another school-boy response to Dublin's punk scene," they went through a number of phases, becoming music press darlings with their first three albums: the 1980 *Boy*, the 1981 *October* and the 1983 *War*, following with a "relatively experimental phase…as the group collaborated with Brian Eno on *The Unforgettable Fire* (1984), backtracking with the stadium sound of *The Joshua Tree* (1987) and the film and soundtrack *Rattle and Hum* (1988)" and then shifting gears again with the 1991 *Achtung Baby*, which some critics have interpreted as "an apologia for the image they had created as (in the words of TIME Magazine) 'Rock's Hottest Ticket'" ("Review" 26). The shift that occurred with *Achtung Baby* is understood by musicologists as "particularly decisive" (Fast 34). As Susan Fast has shown, "[n]ot only did the band's music change significantly, but with this album and the tour in support of it, U2 moved from a sound/text/image that presented their politics on the surface to one that filtered them through the distancing lens of irony" (34). This is not to deny that the music and the spectacle of the tour "were as politically charged – if not more so – than ever" (43), but rather to point to the more sophisticated, technologically and representationally aware quality that accompanied the entirety of the band's production with this album.

What did Berlin contribute to *Achtung Baby*? A desirable darkness that allowed the band to reinvent itself as not only separate from, but critical of, the materialist 1980s culture that had made them "rock's hottest ticket." While U2 was only in Berlin for two months, and only began recording the album there (the rest was completed back home in Dublin), they arrived at a momentous moment: 3 October 1990, the day of German reunification. Drummer Larry Mullen Jr. denied that the band had gone to Berlin for any political reasons, commenting that "it just seemed like a place to be before it all changed," while lead singer Bono averred in an interview, "There was this sense of Berlin as where it was at. You're not just being dedicated followers of fashion. It's more than just style. I mean, we don't have any style anyway. Swagger, no style."[9] Despite the attitude this self-fashioning exudes, it should not be seen as the kind of opportunism evidenced by Pepsi's reaction to the falling of the Berlin Wall: "On the day the Berlin Wall fell, we decided to send a film crew to the scene immediately.... Our immediate concern was that something important was happening that would have a direct and immediate impact on millions of lives, and that would directly influence millions of others around the world in a positive way. We knew there would be value in that linkage for Pepsi.... We made a commercial that celebrated the moment and closed with the words "Peace on Earth," joined tastefully to a small Pepsi-Cola logo" (cited in Rectanus, 22). U2's interest in Berlin was not as ephemeral and news-oriented as Pepsi's. Rather, the city, its history and musical reputation were integral to the change in direction the band wanted to make, as producer Brian Eco made clear in an interview for *Rolling Stone*: "Berlin itself, where much of the early recording was done...became a conceptual backdrop for the record. The Berlin of the Thirties – decadent, sexual and dark – resonating against the Berlin of the Nineties – reborn, chaotic and optimistic.... Buzzwords on this record were trashy, throwaway, dark, sexy, and industrial (all good) and earnest, polite, sweet, righteous, rockist, and linear (all bad). It was good if a song took you on a journey or made you think your hi-fi was broken, bad if it reminded you of recording studios or U2...."[10]

Both the title *Achtung Baby*, to whose wonderful polysemy we will return, and its first track "Zoo Station," with which every show except one on the almost two-year long tour opened, evoke the Berlin context from which the band's reinvention sprang.[11] Zoo is short for Zoologischer Garten, that is, the same train-station Christiane F.'s story had catapulted to global consciousness. It is a name, Susan Fast claims, that English speakers, "for whom 'zoo' also connotes craziness or chaos," find particularly appropriate for "this vibrant, noisy, wild urban area" (41). It might indeed, as Elizabeth Wurtzel commented in a piece on the band in the *New Yorker* (17 Feb. 1992), "seem odd that this is U2's 'love' album" (97) until one realizes that this is love, Berlin-style: "[I]t is precisely the harsh sound that keeps the romantic urges expressed here from degenerating into sappiness" (97). The first song to emerge during their recording session at Hansa Studios, and the one that has gone on to be ranked as one of the best songs of the 1990s and #36 on the Rolling Stone's 2003 list of 500

"Greatest Songs of All Time," is such a love song: "One." Someone who hasn't heard the song but knew of its genesis might think it was about German reunification, at least until viewing the original video for the song, made by Dutch photographer and director Anton Corbijn. About a gay son and his stodgy, conservative father, Corbijn's video features the band in drag, something that, it occurred to them after the video had already been completed but before it was released, might have unintended negative consequences for the AIDS cause they were trying to support, so two more videos were hastily produced: one set in an American bar with the band playing while a tale of heterosexual romance gone wrong between Bono and a supermodel emerges, the second featuring buffalos and flowers in honor of the New York-based artist-activist, David Wojnarowicz, who died of AIDS in 1992.[12]

Corbijn's sepia-toned video most directly engages with the conceptual, historical backdrop U2 came to Berlin in search of. Not only is it clear from the opening sequence of the band performing the song in the main Hansa recording studio, the same one in which Bowie recorded "Heroes" and which is said to have served as a ballroom for the Nazis (Greco 92), but also from the interior shots of a drawing-room, in which the father-son non-confrontation takes place, with Bono sitting on a dark, centrally-placed divan singing through shots of both father and son. It is an "old world" apartment, with high ceilings, dark drapes, a Persian carpet and vaguely art-nouveau furnishings, while the outdoor shots of the drag-queen son and his presumed partner leaving the building à la Elvis and driving off in search of each other in East German "commie" cars called Trabants, or more colloquially "Trabis," incorporate well-known landmarks, with the vehicles first missing each other (to the lyrics of "we are one, but we're not the same") and then coming to meet in the final shot front-bumper to front-bumper in front of the Olympic Stadium. In Corbijn's interpretation, "One" is the first of an ambiguous but positive generational shift implying "two," something he depicts in a series of shots with the father and a teeter-totter. First, they are in front of a surface upon which the large white numbers "1" and "2" have been stenciled. In a second shot from a medium distance, the surface can clearly be identified as a Berlin-like wall divided into concrete slabs. The father is framed by a slab in a series before a slab marked by the "1" and 1955 and followed by a slab with "2" and 1956 on it (the date most likely to be associated by a global audience with Soviet violence – better known than the 1953 Berlin uprising and less polysemous than Prague 1968). The next shot in which the father appears is from the perspective of the wall and shows the father standing on one end of the teeter-totter facing away from the camera towards a no-man's-land with a path that leads towards a railway track. Next, to the lyrics "love is a temple, love the higher law," the father appears framed by the Brandenburg Gate. He and his teeter-totter then appear in front of a portion of the Wall decorated with upside-down figures and a tenement house. A final scene shows him first sitting down on the now-empty divan, as the Trabis the son and his partner are driving touch. There is then a rapid cut back to him as he steps off the teeter-totter, which is again in front of a portion of the wall with upside-down shadows painted on it; the teeter-totter falls to screen right as he exits screen left; and there is a final rapid cut to a shot of the two Trabis steaming in front of the Olympia rings. Associating the "deviant" son with painted Trabis prevents the easy association of the father with the East, despite any superficial resemblance he might bear to Honecker or Brezhnev. With its careful use of imagery, Corbijn's video forces viewers to consider in how far the intolerant, inflexible father generation should be associated not with the East but with the West, and also to imagine what the next generation in the series, generation three – the generation without any personal experience of East and West – will be like. Trabis have come to figure as global signifiers of "Berlin-ness" and are on display in central tourist spots in the city (Figs. 5.3 and 5.4). Therefore, it is not insignificant that several of them, all painted up in the same playful spirit as in Corbijn's video, featured prominently in the stage-set for the Zoo TV tour (four of them are now suspended from the ceiling of the lobby in the Rock and Roll Hall of Fame and Museum in Cleveland, Fig. 5.5). Nor is it inconsequential that both Nazi and communist signifiers featured prominently in the Zoo show. As Fast recounts, "[i]n the film *U2 Zoo TV Live from Sydney*, the Fly appears after the arresting opening video montage [which included powerful images from Leni Riefenstahl's *Triumph of the Will*] and

Figure 5.3: Trabi Safari in front of the Memorial to the Murdered Jews of Europe. (Photo: S. Ingram)

Figure 5.4: Trabi Safari down the street from Checkpoint Charlie. (Photo: S. Ingram)

Figure 5.5: Trabis from the Zoo Tour at the Rock and Roll Hall of Fame and Museum, Cleveland. (Photo: S. Ingram)

sonically to the strains of the climactic moment of Beethoven's 'Ode to Joy,'" while "[j]ust before the encore, one of the video screens sported the hammer and sickle of the Soviet flag and a cartoon figure… who sings a 'Fanfare' from a recording called *Lenin's Favourite Songs*" (Fast 41). In a move typical of the triumphalist, typically monolingual North American academy, Fast reads the symbols of communism to be in consonance with the adding of "baby" to the German imperative of the title, that is, as having been weakened them "to the point of absurdity" (41). However, as our reading of Corbijn's video indicates, as well as the fact of there being three videos for the song and both Nazi and communist imagery incorporated into the tour, one must be extremely attentive to polysemy in the case of *Achtung Baby*. Even the title begs the question about what one should pay attention to, but also be aware and respectful of (in addition to "attention," *Achtung* means "respect" in German) – the band itself and the meaning of its new look and sound? The capitalism they saw poised to roll over the newly vulnerable East? The dangers of untrammeled sexual promiscuity? Clearly, the answer has to be all of the above, and no doubt more.

U2's connection with Berlin was further cemented by their work with Wim Wenders, the film director who has arguably done the most to fashion an international soundtrack for Berlin-associated images.[13] Sound and music are prominent features and themes in Wenders's oeuvre, which includes music videos and documentaries like *Willie Nelson at the Theatro* (1998), *The Buena Vista Social Club* (1999), *Viel Passiert: Der BAP Film* (*Ode to Cologne: A Rock'N'Roll Film*, 2002), and *The Soul of a Man* (2003). His Berlin films – *Der Himmel über Berlin* (*Wings of Desire*, 1987) and the post-reunification sequel *In weiter Ferne, so nah!* (*Faraway, So Close!*, 1993) – are no exception. In both, concerts feature prominently. In the first, Damiel, the angel who decides to become human to experience love, for the first time meets Marion, the circus-performing object of his desire, in the flesh at a Nick Cave concert.[14] In the sequel, his partner Cassiel, who becomes human accidentally by rescuing a child, attends a Lou Reed concert at which Reed performs "Why Can't I Be Good?," the lyrics of which frame Cassiel's later experiences as a human. U2 wrote "Stay (Faraway, So Close!)" especially for the film (Wenders directed the video for it) and included a version of it on the *Zooropa* album. They came up with the idea for the single "Until the End of the World," which first appeared on *Achtung Baby*, when Wenders suggested, on the basis of his having directed their single "Night and Day" for the concept *Red Hot + Blue* AIDS benefit album, that they provide a song for the film he was working on at the time (the 1991 *Bis ans Ende der Welt*).[15] The soundtrack for *Until the End of the World* also features, among others, Lou Reed, Nick Cave and the Bad Seeds, Depeche Mode, and Jane Siberry and k.d. lang singing "Calling All Angels," thus giving firmer shape to the images of lost, wandering souls and dark, industrial-inspired sound associated with Berlin that helped make it possible for Berlin to emerge for the generation that followed as the center of an edgier, more pulsating scene.

Techno: Love Parades, Tillmans Shoots, Lola Runs, and Berlin Calls

"Techno in Berlin…that's like Reggae in Kingston Town."

(Rapp 151)

"The dance floor has always offered a safe haven for the socially marginalized."

(Ross 10)

The spirit of change and possibility that U2 tanked up on in reunified Berlin, as well as the tightrope they found themselves trying to cross with *Achtung Baby* to escape the commercialization that had come with their previous success, also characterize one of the events most responsible for giving the Germans the concept of *Eventkultur*: the Love Parade. Events in the German context are understood as something out of the ordinary, but not necessarily in the sense intended by Foucault and other French theorists, for whom an event is a seismic turning point that irremediably alters the order of things (cf. Rectanus 132). Rather, German sociologists understand events as connected with fun, enjoyment and entertainment (Opaschowski), something they do not necessarily approve of because of the major shift events signal in the structure of society, namely towards what has been termed an *Erlebnisgesellschaft*, or "experience-oriented society" (Schulze). Gerhard Schulze not only noted but gave this name to "the search for happiness and the intensification of experiences" that became increasingly mediated by experiential forms of consumption in 1980s yuppie culture (D. Anderson 41). The Bowie concert in *Christiane F.* is a good example of how the German sociological and French philosophical understandings of an event can overlap. The concert was a life-altering event for Christiane; it completely changed her understanding of what it meant to be "clean." Her life could never be the same as it had been after her first hit.[16] But it was also a result of her search for happiness. Having fallen in puppy love with the addicted Detlef, a young man she meets in a club a school friend takes her to, the film depicts her deciding to take heroin in order to share in the intensity of his experiences. The four characteristics of events that Schulze identifies – uniqueness, singularity, community and participation (Schultze 308) – all apply to Christiane's experience of the concert and its aftermath. However, while "Schulze argues that the uniqueness of events makes them attractive to consumers" and considers participation "mandatory because events are only there for a short time and then they are over," leaving consumers seeking to recapture the remembered experience via consumption (D. Anderson 41), the depiction of Christiane's experience of the Bowie concert in the film calls for a nuancing of this sociological analysis. Participation in events is not mandatory but rather, crucially, involves a choice to participate, and that choice involves making a commitment, which one makes in anticipation of deriving pleasure from the event. This helps to explain why events lend themselves so readily to marketing: they offer a captive market that has *voluntarily* made itself available to whatever influences accompany the experience of the event. Their choice to participate renders them far more vulnerable than were participation required by any kind of authoritarian regime.

The first Love Parade, which took place in the summer before the fall of the Wall (1989), was an event in all respects. A local DJ known at the time as Motte, together with his girlfriend at the time, the American multimedia artist Danielle de Picciotto (who has since married the bassist of the Einstürzende Neubauten, Alexander Hacke, and become half of one of Germany's leading avant-garde artistic couples) organized a demonstration to celebrate his birthday on the main shopping street in West Berlin, the Kurfürstendamm. Taking place under the motto of "peace, joy, and pancakes" (*Friede, Freude, Eierkuchen*), the event attracted 150 people, who gathered to dance to the pulsating beats emanating from an old VW bus.[17] By the following year Motte had upgraded his pseudonym to Dr. Motte and the parade had become the stuff of legend. That the Love Parade struck more than just a chord is evident in its exponential growth: it attracted 2,000 participants in 1990, 6,000 in 1991, 15,000 in 1992, 30,000 in 1993, and then exploded with 120,000 in 1994, around half a million in 1995, three-quarters of a million in 1996; and a million in 1997, before peaking with a million and a half in 1999.[18] Berlin thus became the epicenter of the global musical youth culture phenomenon of techno, a unique development for a place that has tended to import Anglo-American popular culture rather than pioneer it itself (Robb 131).[19]

The Love Parade's enormous success, like the presence of commercial art in the Kreuzberg club SO36, inevitably led to its downfall and regrouping. In 1997 a demonstration was organized against the Love Parade, its sponsorship practices, TV broadcasts, high cost of floats, suppression of more radical forms of techno, lack of political direction, the environmental damage it inflicted on the Tiergarten area, and the crass commercialization of culture and public space it had come to represent (cf. Rectanus 148, Robb 138–9). Called the Hate Parade in its first year, the name was quickly changed when organizers realized how open it was to misinterpretation and how real the possibility that they could be depicted as hate-filled neo-Nazis; since then, the demonstration has been known as the Fuck Parade, short for "Fuck the Love Parade," and each year its route is chosen to reflect its cause and the object of its protest. Popular issues have been police brutality against ravers, such as those that marred the 2005 Czechtek festival and led the parade to troop past the Czech embassy in Berlin, and gentrification, the "becoming fashionable" of central areas which used to be in East Berlin, such as Prenzlauer Berg,[20] and large investment projects, most prominently the Mediaspree conglomeration that has gobbled up property along the banks of the Spree from the Jannowitzbrücke in the west to the Elsenbrücke in the east, turning it into facilities like the O2 World arena as well as hotels, apartments, and office towers housing the likes of Universal Music, MTV Central Europe, and BVG (*Berliner Verkehrsbetriebe*, the company in charge of Berlin's public transportation). The Love Parade itself lost its status as a political demonstration in 2001, which meant that, as a commercial enterprise, it became responsible for all clean-up costs. The dates had to be changed at the last minute, and attendance fell substantially. The 2004 and 2005 parades were cancelled, and in 2006 Berlin's Love Parade went out in style, with over a million participants and the retrospectively ironic motto "The Love is Back," leaving it to other cities to carry on the tradition.

The "Love Parade" aesthetic was captured most programmatically in the photographs of Wolfgang Tillmans, whose 1992 series entitled "Love Parade" hit a market that, as Val Williams explains, was experiencing a "sea change…in the way in which fashion photography was regarded both by the museum and gallery establishments, but, most importantly, by an energized visual arts sector across the Western world. Photography was increasingly absorbed into the fine arts system, photographers became increasingly interesting to collectors and private dealers, works began to be editioned and acquired value" (211). Leading the way were the London style magazines *i-D* and *The Face*, which were joined in 1992 by *Dazed and Confused*. As Williams details, "From the early 1990s, the style magazine *i-D* had promoted the work of a group of photographers who would make their way into the art arena, via fashion photography, fairly effortlessly. Chief among these was the photographer Wolfgang Tillmans" (212), who documented the thriving rave subculture in which he had gotten involved in Hamburg in 1988, where he "worked as a switchboard operator at a community help organization"[21] before attending the Arts University College at Bournemouth from 1990 to 1992, "where he was able to keep up with rave culture in a different setting" and learn the skills to establish himself as the artistic chronicler of his generation and the techno movement (Hoch).

Tillmans' work first appeared in the January 1992 "Think Positive!" issue of *i-D*, their 100th issue AIDS special. As though in anticipation of it were articles on "Techno, the new sound of Europe" in the December 1991"international" issue, on Kraftwerk in the July 1991 issue, and on "Berlin's booming house scene" and "a guide to global clubbing" in June 1991. From the twenty-six issues of *i-D* that Tillmans and his work have appeared in since, one can see the specificity of the niche he carved out for himself.[22] The July 1992 "destination" issue carried a piece on German techno fashion, the September 1992 was a special "parade" issue dedicated to Berlin's Love Parade and London's Gay Pride, while the November 1992 "sexuality" issue included "the Wolfgang Tillmans story that got *i-D* banned." Unlike other photographers who were content to be included in the "fashion photography by…" section, Tillmans' work appeared as its own story, such as "camouflage fashion by Wolfgang Tillmans" (July 1993 "open air" issue, which also included a report "with U2 on Zooropa"), "Moby photographed by Wolfgang Tillmans" (August 1993 "festival" issue), "Erasure photographed by Wolfgang Tillmans" (July 1994 "fun" issue), "International street fashion special photographed by Wolfgang Tillmans and others" (Sept 1994 "street" issue), "Hollywood outsider Gus Van Sant photographed by Wolfgang Tillmans" (November 1994 "underground" issue), "techno legend Carl Craig photographed by Wolfgang Tillmans" (April 1995 "tough" issue), and "Wolfgang Tillmans shoots Gay Pride" (Sept 1995 "fun & games" issue). By *i-D*'s October 1995 "fifteenth anniversary" issue, one had come to expect Tillmans to be included in the "Celebrating 15 years of youth culture with a little help from our friends" section, which he is. He is also in the "200 for 2000" issue, which celebrated the magazine's 200th issue "by incorporating the best of the past with a wink towards the future." Similarly, it would have come as a great surprise had anyone but Tillmans shot the feature on the Berlin Love Parade that appeared in the September 1996 "pioneer" issue. As Tillmans' career progressed artistically and he became the first non-Brit to win the prestigious Turner Prize in 2000, he continued to be featured in *i-D* in such pieces as "How a German fashion photographer became the new face of British art: Wolfgang Tillmans interviewed" in the November 2000 "white" issue. Even as a more established artist, Tillmans has managed to maintain his reputation as a uniquely placed voice of societal critique: "As fashion editors, curators, and artists courted each other, there were, of course, dissenting voices. Wolfgang Tillmans, who had experimented with fashion but who, by the late 1990s, was firmly established as a visual artist working with galleries and museums, remarked in 1998:

There's a continual so-called rebellion. But fashion photography is completely conservative. Take Alexander McQueen's garments printed with war victims. His brand of shock value was rewarded with a job at Givenchy. Images of real girls who don't follow fashion became the fashion rule. Fashion photographers can be incredibly naïve and one-dimensional. They think only of cause and effect, forgetting that the market constantly changes. When a story is published in *i-D*, it's seen by *The Face*, then *Vogue*, seen by advertisers and becomes the new dominant fashion.… I don't like the pretence that we're all doing something radical. However grand the proclamations from photographers such as Juergen Teller or Terry Richardson that they don't want to be 'in fashion', that their work is subversive, they take a look and propel it into fashionability. The substance of their work is essentially the same as David Hamilton's young girls in knickers. The work doesn't question gender roles, or why we buy into fashion, it gives you a series of feelgood factors." (Smith 1997 unpublished interview, cited in Williams, 212–13)

Tillmans has thus remained true to the queer values that motivated his initial work on the Love Parade. As he told a *Spiegel* reporter at the conclusion of their 2 June 2007 interview: "The liberalization of the '90s in Europe is in danger of being turned back. One has to be clear that that was also simply a moment when the reactionary forces were catching their breath. That's why being queer continues to be a political issue."

While the Love Parade as a nexus of Berlin, techno and toleration for the performance of alternative identities could not sustain the commercializing pressures its popularity brought with it, the city's techno scene seems to be managing more successfully, at least according to Tobias Rapp.[23] In order to counter the prevailing mainstream impression that Berlin's techno scene had died, as the loss of the Love Parade and the problems experienced by clubs like Tresor, E-Werk, WMF, Ostgut or Matrix had led many to assume, Rapp wrote *Lost and Sound: Berlin, Techno und der Easyjetset* (2009). The book is smartly structured around a week in the life of the Berlin techno scene, which allows Rapp to map out the main factors, players and places that have contributed to the scene's increasing vibrancy. The city's current status as the global epicenter of techno Rapp sees as ironically based on historical coincidence: "Economically, Berlin never really fully recovered from the fall of the Wall. None of the greater expectations of the early nineties turned out the way they were meant to. The city hasn't become a centre of commerce with Eastern Europe. And instead of increasing, the population is actually declining. In terms of subculture, the opportunities afforded the city after the fall of the Wall – free space widely available, cheap rent – are still being taken advantage of. You can still live for less in Berlin and open clubs without the hassle you get anywhere else" (Gutmair). The growth of discount airlines in Europe was also, as the title suggests, a major enabler, but it was importantly matched by growth in Berlin's hostelling infrastructure, the development of internet portals that offer detailed information about the techno scene, such as the local "restrealität.de" (Rapp 183–7) and Resident Advisor, the online dance and electronic music magazine (www.residentadvisor.net) (187–9), as well as the flexibility in lifestyle that is the hallmark of most of its participants. The response Rapp gave when asked by a *Tagesspiegel* reporter to describe the demographics of the raver scene is enlightening in this regard:

> Without a common denominator. There's the woman from Stockholm, who is currently between two jobs and comes to Berlin for two months and stays in the apartment that friends of hers have bought here. There is the gay computer programmer from Milan, who has been making week-long trips to the city for years. There is the 20-something young Brit, crazy about music, who knows far more about the scene than most Berliners and knows about illegal clubs from the internet. And then people are also interested in the nightlife, for whom "Berlin Chic" is above all an appealing fashion statement. They fly here to study what people are wearing. (Müller 2009)

With this answer, Rapp is not only putting faces to the "Easyjetset," for the most part reasonably young, cosmopolitan-minded adults with reasonable incomes in lines of work that tend to involve the irregular rhythms that capital increasingly tries to demand. He is also setting key parameters of Berlin's "poor yet sexy" image. It corresponds to information gathered on the Anglo rave and techno scenes in the early to mid 1990s, according to which "a significant portion of participants both come from middle-class backgrounds and tend to be employed in middle-class positions (e.g., as a bank teller)" (Rectanus 147). What sets the participants of this scene apart is their uneasy relationship to consumption. While they may, as Rectanus makes clear, "attempt to resist the commercialization of a 'carnival tradition'... and are frequently more interested in producing their own performances and utilizing music they can dance to than listening to a group on stage" (146), consumption is nonetheless a constituent part of their activities, and often their downfall. However, given that Berlin's techno scene is not likely to become as super-sized and overdetermined as the Love Parade became, and given its current strategy of staying in the underground, it seems at least at present to have found a way of being self-sustaining without becoming self-destructive.

One can get a sense of the changes the Berlin techno scene has undergone over the past decade by comparing Tom Tykwer's 1998 surprise smash-hit *Run Lola Run* (*Lola Rennt*) with Hannes Stöhr's more recent *Berlin Calling* (2008). The musical dimension of Tykwer's film has not escaped the attention of critics and scholars. Certainly, as Randall Halle has noted, "[t]he success of the film has much to do with the pulsing energy of its music and motion" (2002, 41), while Bordwell identifies "the techno rush of *Run Lola Run*" (101) as setting it apart in the series of films that appeared towards the end of the 1990s characterized by storylines that repeat or otherwise disrupt linear narratives, such as *Too Many Ways to be #1* (1997) and *Sliding Doors* (1998). Tykwer's film is usually read as a "celebration of youth culture," as Paul Cooke does in contrasting it with Oskar Roehler's lesser known 1996 *Silvester Countdown*:

> Featuring a world that has much in common with the techno-filled, fast-paced environment of *Lola Rennt*, *Silvester Countdown* narrates the whirlwind romance of a couple of fashion-

obsessed twentysomethings as they travel through Germany's party scene. But whereas Tykwer's *Lola Rennt* can be seen as a celebration of youth culture, by the end of *Silvester Countdown* it becomes clear that Roehler is more concerned to show this culture's emptiness. In the film's graphic last sequence, for example, we see the young man, having been left by his girlfriend, masturbating over her image. The pumping techno that accompanied their earlier lovemaking scenes is now gone, and we are left instead with the desperately insistent rhythm of the man's heavy breathing as the film's only soundtrack. Although he no longer has this woman, he has her image and so can continue to simulate a relationship with her. Human contact has been eradicated in favour of solitary gratification. Thus, while Roehler may be aping the fast-paced pop aesthetics of *Lola Rennt*, he is doing so in order to point out what he sees as the self-obsessed vacuity of the world it presents. (33–4)

Tykwer's use of music in *Run Lola Run* is similarly sophisticated, or as Caryl Flinn puts it, "instructive and canny" (197). Both Flinn and Christine Haase note that Tykwer's music is part of larger patterns. Technically, it "moves from minor to major modes…[and to] much more of an overall sense of formal stability" (Flinn 203), which lends itself to being read symbolically; at the same time it inverts the usual national associations of high and popular culture: "[t]he ironic fusion of German/American, that is, serious/popular culture dichotomies as well as the equally ironic representations of the economic influences underlying and connecting theses issues can be found everywhere in *Run Lola Run*" (Haase 402). That is, Tykwer "aligns popular culture primarily with Germany (Sepp Herberger, soccer, and techno), whereas high culture seems to come from 'outside,' and from primarily the U.S., (e.g., T.S. Eliot and classical music)" (Halle 2002, 41); Tykwer can thus be seen to be shifting "preconceived cultural notions: Germany, the supposed home of poets and philosophers, is represented by a popular soccer coach, whereas the United States, home of Michael Jordan, the genre of the sports movie, and self-help bestsellers, is introduced by a demanding poet" (Haase 403).[24]

Music has a special role to play in this postmodern overturning of values: namely, it is its motor. As James Tobias points out, *Run Lola Run* "foregrounds musical values as it incorporates conventionally distinct media as narrative tropes proper" (29). Reading *Run Lola Run* in terms of its musicality, Tobias shows how this approach "emphasizes the ways rhythmic texturing moves audiences through cultural and gender politics, psychic imaginaries, and transnational reconfigurations of competing media forms" (31), drawing attention to the way the "action-oriented musical sequences vary with interaction between Lola and supporting characters that turn out to be pivotal in her last successful go-round through the urban obstacle course.… Once Lola decides – on anything – the action begins again, and as the music fades up from the background, the beat-driven soundtrack drives the narrative flow for long sequences at a time" (30). The main point of the film, as its title makes clear, is that Lola runs; in the trajectory of our chapter, she runs from punk to techno. What Tobias wants to draw our attention to, if we understand his argument correctly, is the rhythmicality of this action: "This explicitly musical gesturality is aligned with action and urgency against the unknown, the accident, and death; it is motivated, in turn, by underscored sequences which present failed intention, narrative dead-ends, or transgression that ultimately doesn't pay" (30). Tykwer thus makes "musicality and narrativity operate together as elements in rhythmic disintermediation: effectively, the articulation of female desire as medial action supersedes both the conventions of the univocal cinematic text and the tendencies of the masculine reception of the competing video game form which Lola outpaces" (31). The throbbing beat that accompanies Lola's action – and Tobias points out that even her famous scream in the casino is a "looping, sampled" scream (30) – expresses "a female insistence on agency in the face of senior figures whose power is undesirable, and of peers whose impotence is unacceptable" (31). Music is thus depicted as (em)powering Lola; it is what keeps her going.

In contrast, Hannes Stöhr's 2008 *Berlin Calling* charts the travails of a Berlin DJ/producer as he is consumed by and treated for the effects of his excessive lifestyle. The character's name, Ickarus (his friends call him Ikka), hints at the film's allegorical dimension. Unlike Lola, who is depicted as coming out of the tradition of punk, with rugged clothes, crazy hair, a small-time drug-runner of a boyfriend, and a generally rebellious nature as far as her parents and society are concerned, Ikka is part of the post-Love Parade electronic music scene and has to worry about record contracts and paying rent and back taxes. Unlike Lola's, however, Ikka's feet are nowhere near the ground, and it is only a matter of time before the drug-induced heights he reaches bring him crashing down and he finds himself half-naked in a ritzy restaurant incongruously smearing himself with the toppings for blueberry pancakes before being taken to a rehab clinic. Whereas Lola is mostly in motion and is only brought to a standstill by male forces (she runs past or through female ones – her mother, the nuns, etc.), Ikka is surprisingly stationary, suspended by, and in front of, the music he spins or otherwise creates (he is one of the newer brand of DJs who performs his mixes live – hence the German term for this profession: *Liveact*). What action Ikka does undertake is for the most part to either escape or confront the powerful women in his life: his girlfriend Mathilde, the head of his record label and the doctor at the clinic. Even when he travels, he is shown not to be in motion himself, as in the shots of him and Mathilde at airports, looking übercool in their sunglasses as they wait for flights with their feet perched on their luggage. Unlike Lola, who crosses the city not just one but three times in her attempts to rescue Manni, Ikka never really goes anywhere. Played with great bravado by DJ/producer Paul Kalkbrenner in his film debut, Ikka keeps returning to a series of favorite haunts: clubs, Mathilde's girlfriend's apartment, his supplier's apartment, the record label's office, the clinic and his father's church, the sites thus repeating like the music he creates.

While a sympathetic, non-moralizing depiction of the Berlin techno scene (Stöhr is a self-confessed fan), the film nevertheless draws some sober, informed conclusions about it. After all, none of the characters in the film is depicted as being particularly young; rather, they are all thirtysomethings who would have come of age during the 1990s, when techno was just taking off in Berlin. (Kalkbrenner, for example, was born in 1977; Rita Lengyel who plays Mathilde was born in 1973; her girlfriend is played by Araba Walton, born in 1975, while the doctor, the record-label producer, and the club owner are of an older generation, born in 1954, 1967 and 1969 respectively.) So what we have here is not the straightforward generational confrontation of post-Wende youth against their elders ('68er hippies turned conservatives), which structures, for example, Hans Weingartner's 2004 *The Edukators* (*Die fetten Jahre sind vorbei*). Rather *Berlin Calling* is a portrait by a director, born in 1970, of a scene for whose future he fears. Stöhr's concerns are understandable: "Being a DJ, rocking on a different stage every week, is a tough job.... If you have a look at Paul Kalkbrenner's calendar, he plays over 80% of his shows abroad. So you spend a lot of time in airports, jetlagged."[25] Implied is the question: how much longer can he keep it up, especially given the unhealthiness of the lifestyle? How will Berlin's beat manage to go on?

Coda: The Ramones Museum

Unlike the punks of the 1970s, today's Berlin technoculture may feel it has a future, but that this future is a most precarious one is illustrated by the Ramones Museum. In what remains of the chapter, we explore how Berlin came to house the only museum thus far devoted to that group of lads from Queens, whose expression of the wish to be sedated took them to stardom and a place in the Rock and Roll Hall of Fame.[26] Given what has been established so far about the kind of musical location Berlin represents and the type of soundtrack that accompanies its poor but sexy image, it should not come as a surprise to learn that the one of the four founding Ramone members who did not grow up in the Forest Hills area of Queens (Dee Dee, whose real name was Douglas Colvin) spent his childhood in Berlin, where his soldier-father was stationed. Colvin's returning to America at age 15 – and specifically to Queens, with his sister and German mother to get away from their father – led to the band's formation. It should also not come as a surprise to learn that the music the four original band members bonded over included that of Iggy Pop and the Stooges. Nor, given Stratton's work on the Judeocidal tendencies in punk, should one wonder that the title of the Ramones' first hit, which is attributed to Dee Dee, is "The Blitzkrieg Bop," or that the last track on their final studio album, the 1995 *¡Adios Amigos!*, is "Born to Die in Berlin."

Much connects the Ramones with Berlin, including Nina Hagen.[27] But it took a young German Ramones fan from Helmstedt, a town of around 25,000 between Braunschweig and Magdeburg on the former border that separated East and West Germany, to not only assemble enough memorabilia to fill a museum, but also to go to the trouble of making it publicly available on a permanent basis. The Ramones Museum is the brainchild of Florian Hayler, who also serves as the acting chief editor of *unclesally's*, a free monthly underground lifestyle magazine published in Berlin that celebrated its 150th issue in October 2009. If there was ever a poster boy for "poor but sexy," Hayler has to be it (Fig. 5.6). A prototypical punk-rock fan as a teenager, Hayler found in the Ramones a welcome escape from his firmly middle-class WASP-ish background, something coming of age helped enormously.[28] After graduating from *Gymnasium*, Hayler channeled all of his independence, energies and earnings into fandom. When asked by an interviewer how many times he had seen the Ramones play live, he replied:

Figure 5.6: Ramones Museum founder, Flo Hayler.
(Photo: F. Hayler)

One hundred and one, and that just about everywhere, except in South America, Japan and Australia. But in Europe we were actually always part of it. We flew to Greece, to England, to Scandinavia, and to concerts in France, Holland, Belgium and, of course, Germany. Things really kicked into gear in 1993; the last three Ramones years were very, very intense. With the Lollapalooza Festival and the White Zombie tour in North America, or the 20th anniversary celebrations in New York in 1994. All of life simply revolved around the next Ramones tours. And everything else, whether school or work, was just down time. All that mattered was the Ramones.[29]

After the Ramones disbanded in 1996, Hayler soon discovered that his knowledge of and connections in the punk-rock scene could be mobilized to help cover his living expenses. In 1997 he did his first interview for *unclesally's*. By 2005 he had worked up enough courage to open the first iteration of the Ramones Museum, in Kreuzberg, but as he notes on the museum's website, it did not take long for the economic realities of the new Berlin to make themselves felt: "After 2 years and attracting more than 10,000 visitors from all over the world, the first Ramones Museum had to close because the landlord tripled the rent. *In*

November 2007, the Ramones Museum had to leave in order to make place for a soap shop."[30]
Rather than giving up on his venture, Hayler channeled his sense of outrage into finding
a workable alternative. In July 2008, he found "the new place" in Mitte, around the corner
from the Synagogue, which he opened together with "his friend Svana, who is now in charge
of the place and runs the excellent museum café, Café Mania."[31] It does not take more
than a quick glance down the Krausnickstrasse to determine the building that houses the
Ramones Museum and the circumstances that made Hayler's new landlord keen to have a
commercial tenant on the ground floor. In a row of the solid stone *Gründerzeit* buildings that
Equilibrium producer Lucas Foster and director Kurt Wimmer so admire (Fig. 5.7), a shiny
new section with ceiling-to-floor glass fronts and two arched roof extensions stands out
as though transmuted directly from the glossy pages of a design magazine (Fig. 5.8). Even
should the sale of the condo units on the property have been enough to recover the costs of
the renovation, there are still ongoing expenses that a tenant can help to meet. One can only
wonder how long it will be before Hayler once again faces rent increases and whether Café
Mania will provide enough revenue to prevent the Krausnickstrasse from becoming home
to yet another soap shop.

Hayler's experiences with the Ramones Museum have influenced his view of Berlin.
While the city may be "so big and cheap you can find your own niche and hide out and do

Figure 5.7: Ramones Museum, Krausnickstraße 23. (Photo: F. Hayler)

Figure 5.8: Ramones Museum, Krausnickstraße 23. (Photo: S. Ingram)

your own thing," the situation is not nirvana. The problem? As Hayler sees it: "we have too many creative people and no money. The artists don't make any money. But the people with money want to invest into that creative potential, and that's what happens in every city – it happened in NY in the '80s. We're right in the middle of it, and it's just a matter of time before everything's bought" (Hartwig 40). While the lessons of urban gentrification have not been lost on Hayler, they have not translated into an equal appreciation of historical distance and cultural specificity. Berlin has certainly gentrified since reunification, but the Berlin of the "naughts" differs considerably from the New York of the 1980s. Much separates, for example, Hannes Stöhr (1970 in Stuttgart) and Paul Kalkbrenner (1977 in Leipzig) from Andy Warhol (1928–1987) and Jean-Michel Basquiat (1960–1988). To try to gauge the distance between them in terms of entrepreneurial practice, we turn in our next, and final, chapter to the struggle of Hayler's "creative people" to continue to be able to do their own thing, and see how the creative industries, and fashion in particular, have influenced how Berlin has been reconstructed and reimagined since reunification.

Notes

1. As Diederichsen discusses, there has been an ongoing struggle in music between *Noten* and *Töne* (notes and sounds), in which John Cage's methods for breaking away with traditional harmony proved decisive: "Noise, chance sounds and the world's sound were to supersede old European composers' subjects" (2008, 152). One can thus read in the studio's name a gesture towards the kind of sound-oriented music, mostly varieties of punk and electronica, that it made its reputation producing.
2. Its website (http://www.hansatonstudio.de/) provides the following list of recording credits in the section on "yesterday": Snow Patrol, Supergrass, Aloha from Hell, Herbert Grönemeyer, Wyclef Jean, Depeche Mode, David Bowie, U2, Revolverheld, Iggy Pop, Nick Cave, David Byrn, Bon Jovi, Marillion, Boney M., Bronski Beat, Rosenstolz, Alphaville, The Hooters, Daniel Lanois, Anne Clark, Killing Joke, Little Steven, Leningrad Cowboys, Wire, Brian Eno, Real Life, N'Sync, NKOTB, Elektric Hippies, Beatitudes, The Other Ones, Crime and the City Solutions, Diamand Galas, Rainbirds, Water Congress, Just Friends, Eartha Kitt, Maggie Reilly, Paul Anka, Toni Christie, Wanda Jackson, Naomi Campbell, Rudy Stevenson, Tom Cunningham, Rattles, PVC, Skew Siskin, Mitch Ryder, Hikasu, Masami Sakide, Lesiem, Sarah Connor, Neonbabies, Guano Apes, Humpe & Humpe, Diether Krebs, Iris Berben, Geier Sturzflug, Gebrüder Blattschuss, Hans Werner Olm, Achim Mentzel, Hoerstuatz/Madsen, Udo Jürgens, Peter Maffay, Pavarotti, Julio Iglesias, Monserat Cobalie, Roland Kaiser, Nina Hagen, Udo Lindenberg, Tim Fischer, Zarah Leander, Hildegard Knef, Johannes Hesters, Freddy Quinn, UVM.
3. This material is from Greco 93 and http://en.wikipedia.org/wiki/Lou_Reed.
4. For an account of the changing vicissitudes of the Bahnhof Zoo area as the Wende approached and it became Eastern Europeans' portal to the city, see Schlögel 2009.
5. One should also note the ongoing popularity of Bowie in Germany, something no doubt influenced by his Berlin trilogy. The decision of Vodaphone to use the music of "Heros/Helden" in a lifestyle ad is a good example of this ongoing popularity (the ad is available at http://www.youtube.com/watch?v=kSgHB6E92ZQ).

6. This phrasing is on the Rock and Roll Hall of Fame and Museum's website (http://www.rockhall.com/inductee/sex-pistols).
7. The 1985 interview with David Letterman is available on YouTube under "NINA HAGEN ON LATE NIGHT WITH DAVID LETTERMAN IN 1985" (http://www.youtube.com/watch?v=0WvNYACnkI8).
8. Part of this chapter is also available in English translation (Diederichsen 2007, 149). What is cited here is our translation of the original.
9. Part of "U2 Story Part 3" (http://www.youtube.com/watch?v=HTLtx5oM6xE&NR=1). Larry Mullen's comment is from "Part 2 of U2 – ACHTUNG BABY – THE VIDEOS, THE CAMEOS, AND A WHOLE LOT OF INTERFERENCE FROM ZOOTV (http://www.youtube.com/watch?v=NKUGdFTNjzg&feature=related).
10. In the 28 November 1991 issue of *Rolling Stone*, also cited in Greco 92–3 and in the Achtung Baby entry on the English Wikipedia site.
11. The city also figures prominently in the video for "The Fly" as well as in the one for "Stay," the song U2 did for Wim Wender's 1993 sequel to *Wings of Desire*: *Faraway, So Close! (In weiter Ferne, so nah!)*.
12. For an account of the making of Corbijn's "One" video, see "The Story Of One (Part 1 HQ)" (http://www.youtube.com/watch?v=2azPOGI7e-Q&feature=related).
13. Wender's presence on the "Metrobranding" panel at the 2007 Berlinale as the representative of Berlin, together with Tata Amaral (Sao Paulo) and Ning Ying (Beijing), speaks to his influential standing in this regard (http://www.berlinale-talentcampus.de/story/11/2011.html).
14. The concert takes place in the remains of the Esplanade Hotel Kaisersaal, which used to be one of the two remaining buildings in the no-man's-land of Potsdamer Platz, and which is now cleverly integrated into the Sony Centre as a dining and banquet facility.
15. Other filmic collaborations between Bono and Wenders include the 2000 *Million Dollar Hotel* and the 2005 *Don't Come Knocking*.
16. That her life is still affected by drug use is indicated by newspaper headlines in August 2008, such as the August 11th one in the *Spiegel* claiming that "Christiane F. can no longer look after her son" ("Christiane F. kann sich nicht mehr um Sohn kümmern" (https://www.spiegel.de/panorama/gesellschaft/0,1518,571293,00.html).
17. Dr Motte recounts the Love Parade's genesis as follows on his website: "It's 1989. The british music-scene declares the 'Summer of Love,' Raves and Acid-House are hot themes in current music-magazines. In these times, Motte already lived for 7 years on his music and he operated with some pals the club 'Turbine Rosenheim,' a legendary underground location in Berlin. By that he became one of the founders of the electronical music-scene in germany. Inspired by the british movement, Motte organizes and originates a demonstration for 'portrayal of contemporary dance music culture in terms of a parade,' which will get famosity worldwide by the name 'Loveparade.' And with it, of course his originator, Dr. Motte." (http://www.drmotte.de/wordpress/about-dr-motte/). Many characteristics of the Berlin-led techno culture are evident in this passage, among others the casual, email inflected use of English as a lingua franca.
18. These figures are the organizers'; police estimates are some 30% lower. Exact attendance is impossible to determine as attendance was both free and free-flowing.
19. Robb does not deny the origins of house music in Detroit and Chicago, something Harley has established, but rather stresses the unique development of techno in Berlin and the exportation of the Love Parade to cities around the world. Cf. Rectanus, "Youth Scenes," 146–51.
20. For an account of the social problems that gentrification has brought to Prenzlauer Berg, see Sußebach.

21. This is taken from the biography available on the Guggenheim Exhibition site (http://www. guggenheimcollection.org/site/artist_bio_213.html). One presumes that this work was part of Tillmans' social service, which he had chosen to do instead of military service.

22. They are available on the i-D website (http://www.i-dmagazine.com/icollectframe.htm).

23. Unfortunately, Graham St John's *Technomad: Global Raving Countercultures* was published too late in 2009 for us to be able to deal with it adequately here; however, from the generous overview provided online (http://www.edgecentral.net/technomad.htm), it seems to situate Berlin's Love Parade in the larger context of "new tribal gatherings" and to establish the phenomena of "European tekno sound systems" and "European tekno-travelers and teknivals" as part of a global mapping of techno as one of the key cultural phenomena of the late 20th and early 21st centuries.

24. This reading can be complicated by a consideration of the music video for "I Wish (Komm Zu Mir)," one of the hits to emerge from the soundtrack. In it Franka Potente sings the chant-like lyrics from the film in English, while Thomas D of the German hip-hop group Die Fantastischen Vier adds a matching, alternative set of lyrics in German.

25. From "Interview mit Hannes Stöhr" on the film's website (http://www.berlin-calling.de/de/interview-mit-hannes-stöhr).

26. The Ramones were inducted into the Rock and Roll Hall of Fame in March 2002, less than a year after Joey had died of lymphoma. In June 2002, Dee Dee died of an overdose, while Johnny died after a protracted battle with prostate cancer in 2004. Only one of the four founding Ramones has survived: Thomas Erdelyi, better known as Tommy.

27. Hagen performed on one of Dee Dee's solo ventures in the 1990s (the 1994 album *I Hate Freaks Like You*), while he featured on her 1995 *Freud Euch*.

28. In an interview, he recalls: "It was the beginning of the '90s. I had just reached the age of majority and had gotten my first car and with it, the possibility to travel a bit.... Then one no longer travelled to Brittany with one's parents but rather to Italy with one's friends" ("Das war Anfang der 90er Jahre. Ich war gerade volljährig geworden, hatte mein erstes eigenes Auto und dadurch die Möglichkeit, ein bisschen zu reisen.... Man ist dann nicht mehr mit den Eltern in die Bretagne gefahren, sondern mit den Freunden nach Italien.") From an interview conducted in November 2006 on Die Toten Hosen website in the section "All die ganzen Jahre" (All These Years). Hayler is among the band's friends (http://www.dietotenhosen.de/alldieganzenjahre_freunde_flo_hayler.php).

29. "101 Mal – und das fast überall, außer in Südamerika, Japan und Australien. In Europa haben wir aber eigentlich alles mitgemacht. Wir sind nach Griechenland geflogen, nach England, nach Skandinavien, und zu den Konzerten in Frankreich, Holland, Belgien und Deutschland sowieso. 1993 ging es dann so richtig los: Die letzten drei Ramones-Jahre waren sehr, sehr, sehr intensiv. Mit dem Lollapalooza-Festival und der White-Zombie-Tour in Nordamerika oder dem 20. Ramones-Jubiläum 1994 in New York. Da hat sich das komplette Leben einfach nur um die nächsten Ramones-Touren gedreht. Und alles andere, wie Schule oder Jobben, war nur zwischendurch. Es ging eigentlich nur um die Ramones" (http://www.dietotenhosen.de/alldieganzenjahre_freunde_flo_hayler.php).

30. This is the account Hayler offers on the Ramones Museum website (http://www.ramonesmuseum.com/History). He put in bold lettering what we have here in italics.

31. This quote is also from the Ramones Museum website.

Chapter 6

Becoming Berlin: The Flux of Corporate Luxe

"Between 1989 and 1999, the slogan 'Berlin is becoming' was adopted by the newly united city.... It spoke of becoming amidst ruins and construction sites, tracing new maps between nostalgia and history."

(Boym 175–6)

"The original notion of the brand was quality, but now brand is a stylistic badge of courage."

(Tibor Kalman, cited in Klein, 24)

Sony's announcement on 28 February 2008 that, "as part of its streamlining efforts, it would be selling the Berlin Sony Center to a group of German and U.S. investment funds, including investment bank Morgan Stanley, Corpus Sireo and an affiliate of The John Buck Company," would seem to confirm suspicions of "waning confidence in the Potsdamer Platz project – especially given that Sony was allegedly unable to find a buyer willing to pay its initial asking price of 800 million Euros."[1] This sale followed on the heels of the one in December 2007 of the nineteen buildings that make up the Daimler section of Potsdamer Platz to the Swedish banking group SEB, which followed on the heels of Daimler-Benz's selling off the Chrysler Group to Cerberus Capital Management in August 2007, and shortening its name in the process. When the Berlin Senate announced a design competition for the reconstruction of Potsdamer Platz in 1991, it was hailed as one of the most ambitious development projects in post-reunification Germany, and the two largest sections – then Daimler-Benz's, overseen by the Italian architect Renzo Piano, and Sony's entertainment complex, featuring a spectacular domed building designed by Helmut Jahn – opened with great fanfare in 1998 and 2000 respectively. However, the complex failed to help turn the neighborhood into the capital's new commercial district, just as the "boosterist ambitions" of the massive New Berlin rebuilding program failed to catapult "the former Cold War outpost into the top tier of contemporary global cities; rather, the regained capital is languishing under bankruptcy and high unemployment" (Ward 2004, 239). This situation was not aided by the decision of the German Constitutional Court in October 2006 that Berlin "had no right to a single Euro of federal funds to offset its huge budget deficit of 61.6 billion Euro" (Schwarz). The judges' decision, based on their view that the city was still in a position to reduce its expenditures and increase revenues despite the drastic austerity program it had already adopted, seems to have cemented Berlin's poor but sexy status.

As we have seen in previous chapters, the consequences of reunification and Berlin's not having met post-reunification expectations have not been wholly devastating for the cultural sectors. In addition to the city's much vaunted high-culture scene – its over 150 theatres and museums, three opera houses, seven symphony orchestras, eight choirs, etc. have come under considerable scrutiny on account of the city's grave financial plight and must have been a factor in the Court's refusal of a bailout –, one can also point to the city's currently thriving techno scene, the ongoing success of its international film festival, the new ownership that has invigorated the Babelsberg film studios, the reorganization of the museal sphere that has encouraged the sprouting up of new private museums like the ones which commemorate Heinrich Zille and Helmut Newton, and the fact that the *Kunstgewerbemuseum* was in a position to make a major acquisition like the Kamer/Ruf collection. We would not, however, as this chapter is intended to make clear, want the accomplishments charted in the previous chapters to be mistaken for the kind of boosterism that led the New Berlin rebuilding program. Rather, we take the opportunity here to revisit the transitions that Berlin has made as "Berlin is Becoming" became first "New Berlin" and then "be Berlin." We find that the presence of fashion in Berlin has intensified tremendously since reunification. The extent of this intensification is such that Nadine Barth found, in attempting to document the state of fashion in the city in 2007, that she could barely keep track of all of the openings and closings (314); even the staid Goethe Institute (whose name reveals its typically traditional approach to culture) now has a "Fashion Scene" section on its online magazine.[2] Noting how the growth of fashion retail and the fashion trade has figured in the city's current reinvention of itself as an anti-establishment glurban brand, we also probe the issue of corporate involvement and find that global corporate players, such as Daimler, have found it necessary to shift their strategies in order to keep up with the city's frenetic pace of change.

The Reemergence of Retail: Potsdamer Platz, Friedrichstraße, Hackesche Höfe

How and why was it that fashion-oriented retail moved into the central sites of Cold War confrontation? There was a general feeling that, as Mattias Frey notes, reunified Berlin "lacked a center, and thus by extension, so did Germany. Even the 1999 Berlin Architectural Chamber's yearbook – a promotional publication meant to put a positive spin on the year's urban designs – featured an article by French architects who claim they are 'confused' by Berlin's 'lack of an old city core and on account of a clear division between "center" and "edge district"'" (69–70). The city's former center, Berlin-Mitte, became the focus of interest and, in Ward's graphic description, was treated like "a piece of play-dough" by post-Wall planning commissions, architectural organizations, and speculative investors and developers (2004, 247). Pushed and pulled into shape by competing forces, Mitte was supposed to evoke "the densely structured prewar ensemble of churches, museums, theaters, department stores, and popular entertainment venues in the vicinity of Unter den

Linden, Friedrichstraße, and Potsdamer Platz, the districts that contributed much to Berlin's continuing aura as a vital metropolis since the late nineteenth century" (Goebel 1269).

Not only did the new Berlin's post-reunification rebuilding plans thus lend it a "putative centre" (Goebel 1269), and not just any center but the one that had already served as center during the city's "golden age," this development supported another tendency, namely, the erasure of East German memory. Key sites were dismantled that could have contributed to its reproduction:

> Following the fall of the Wall...landscapes of the postwar division quickly began to disappear in the public spaces of Berlin.... [M]emorials dedicated to socialist leaders were torn down, street names celebrating communist resistance fighters were changed, and many historical buildings were renovated. Former German Democratic Republic (GDR) government buildings, including the Palace of the Republic (the People's Parliament), the Marxist-Leninist Institute, and the Museum of German History were closed. (Till 2001, 273)

Figure 6.1: The Palace of the Republic, viewed from the Spree, 2005. (Photo: S. Ingram)

Figure 6.2: The razed site where the Palace of the Republic once stood, November 2009. (Photo: K. Sark)

Because these sites were understood by Western officials as "places of GDR memory that promoted Eastern values, pride and truths," they "were perceived as a threat to the legitimacy of a new Germany" and so had to be re-signified via reconstruction (Till 2001, 273), something which has not gone unnoted and unmourned (Figs. 6.1 and 6.2). Another example is the razing of the former socialist-chic Hotel Unter den Linden, on the corner of Friedrichstraße and Unter den Linden (Fig. 6.3), to make room for the newly opened Upper Eastside Berlin complex, which includes offices, apartments, retail along the lines of Zara and Marco Polo, and a Mercedes-Benz showroom.

Reaching back to the glorious pre-Nazi period of the city's history in the post-Wall redevelopment of Mitte was a way of shaking off unwanted ideological elements that might hurt Berlin's chances of attracting the global capital necessary to catapult it to world-city status. The vision shared by government and business leaders was "that Berlin would become a major player in the global economy, *a world city*, a service metropolis, a bridge between East and West, and the old/new capital city of the reunified Germany"

Figure 6.3: Corner of Unter den Linden and Friedrichstraße after *Hotel Unter den Linden*; was torn down to make room for the Upper East Side shopping mall, June 2006. (Photo: K. Sark)

(Lehrer 333, italics added). That is, suddenly at the mercy of the global forces that had been transforming cities and regions since the 1970s, Berlin found itself part of a post-industrial world-system in which cities operate, as Friedmann has argued (21–6), "as the 'organizing nodes' of world capitalism, as 'articulations' of regional, national and global commodities flows, and as 'basing points' in the 'space of global capital accumulation'" (cited in Brenner and Keil, 9). Because of "the consolidation of this truly worldwide urban hierarchy that has significantly expanded the scale of major cities' command and control functions within the capitalist world system as a whole" (Brenner and Keil 20), Berlin could not avoid the tough competition reunification confronted it with. What could it offer to companies already prosperously settled in Hamburg, Munich, Cologne and Dusseldorf to make relocation worth their while? How could it displace Frankfurt as the financial and transportation center of Germany when that city was already the largest financial center in continental Europe? How could it establish itself as a gateway to either Russia or Central Europe with Helsinki and Vienna vying for those positions and not facing the considerable challenges it was?[3]

The city's response was to encourage projects that would provide it with not only an initial transfusion of global capital but also an ongoing supplier. It did so by focusing on central areas already appropriately laden with what one might term historical capital – that is, sites whose histories provided them with appropriate connotations, in this case to histories of burgeoning consumerism: Potsdamer Platz, Friedrichstraße and Hackesche Höfe. That all three see the historical success of their locations as a valuable selling point is evident from the mention it receives on their websites, as though this invocation of past prominence were enough to make history repeat.[4]

All three projects were developed, like Upper Eastside Berlin, with an emphasis on mixed usage (retail, residential and office), only differing in the percentage of the mix and the class of establishment. Most mundane in this regard is the Daimler portion of Potsdamer Platz. It contains a mixed usage with 50% offices, 20% apartments and 30% special purposes; the latter includes, in addition to theatres and cinemas, a casino, a nightclub, two hotels and a panoply of restaurants and bars, a shopping mall called the Potsdamer Platz Arkaden, which has been described as a "standardised, monotonous reproduction of the mall form found around the world" (Färber 2005, 9). Among its 50-odd shops are such recognizable specialists of middle-market affordable fashion as Esprit, H&M, Mango, Marc O'Polo, Puma, Swatch, Tommy Hilfiger and Zara. That it aims at a lower-end market is confirmed by the presence of an Aldi discount supermarket in the basement. In contrast, the Sony Centre across the street from the Potsdamer Platz Arcades distinguishes itself from its neighbor by its lack of retail. The only retail tenant in the Forum is the multi-story Sony Style Store.[5]

More *mondain* shopping is to be found in the FriedrichstraßePassagen, which consist of three buildings connected via underground passages: "Quartier 205 houses low-end stores and restaurants, Quartier 206 forms the luxurious centerpiece of the complex, and Quartier 207 sports a branch of the French department store Galeries Lafayette" (Goebel 1279). The 1991 decision of the Galeries Lafayette to open up a second store on one of the main thoroughfares in Berlin's reemerging core was a monumental one for the company, on a par with Sony's decision to purchase Columbia Pictures Entertainment from the Coca-Cola Company for US$3.4 billion in 1989 and follow it up by investing in the Potsdamer Platz complex. Galeries Lafayette were part of the late nineteenth-century expansion of French department stores that saw them become temples of commodified consumerdom. While Le Bon Marché, Printemps and La Samaritaine were originally founded as small shops in 1838, 1865 and 1869 respectively, their initial success led them to undertake expansion, which involved the construction of lavish buildings specially designed to provide sumptuous, for the most part art nouveau settings for the goods on display. The Galeries Lafayette got into the game in 1893 and by 1905 had purchased property slightly to the north of the Opéra at the intersection of the rue La Fayette and the Boulevard Haussmann. The decision to expand to Berlin seems to have been a canny one as it allowed the company to remain solvent during the 1990s, a period of great hardship for department stores in general and French ones in particular. (In 1998, Le Bon Marché fell victim to the predatory LVMH, the luxury-goods conglomerate whose name comes from the merger of Louis Vuitton, champagne producer Moët et Chandon and cognac manufacturer Hennessy,[6] while La Samaritaine was bought out by LVMH in 2001 and closed in 2005, ostensibly for renovations; its reopening is scheduled for 2011.) The Galeries Lafayette understood the Friedrichstraße opportunity as a chance to escape this fate by tapping into historical precedent: "the FriedrichstadtPassagen cite the prewar Friedrichstraße, together with its famous shopping arcade, the Kaisergalerie, to celebrate themselves as a luxurious symbol of the reunited capital's political power, cosmopolitan culture, and international competitiveness. The new arcades, like Benjamin's icons of nineteenth-century iron construction, reflect a collective wish to overcome the recent past and return to a supposedly more glorious chapter of history" (Goebel 1282). Expanding to the Friedrichstraße also allowed the Galeries Lafayette to reinforce its reputation for trendsetting luxury. It understands itself not only as a retailer of jewelry and watches by "Cartier, Hermes, Bulgari, Tiffany, Chopard, Chanel, Fred, Chomet, Boucheron, and Din Van," bags and leathers by "Louis Vuitton, Furla, Coccinelle, Hervé Chapelier, Chanel, Dior, Gucci, Prada, Sonia Rykiel, Céline, Longchamp, Lancel" and "Clothing: Vivienne Westwood, Agnès B., Burberry, D&G, Zara, Paul Ka, Diesel, Chloé, Sonia Rykiel, Max Mara,"[7] but also as an attractive tourist destination. The original Parisian location boasts on its website that it is:

> not only well known for shopping, but also has a reputation for being one of the best sightseeing spots in Paris. The splendid glass dome of Neo-Byzantine style has been classified as a historical monument. It is an architectural landmark which attracts people from all over the world. The terrasse of the building offers a splendid panoramic view of the city. The newly renovated building of the Opera Garnier House lies beneath your eyes, and if you look up, you will see in the distance the Basilica of the Sacred Heart atop the Montmartre Hill.

The Friedrichstraße store a few blocks off Unter den Linden was designed in this spirit, as were the company's subsequent attempts at expansion: to Manhattan's Trump Tower, which quickly failed; and to the Dubai Mall, the new world's largest shopping center, at least based on total area (their anchor store there opened in May 2009). Due to its prime location, the Friedrichstraße Galeries Lafayette indeed functions as a tourist destination, much like Harrod's in Knightsbridge or Rodeo Drive in Beverly Hills. Given that retail integration has turned the latter "once-chic shopping streets into tourist attractions and driven luxury brands to look for new, more 'insider' addresses, such as the meatpacking and financial districts in New York and Melrose Place in Los Angeles" (Thomas 2007, 265), one wonders whether (or what) changes of character await the still very highbrow Galeries Lafayette and its surroundings.

For an example of how tourism has already had these kinds of effects in Berlin since reunification, one need look no further than the area between Friedrichstraße and the Hackesche Höfe (or Courtyards). At the beginning of the 1990s, the area behind the Höfe was still known as the "Scheunenviertel" or stall quarters, a moniker it received in the nineteenth century when it overfilled with the influx of poor Eastern European Jews.

Then the Oranienburger Straße that connected it with Friedrichstraße was one of the city's premier scenes.[8] As Nadine Barth remembers in her 2007 documentation of the city's fashion scene: "here was where 'real life' was filmed, a new living arrangement tested, the beginnings of reality TV. With barbecue parties on the roof, visits to the club 'Tresor' and creative discussions about behaviour, friendship and style. In the evening the crew would go to 'Fruit and Vegetables,' a bar in the Oranienburger Straße, across from it the 'Tacheles' held its first wild art exhibitions" (314). However, just as the Fruit and Vegetables bar had once been a store that sold fruit and vegetables, by the end of 2007 the bar had again changed, this time mutating into an "awful tourist dive with tropicana cocktails" (314), while the creative scene of interest to Barth crept progressively northeast up Kastanienallee, before decamping for the newly hip Kreuzberg-Friedrichshain areas.[9]

The Höfe themselves were originally built in 1906 across from the Hackesche market and contained a mix of businesses, reform-style apartments with access to light and green space, restaurants like the leading Neumannsche Festsäle in the front courtyard, and cultural activities. In addition to theatres and cinemas, an expressionist poet society met in one of its ballrooms before WWI, while the Girls Club of the Jewish Women's Organization (*Mädchenclub des jüdischen Frauenbunds*) rented space there between 1916 and 1933. The area, known as the Spandauer Vorstadt, housed the textile manufacturers and homeworkers who supplied the fashion houses in the reasonably close Hausvogteiplatz and its vicinity. A company called Kurzberg, located in the front courtyard along the Rosenthaler Straße, sold elegant men's ready-to-wear, while furs by Joka & Co, gloves by Baermann & Schuster, women's coats by Ahrndsen, shoes, aprons and hats were all produced in the inner courtyards (Siebel). This legacy still makes itself felt in the choice of tenant that the Höfe solicit: "A diversity of uses and high level of products on offer, thereby avoiding the mainstream. Tenants of relevance for these shops have an individual and distinctive profile. All shops are run by their owners and sell products that have been designed, manufactured or finished in the courtyards. To foster diversity individual shops are deliberately no larger than 100 m^2."[10] In other words, franchises are not welcome while avant-garde evenings like the "Por-Yes" one moderated by filmmaker Margaret von Schiller, at which the first feminist porno film prize in Europe was awarded, are.[11] Trippen, the innovative German manufacturer of funky leather shoes, is ideal.[12]

What we have here, then, in Potsdamer Platz, Friedrichstraße and the Hackesche Höfe are three attempts to develop lifestyle-oriented centers of consumption that, in order to achieve sustainability, cater to well-heeled, lifestyle-seeking visitors as much, if not more, than locals. What success Berlin has had is due to its establishing itself as a "cheap, yet cool, destination for holidaymakers."[13] In 2008, the city attracted 7.9 million visitors, "breaking its own record for the fifth consecutive year with a gain of 4.2 percent from 2007," while 2009 proved the best tourist year for Berlin on record with 8.3 million visitors. Moreover, as one can read in *Fashion in Berlin: The Place to Be*, the 2008 publication of Berlin Partner, the self-described "chief contact agency" for businesses interested in establishing themselves in the city (21), Berlin has been able to attract "a significant number of international consumers with above-average spending power" (2). Unlike the modern approach to tourism, in which travelers expect to visit a noteworthy locality only once and therefore attempt to soak up as much of its unique history and culture as possible (a legacy of the Grand Tour, which is also still a factor in Berlin tourism), what we might term postmodern travelers visit repeatedly, and sometimes even decide to live and work for periods of time in, places with amenities they like. Hence the prevalence of restaurants, movie theatres and hotels as well as shops and apartments in these complexes and their immediate vicinities. If, as Lehrer reminds us, "the social construction of these images…represents a strategic attempt to position the city within the accelerated global interurban competition" (333), we can see from the three sites examined here that Berlin's strategy has involved a canny expansion of its fashion retail sector.

Fashion: Berlin's Bread and Butter?

"If Paris' fashion week is a symphonic concert in a philharmonic, Berlin is slowly becoming the rock venue – with wild productions and intentional wrong notes."

(Lippitz 92)

Following in the footsteps of its expansion in fashion retail, Berlin has also begun to see a matching development on the fashion trade front. Momentum has been building since the Street and Urbanwear trade show Bread & Butter moved from Cologne to Berlin in 2003.[14] Having started out in 2001 with a concept for "an innovative trade fair event for the progressive, contemporary clothing culture" that ran biannually as a parallel event to Cologne's "*Herrenmodewoche* (Men's Fashion Week)/InterJeans," its immediate success (with an increase from the initial 50 exhibitors and 5,000 visitors to 180 exhibitors and 10,000 visitors by the summer of 2002) encouraged organizers to become more internationally oriented and move to the capital. Two years later, the trade show was set to expand again. Barcelona, one of the major contenders in the battle for capital of Eurochic, was very interested in hosting Bread & Butter and made it an attractive offer it hoped couldn't be refused, involving "much space in a central location and sunshine" (Drier 27), However, instead of committing to Barcelona completely, Bread & Butter decided to hold back-to-back events, with the first in Barcelona followed by another in Berlin two weeks later. Not only did this allow the trade show to boast of being able to cover "the complete European market by establishing a north-south axis," but it also doubled the number of exhibitors and visitors. However, the coordination of two events proved too much, and Bread & Butter decided for the winter 2007 event to concentrate its activities on Barcelona, holding a scaled-down event at the Berlin Kraftwerk. By summer 2009, however, Barcelona was no longer considered competitive, and the Bread & Butter slogan was "Bread & Butter is coming home!" – in other words, back to Berlin.

These shifts point to the volatility of the fashion industry and the multitudinous factors that affect the coordinating and orchestrating of trade shows. In the case of Bread & Butter, what they discovered in moving to Berlin in 2003 was that they were not alone in sizing up the city as an untapped market. Norbert Tillman and Anita Tillman also had the idea of starting up a fashion trade show, whose name – Premium – embodies its aspirations to provide "a contemporary trade platform for choice collections, international newcomers and exclusive trend products."[15] Thus not one but two fashion trade shows premiered in Berlin in January 2003, in venues reflecting their very different orientations and images: Bread & Butter in a derelict, crumbling factory on the outskirts of the city in Spandau; Premium in a conversation-worthy section of an underground U-Bahn tunnel beneath Potsdamer Platz that was no longer being used. This impetus proved to be precisely the breath of fresh air Berlin had been waiting for. In January 2005, ten fashion-oriented trade shows took place in Berlin, of which several were "short-lived and/or badly run" (Drier 26). Bread & Butter's decision to move to Barcelona is indicative of the energy that was dissipating from the city by 2007, while their move back in 2009 is indicative of how much the launch in July 2007 of an IMG- and Mercedes-Benz-sponsored Fashion Week that runs parallel to the Premium shows has reinvigorated Berlin's fashion industry.

Mercedes' sponsorship of Berlin Fashion Week did not come as a surprise to industry insiders. The German luxury automaker had been assiduously associating itself with fashion for a decade, taking every opportunity to point out how much "the brand with the star" and fashion have in common (Fig. 6.4), namely that: "Both are driven by the passion for creating something that is without parallel. The cornerstone of the Mercedes-Benz allure stems from combining technical innovation with timeless, elegant design. So by getting

Figure 6.4: Bebelplatz, Fashion Week 2009. (Photo: S. Ingram)

involved in the world of fashion, Mercedes-Benz is simply being consistent."[16] Mercedes' first involvement in the fashion industry came with its sponsoring of Australian Fashion Week in 1996, the year after the event was founded by Simon Lock. Mercedes then entered the American fashion scene, sponsoring the New York Fashion Week in the spring of 2001 and a show in Los Angeles in 2002 that merged the following year with its competition, the Smashbox Fashion Week Los Angeles, to become known as Mercedes-Benz Fashion Week at Smashbox Studios in Los Angeles and the "foremost fashion show in the United States outside of New York City"[17] In 2007, the Miami Swim Fashion Week, the Mercedes-Benz Fashion Festival in Brisbane, and Mercedes-Benz Fashion Mexico, which was established in collaboration with Vogue magazine and Fashion TV, were all added to the Mercedes stable,[18] while the Mercedes-Benz Dutch Fashion Awards were established in cooperation with the Dutch Fashion Foundation (DFF) to encourage talented new fashion designers in the Netherlands.[19] Starting up Fashion Week in Berlin in 2007 can thus be seen to be part of a larger corporate expansion, a strategy that continued with Mercedes' title sponsorship of Stockholm Fashion Week in 2009[20] and the announcement in September 2009 that the Mercedes-Benz had become the official car for the Milan, Paris and London Fashion Weeks.[21] There is thus every reason to believe that the extremely Limited Edition (100 vehicle production) of the 2005 Mercedes-Benz CLK Cabriolet by Giorgio Armani, the idea for which arose from the automaker's five-city tour sponsoring of the Salomon R. Guggenheim's "Giorgio Armani: Retrospective" exhibition was not an anomaly but the first in a series of fashion designer-designed vehicles.[22]

Mercedes seems to have found an ideal partner in their fashion venture: IMG, which originally stood for International Management Group. Describing itself as "the world's premier and most diversified sports, entertainment and media company" and "the global leader in event management and talent representation across golf, tennis and fashion," IMG is a phenomenon of global corporate sponsorship. It defines the service it offers as being able to "partner with the world's leading marketers and media networks to help them grow their businesses through our event properties, media production and distribution, talent brands, sponsorship consulting, brand licensing, sponsorship sales and other services."[23] One can better understand the implications of what this means by turning to the example of Mercedes Australian Fashion Week founder Simon Lock, who in 2005 sold MAFW and its parent company Australian Fashion Innovators to IMG and became the Managing Director of IMG Fashion Asia Pacific.[24] Lock explains his motivation to join IMG as follows:

> It was great being a well-meaning entrepreneur owning the event [MAFW] and operating the event as I saw fit, but it didn't really enable us to get connected globally as I wanted. So the ultimate for me was that our organisation, Australian Fashion Innovators, had become an acquisition target for [U.S. company] International Management Group to complete their global footprint of fashion weeks by bringing in the Asia Pacific region. When it was explained to me the value that IMG Fashion could add to the Australian fashion industry, it was a no-brainer to sell the company. (Traill-Nash)

Lock has gone on to launch Fashion Weeks in Hong Kong, India and Pakistan and sponsor designers to show in New York and Europe (cf. Gilewicz), while IMG's stable of fashion events now includes the Mercedes-Benz Fashion Weeks in New York, Miami and Berlin, Volvo Fashion Week presented by Visa in Moscow, the Rosemount Australian Fashion Week and the Rosemount Sydney Fashion Festival in Sydney, Swim Fashion Week at Sanctuary Cove on Australia's Gold Coast, MasterCard Luxury Week in Hong Kong, ecoStyle in Kuala Lumpur, Lakme Fashion Week in Mumbai and Fashion Fringe at Covent Garden in London. IMG also represents commercial rights at Milan Fashion Week, LG Fashion Week Beauty by L'Oreal Paris, London Fashion Week presented by Canon, and the British Fashion Awards. Its CEO, Theodore J. Forstmann, was #321 on the Forbes list of the 400 richest Americans in 2008 and is a noted Republican fundraiser.

Branding Berlin with Fashion

Propelled by the growth of fashion retail and trade shows in Berlin, there is a growing market for everything Berlin-esque, beginning with the city itself. Such marketing campaigns as the "Be Berlin" one launched in spring 2008 have helped to create a Berlin brand that sells freedom and creativity (Fig. 6.5). Although expensive, tax-draining and therefore heavily criticized, one should not underestimate their value. While commissioned to attract more capital investors, small entrepreneurs, artists and designers, city branding campaigns also function as communication platforms and media vehicles for collective identity and image projection and formation and act as multipliers for events such as Fashion Week (Fig. 6.6). For example, out of the campaign slogan "be creative, be curious, be berlin!" emerged a young designers' fashion show featuring the work of Beate Richter, Behnam Samrad, Xiao Mial, BEASBERLIN, Atelier Mohr, Lucilux, Frikant, kvast, kidneykaren, Rasselbande and Urban Speed/stadtkluft. Sponsored by the city campaign and held in the city-store (for young designers who are not yet part of the Mercedes Fashion Week selection at Bebelplatz), it allowed the young designers to not only establish their labels but to become part of a recognized, and often Senate-supported, community of entrepreneurs and creators.

Besides the city itself, Berlin's name and history are mobilized to increasing effect to sell clothing, accessories, souvenirs and design articles by both local designers and international chains. Thirty-nine stores listed in the 2009 *Tip* have Berlin in their title, including shoe stores (*Black Roses Berlin, Shoes-Berlin.de,* Figs. 6.7 and 6.8 respectively), specialized sneaker and skater stores (*BerlinBurns*), vintage clothing stores (*Made in Berlin*, Fig. 6.9) as well as the latest in fashionable clothing (*Skunk Funk Berlin*, Fig. 6.10), department stores (*Carré Berlin*) and concept stores (*Berlinomat,* Fig. 6.11; *Waahnsinn Berlin*, Fig. 6.12). Among the striking features of these stores are their collaborative qualities and that they are usually designed to be scenes, places to hang out, read up on the state of fashion over a cup of organic coffee, discuss the scene with young designers, and feel included in it. For example, Berlin designers like Claudine Brignot of Urban Speed (www.urbanspeed.de) collaborate

Figure 6.5: Be Berlin poster. (Photo: S. Ingram)

Figure 6.6: Be Berlin as a sponsor of Fashion Week 2008. (Photo: S. Ingram)

Figure 6.7: Black Roses Berlin, Alte Schönhauser Strasse 39. (Photo: K. Sark)

Figure 6.8: Shoes Berlin, Rosenthaler Strasse 50. (Photo: K. Sark)

Figure 6.9: Interior of Made in Berlin, Neue Schönhauser Strasse 19. (Photo: K. Sark)

Figure 6.10: Interior of Skunk Funk Berlin, Kastanienallee 19.
(Photo: K. Sark)

Figure 6.11: Interior of Berlinomat, Frankfurter Allee 89. (Photo: K. Sark)

Figure 6.12: Waahnsinn Berlin, Rosenthaler Strasse 17. (Photo: K. Sark)

Figure 6.13: Eastberlin, Alte Schönhauser Strasse 33–34.
(Photo: K. Sark)

Figure 6.14: Sophienhof with sewing machine.
(Photo: K. Sark)

Figure 6.15: All Saints display with sewing machines, Rosenthalerstrasse 52. (Photo: K. Sark)

on new creations with graphic and interior designers like Sandra Siewert of s.wert design (www.s-wert-design.de) and integrate Berlin themes into their designs, bridging the city and fashion (under the name *Stadtkluft*). Their goal is to create highly creative and original designs with a particular Berlin feel that encourages the wearer to identify with the city's associating itself with freedom and independent-minded creativity. Stores like Eastberlin (www.eastberlin.net) at Alte Schönhauser Straße 33-34 (just a block away from where Marco Wilms, Sabine von Oettingen, and Frank Schäfer recreated their *Erdbeerfolie* fashion show) play on the curiosity and *ostalgie* of shoppers, offering casual street wear and accessories with "Eastberlin" inscriptions that promote their logo and a sense of nostalgia for a part of the city that no longer exists (Fig. 6.13). Similarly, old Singer sewing machines pop up in unexpected places in the city. They decorate shop windows and restaurant entrances, such as the *Sophienhof* at Sophienstrasse 11 (Fig. 6.14) and remind the city's inhabitants how far back its fashion history stretches. Even übercool specialty chains like *All Saints* (www.allsaints.com) have lined the window of their Berlin location at Rosenthalerstraße 52 with Singer sewing machines, linking their stylish urban wear with the city's manufacturing history (Fig. 6.15), while designer outlets, like the one near Spandau, advertise brand names as "checkpoint jeans" (*Zitty* Oct–Nov 09, 52). Commemorations specific to Berlin also make their way into fashion. The *Overkill* sneaker and street wear shop (www.overkillshop.com) marked the twentieth anniversary of the fall of the Berlin Wall by teaming up with *New Balance* to launch a limited edition sneaker in three colors: red for the USSR flag, blue for the U.S. flag, and black for the Berlin bear. Each shoe was made with a sketch of the Wall and the dates 89/09 printed on the tongue, and each pair cost 124.90 Euros.[25] It is a safe bet that a pair will end up in the *Deutsches Historisches Museum*, most likely the black ones. The Berlin spirit is thus marketed to tourists and locals alike as something uniquely local, something which cannot be bought in global chains like Nike, Calvin Klein, Miss Sixty and Ugg, which offer the same goods the world over – the retail equivalent of Marc Augé's non-places. "It's not so much about educating the customer, but rather communicating that the work we do is different from, say, H&M," explains Berlin designer Natascha Loch.[26] Her knitwear designs (www.nataschaloch.de) cater to "customers with a taste for the exquisite": her 2009 collection included cashmere and silk wool dresses, cardigans and asymmetrical tops created for "women who are brave and curious, and who want to discover something new, comfortable, and uncomplicated in fashion." One cannot escape the similarity of Loch's designs to those of long-established Berlin knitting avant-gardist Claudia Skoda, who has been "selling her collection in the Alte Schönhauser Strasse since 2002. It is her fourth store in Berlin, after one on the Kurfürstendamm, another on Linienstrasse and one way back, in the '70s and '80s, in a Kreuzberg factory loft. And in 1981 she opened one in New York" (Wahjudi 106). David Bowie is the one credited with having talked her into going to America.

In addition to being scene-ish and collaborative, the spaces in which Berlin fashion is sold are often temporary. Luxux International, a concept store in Kastanienallee 101 (www.luxus-international.de) was established in 2002. The idea for it originated from various events in Berlin's so-called off-scene. Creative designers can rent a display area for 7.50 Euros and sell their products. Since its opening, the store has provided space for 950 "creative types," while at the same time providing customers with innovative trends and articles intended to make life a little better. Another example is CUBE (www.cube-berlin.net), located in the Schönhauser Arkaden mall, a collaboration of eight Berlin designers (Hypnosis-berlin, Cultivate, Aspique, LIAN, Widda, Velibor, Natascha Loch, and B. Weiss) who periodically stage weekend fashion shows and invite local DJs. Its location in the fall of 2009 was its second and most likely not last home, since the lease is on a three-month basis (Fig. 6.16). Many of the designers know each other from fashion school; there are plans for a second CUBE store.

Even more temporary are the popular pop-up stores, which display avant-garde labels for a short time in various locations throughout the city with the goal of attracting a diverse clientele. Pop-up stores hide in not yet renovated courtyards and basements and sport a minimalist, spartan aesthetic devoid of advertisement. Popularized by word of mouth

Figure 6.16: Interior of Cube, Schönhauser Arkaden mall. (Photo: K. Sark)

and with their own websites, they cater to fashion enthusiasts who prefer exclusivity; the items they sell are regarded as the latest thing (*Tip* 34). Examples include 8½ Weeks (www.achteinhalbwochen.com) and Canadian men's fashion designer Campbell McDougall's darklands (http://darklandsberlin.com/site/). Pop-up stores are also increasingly being organized by the Create Berlin network of Berlin designers. The network arranges for different temporary fashion retail locations, such as the temporary showroom in Kastanienallee, which also serves the multiple functions of exhibition hall, shop, and PR agency (*Tip* 37). Create Berlin sees itself as an "ambassador of Berlin Design" and underscores that "Board and members alike are committed to establishing Berlin as the key location for creative industries and as the UNESCO 'City of Design,'" referring to the fact that in 2005, Berlin became the first, and remains the only, European city to be included in the UNESCO Network of Creative Cities as a "City of Design" (Barth 8).[27]

As in the case of the techno scene, with which it, of course, overlaps, this Berlin-specific fashion retail scene makes use of a variety of communications technologies to develop its image and make itself known.[28] Like every city that wants to establish itself as having a fashion Zeitgeist, Berlin has an active blogger culture, of which StilinBerlin (http://stilinberlin.blogspot.com), which specializes in photographing stylish outfits and street trends, is the oldest street-style blog (online since 2006) and, with up to 3,000 daily visits, the most popular. The online site www.fashion-guide-berlin.de, run by the marketing and design company *Merkel Design Berlin,* provides further guidance in locating and mapping the trendy new spots in Berlin, while the online television channel www.berlinfashion.tv features information, reports, and interviews with Berlin fashion and design experts.

Pop-up stores and the new Berlin fashion scene have even found their way into Berlin fiction. In the 2009 *Ein Amerikaner in Berlin: Wie ein New Yorker lernte, die Deutschen zu lieben* (*An American in Berlin: How a New Yorker Learned to Love the Germans*), Ralph Martin portrays Berlin as "the capital of hipness; the creative art and literary factory" (13) and details his attempts to adopt his metrosexual, white-scarfed, New York sartorial sensibilities for Prenzlauer Berg. Adjusting to Berlin, his carefully cultivated New York fashion sense (a mix of Bowie and Isherwood, whose sexual ambiguity did not occur to him in his New York state of mind) forces him on a fashion quest through the boutiques around Alte and Neue Schönhauser Strassen. Martin claims to have spent all his energy in his twenties on developing his self-esteem and a personal style. In Berlin, however, he discovered that the wheel of fashion could turn differently (41). As his costume-designing friend Annie in New York tells him, in Berlin, fashion is particularly "*exigéant*" (demanding, fastidious, heavy-handed). Martin interprets the fashion codes of Prenzlauerberg to suggest a construction-worker look and buys himself a grey, zip-up hoody and yellow Puma sneakers at *Carhartt* (44). Yet, still unsatisfied, he decides to do further fashion research to decode the codes:

My friend Annie in New York knew of a boutique in Mitte that was, as she put it, the 'non plus ultra' of Berlin fashion. When I finally found the address, it looked like the boutique was hidden behind an unmarked metal door in a back courtyard. I pressed the metal door open and followed a cement staircase downstairs into a small, dark basement, which was only illuminated by a purple neon bulb. The walls were painted black, if there were any at all. Behind the counter stood a tall youth with large, black-rimmed glasses and a black zip-up sweatshirt. He had his hood up so that his face seemed to float in space. He ignored me while I groped my way through the store looking for clothes. Finally I found something: a long board made of unfinished wood. On top of it lay a sweatshirt and a pair of sneakers. I bent over and attempted to see something in the purple light. The sweatshirt seemed to be grey, with a blindingly white fleecy lining. After I had stared at the price tag for some time, the floating face with the glasses said in English: "300 Euros.... It's hand-made," said the boy. I held it to the purple light. If I had had a sewing machine, I could have made something like that myself. (Martin 51)

The store Martin describes so evocatively and satirically but does not name actually exists. It is called *Apartment* and is located at Memhardstrasse 8 (www.apartmentberlin.de). From the outside, the building looks like an empty gallery. Owner Christof Rücker seems to be avoiding walk-in customers on purpose, and it is precisely this image that has succeeded in garnering his store a reputation that can now, thanks to Martin, be considered emblematic of Berlin's new fashion scene, and which will live on in Martin's work as such.

Corporate Consequences

How does a city become the kind of fashion space it does? In the case of North American cities, an image sometimes unexpectedly emerges from the culture industries that strikes a chord that can be capitalized on. Perhaps the most successful example is the Versace look for the *Miami Vice* television show, which ran on NBC from 1984 to 1989 and changed the South Beach area of that city from a seedy backwater to a holiday playground for metrosexual style mavens, helped in no small part by Versace's move to the city in 1992 and his creation of a "Miami Collection."[29] As the "Be berlin" and Create Berlin examples illustrate, however, the Versace model seems to have been superseded, at least in Berlin, by one involving multi-modal synergy. The Create Berlin network is an excellent example of the self-organization common to "culturepreneurship," which Bastian Lange has shown to be characteristic of Berlin's creative industries. Culturepreneurs "in structural terms, are communicative providers of transfer services between the sub-systems 'business related services' and 'creative scene' and, in doing so, seem to satisfy a necessary demand by operating in flexible social networks.... [They] create their own relational spaces of interaction where borders blur: competition and cooperation, exchange and isolation, private and public, work and leisure coexist and are hard to tell apart. They invent forms of self-organization to gain access to power structures, based on informal conglomerates and extensive networks" (Lange 13, 22). Contemporary Berlin designers have become, in other words, as flexible, disorganized and alliance-oriented as the capitalism that attempts to structure and define their work (Banks 128–31).

However, despite the increasing status and symbolic importance of the creative industries in the city's refashioning of itself since unification, they still only represented about 20% of Berlin's GDP in 2006 (Lange 3–4). While "the economically and socially transitional Berlin is being promoted as Europe's leading bohemian, creative city with its marginal districts (such as Prenzlauer-Berg) becoming widely touted as epicentres of a renascent European artistic sensibility" (Banks 147), one should not forget that both state and corporate presences have also contributed to the reshaping of Berlin's city-image. In 2004 Ward was struck by the "tirelessly corporate" nature of developments in Berlin and noted similarities between them and those in New York and London: "indeed, Manhattan's Times Square redevelopment under the aegis of Disney can be regarded as a precursor to the purchase and rebuilding of Potsdamer Platz by Daimler-Benz and Sony.... While London's financial center has been effectively moved eastwards by the 1980s development of Canary Wharf out of once deserted docks, Berlin's plans for the Osthafen area [i.e., the MediaSpree development discussed in the previous chapter as a popular target of techno and club culture protest] are perhaps no less ambitious" (2004, 247, 252). And likely also no less volatile. Sir Howard Stringer, for one, has had the opportunity of experiencing the volatility of Berlin property since becoming, in June 2005, the first foreign-born CEO of a major Japanese electronics corporation, namely Sony. Potsdamer Platz turned out to be the site of a struggle both Sony and Daimler decided they were not likely to win. Sony sold out, while the Mercedes-Benz portion of Daimler decided to shift its chips to *Eventkultur*.

The model Ward is implicitly drawing on in comparing Berlin to New York and London is Sharon Zukin's account of the gentrification of New York's SoHo district in the 1980s, an account that has been shown to speak to the experience of many de-industrialized Western cities, "where grass roots cultural zones in the city fringe have been pervasively gentrified and sanitized by local authorities seeking to attract middle-class residents and consumers" (Banks 142). However, especially European scholarship has been quick to offer alternative models, detailing the success of efforts made in cities "like Berlin, Brussels and Helsinki by artists and 'informal actors' to develop 'free,' creative production spaces." They have been "able to flourish because of the mixed approach taken by (European) planners and governments to their 'strategic' economic development" (Banks 142). Certainly a factor in preventing Berlin from descending into the more brutal neocolonial conditions characteristic of countries with less of a tradition of social welfare is the investment being made in its creative sector by government. One such example is Project Future (*Projekt Zukunft*), an initiative of the Berlin Senate for Economics, Technology and Women's Issues that is funded by the state of the Berlin and the European Regional Development Fund and supports projects identified as building on established expertise in Berlin's creative industries, such as in mobile broadband communication, print media, the art market, design, interactive entertainment software and music.[30]

The fate of the fashion bubble is difficult to predict. Footage of fashion shows seems to have filled the niche created by MTV videos for short, music-driven visual spectacles peopled with desirable young people, and it is increasingly used to create atmosphere on screens in public places, particularly those devoted to lifestyle travel, such as airport lounges and the lobbies of boutique hotels. The pulsating flow of the catwalk seems an adequate reflection of the experience of late modernity, which Manuel Castells has described as "the spatial logic specific to the Information Age," and Appadurai has termed a space of flows (cf. Abbas 250). There are an increasingly number of fashion shows to provide the necessary fodder for an increasing number of fashion channels,[31] and it is hard to fault Berlin for riding this wave when it is in a good position to do so and without more attractive, realistic alternatives. The city succeeded in putting itself "on the map of global cultural spectacle" with events like the Love Parade and by being associated with U2's Zoo TV tour (Lehrer 333), and its ability to stage events as global media spectacles continues to serve it well: the 2006 World Cup and the 2009 celebrations of the twentieth anniversary of the fall of the Wall, with its climactic falling of the domino pieces along the former path of the Wall, were staged for a global spectatorship and meant to be seen on a television screen rather than up-close in person. Moreover, the type of growth the city has seen since reunification has been conducive to the fostering of the city's service and creative sectors. As Ward notes, "despite being a third-tier global city, Berlin actually ranks as a first-tier 'global media city,' according to Krätke's ranking of cities according to their level of networked media company clusters" (2004, 251). Given the synergistic nature of the industry and the level of government support for creative ventures, one could imagine Berlin maintaining this first-tier media status for a considerable while.

Notes

1. The quotations and information in this paragraph are from "Berlin's Sony Center Sells for Bargain Price." Since selling out to SEB, Daimler rents half of the space in the Daimler complex (Lehmphul).
2. Available at http://www.goethe.de/kue/des/prj/mod/enindex.htm. While the magazine is pan-German in its focus, Berlin's status as capital and the rapid growth of its fashion scene translate into a substantial presence.
3. A key lack on Berlin's part was in infrastructure, as Ulrich Kissing, the head of the IBB (Investitionsbank Berlin), noted in a 19 October 2009 *Tagespiegel* interview. His response to the interviewer's comment that "the fulcrum to Eastern Europe is not Berlin but Vienna" was: "That is true, we have much to catch up on. For example, airports. When I've flown with Air Austria [sic], I've often thought that today Berlin also could have all these connecting flights to Central and Eastern Europe if the large airport had been built earlier" (Döbler and Schröder).
4. One reads on the Sony Centre website that: "In the 1920s Potsdamer Platz was one of the most prominent business districts in Berlin with its department stores, government offices and hotels such as the luxury Grand Hotel Esplanade. Café Josty used to be a famous location for Berlin's high society. As one of the most central places, Potsdamer Platz developed into an important traffic junction with up to 20,000 cars per day. At this location the first traffic light system in Europe was installed in 1924.... On this historic ground, a modern ensemble emerged that opened in June 2000 and that fascinates its visitors by its airiness and transparency" (http://www. sonycenter.de/en/center/datenfakten/geschichte). The Galeries Lafayette inform on theirs that: "In 1996 the Galeries Lafayette succeeded in bridging Paris and the Spree. The first German store was built in the Friedrichstraße, on the corner of Französische Straße.... After the seemingly endless work of tearing down, building, excavating and cleaning up, the new Friedrichstraße took shape with the old shopping stretch again with a new sparkle" http://www.galerieslafayette.de/ ueber_galeries_lafayette.html?PHPSESSID=f19d61f9a5646022eef32651f3b1c4c8. A related link announces that "this mixed-use building playfully announces itself on the predominantly staid Friedrichstraße, once the most important shopping street in Berlin" (http://www.galinsky.com/ buildings/f-passagen/index.htm). As for the Hackesche Höfe, there is a separate screen on history on their website, which offers a detailed account of the area's involvement in textile manufacturing that begins "In 1906, when the Hackeschen Höfe was built, Berlin counted as one of the largest fashion metropolises in the world" (http://www.hackesche-hoefe.com/index.php?id=35).
5. http://www.sonycenter.de/en/center/mieterliste. It would seem that Sony did not want any other values to compete with or encroach on the attribute it built into the Forum with the inclusion of cinemas and the Film Museum, namely, quality entertainment. This is in keeping with the Japanese approach to brands: "Branson refers derisively to the 'stilted Anglo-Saxon view of

consumers,' which holds that a name should be associated with a product like sneakers or soft drinks, and opts instead for 'the Asian "trick" of the *keiretsus* (a Japanese term meaning a network of linked corporations).' The idea, he explains, is to 'build brands not around products but around reputation. The great Asian names imply quality, price and innovation rather than a specific item. I call these "attribute" brands: They do not relate directly to one product – such as a Mars bar or a Coca-Cola – but instead to a set of values"' (cited in Klein 24).

6. See Thomas (2007) for a detailed account of how Bernard Arnault turned LVMH into one of the world's largest, and most ruthless luxury-good conglomerates.

7. These are among the brands they list as selling on their website (http://www.galerieslafayette. com/).

8. This scene is illustrative of the point Alan Blum has made in distinguishing scenes and subcultures on the basis that the former is permeated by commercial structures while the latter may not be (Blum 2001, 8 ff.)

9. It should be noted that this kind of creativity does not correspond with Richard Florida's concept of the "creative class," which Stefan Krätke has argued is better termed a "dealer class" as it is constituted of not only of "artistically creative occupations" (of interest to Barth) and "scientifically and technologically creative employees," but also the "creative professionals" of the finance and real estate business (Krätke 2).

10. This is from the "Mieterkonzept" section of their website (http://www.hackesche-hoefe.com/ index.php?id=47).

11. See "Feministischer Porno-Preis 'PorYes' vergeben". See also Kutsche.

12. For Trippen's history and philosophy, see Spieth & Oehler.

13. See "'Poor, but sexy' Berlin is a hit" and Jacobs.

14. Information in this section is from Drier as well as the Bread & Butter website: http://www. breadandbutter.com/winter2010/metanav/about-bb/.

15. From the Premium website (http://www.premiumexhibitions.com/press/).

16. From the "Sponsors" section of the Mercedes Benz Fashion Week website (http://www.mercedes-benzfashionweek.com/sponsors/mercedes-benz.html).

17. "Mercedes-Benz and Fashion: Mercedes-Benz Fashion Week at Smashbox Studios in Los Angeles" (17 July 2008, http://www.emercedesbenz.com/Jul08/17_001270_Mercedes_Benz_And_Fashion_ Mercedes_Benz_Fashion_Week_At_Smashbox_Studios_In_Los_Angeles.html.

18. See "Mercedes-Benz Dives into Mercedes-Benz Fashion Week Miami Swim with Sleek Microsite Featuring Supermodel Tyson Beckford and Honoring Lauded Fashion House Badgley Mischka with 'Mercedes-Benz Presents'" (9 July 2007, http://www.prnewsonline.com/prnewswire/1186. html); the background section of the Brisbane Fashion Festival website (http://www.mbff.com.au/ index.php?id=3); and "Mercedes-Benz And Fashion: Mercedes-Benz Fashion Week Mexico" (17 July 2008, http://www.emercedesbenz.com/Jul08/17_001272_Mercedes_Benz_And_Fashion_ Mercedes_Benz_Fashion_Week_Mexico.html).

19. "Mercedes-Benz and Fashion: Mercedes-Benz Dutch Fashion Awards" (17 July 2008, http://www. emercedesbenz.com/Jul08/17_001273_Mercedes_Benz_And_Fashion_Mercedes_Benz_Dutch_ Fashion_Awards.html).

20. "Mercedes-Benz and Fashion: Mercedes-Benz Becomes the Title Sponsor of Stockholm Fashion Week" (17 July 2008, http://www.emercedesbenz.com/Jul08/17_001274_Mercedes_Benz_And_ Fashion_Mercedes_Benz_Becomes_The_Title_Sponsor_Of_Stockholm_Fashion_Week.html).

21. See "Mercedes-Benz is in the Front Row Seat for London Fashion Week" on the Auto Channel website (http://www.theautochannel.com/news/2009/09/14/477454.html).

22. Specs for this vehicle, which cost when it was launched US$106,000, or €86,884, are available on the Serious Wheels website (http://www.seriouswheels.com/cars/top-2005-Mercedes-Benz-CLK-Cabriolet-Armani.htm).
23. This self-description is from the IMG website (http://www.imgworld.com/about/default.sps).
24. For further details on Lock and IMG, see Huntington and Breen Burns. Mercedes' association with the Australian Fashion Week lasted eleven years and came to an end with the Spring Fashion Week in 2006. Since then Fosters has been the Fashion Week's major sponsor and the Australian and Sydney Fashion Festivals have been known as the Rosemount Fashion Festivals (beer presumably being seen as too déclassé a drink for a fashion week), while the Melbourne Festival, which claims to be the "largest and most successful consumer fashion event in Australia" is a not-for-profit organization sponsored by L'Oreal.
25. Available on the Overkill website (http://www.overkillshop.com/de/product_info/info/6322/).
26. Interview, 18 November 2009.
27. See http://www.create-berlin.de/Profil_en.html for more on the network's self-presentation, which is much more extensive in the English section of the website than in the German one.
28. The same is true of the students who spontaneously decided to occupy the University of Vienna's Audimax lecture hall in October 2009 only to be forcibly evicted by the police shortly before Christmas. Their use of new communications technologies and rejection of traditional organization proved more effective than official, union-led strikes elsewhere.
29. "After moving here in 1992 and creating a palatial estate at Casa Casuarina on a still raw Ocean Drive, Versace distilled the visuals and youthful sexuality he saw on the streets of South Beach into his 'Miami Collection,' a line of bold colors, art deco images, sleek 1950s automobiles, and, as always, mondo sexuality" (Brown).
30. See the Projekt Zukunft section of the berlin.de website (http://www.berlin.de/projektzukunft/english/about-project-future/).
31. See Emling.

Chapter 7

Conclusion – Where Fashion Lives Today, Battleground Berlin

"If Berlin had been a person, it would have been one of us, and not one of them."

Monika Maron (68)

"Chic is when you don't have anything left."

Ines de la Fressange (Livingstone)

From the material presented in this study, we have learned that there are critical distances and conceptual limits that are usefully maintained. Alison Bancroft has astutely pointed out that "the lack of a fixed definition of fashion dogs all of its scholars" (394). Fashion not only pertains to clothing. In Simmel's noteworthy observation, "the domination of fashion is most unbearable in those areas which ought to be subject only to objective decisions: religiosity, scientific interests, and even socialism and individualism have all been the subject of fashion" (cited in Carter, 61). The "lexical disjuncture between fashion as garments that are worn and fashion as something popular" (Bancroft 394) is something we found manageable only from the point of the view of the former. However, it was pleasant to discover time and again how much more broadly illuminating our focus turned out to be. When the history of fashionable Berlin pastimes is written, it will necessarily include material we have uncovered here, whether it be sunbathing, going to the cinema or clubbing. In retrospect, given that there are relatively few fashionable pastimes that one engages in without being clothed in some way, we should have been less surprised.

More pointedly, understanding fashion more broadly in terms of the pleasure humans derive from change, as Claudia Ebner does in her championing of René König's work (143), would not have helped us in determining the specificity of Berlin's contribution to fashion and the counter-hegemonic challenges that fashion-related culture there has been able to mount. What Barbara Kosta claims of Marlene Dietrich, for example, – that Dietrich in her own way "reconciled and challenged dichotomies, broke taboos, violated categories, and projected a sense of freedom, lawlessness and independence" (157) – we repeatedly found to be equally true of the varied aspects of Berlin's fashion-related culture, from the Lipperheides' collecting practice violating the category of "old" art to the underground fashionistas in East Berlin that appear in Marco Wilms' documentary, to Heinrich Zille's sketches and photographs of his "Milljöh" and Helmut Newton's photographs of big nudes, to the music recorded in the Hansa Studios, played at the Love Parade or on sale at the Ramones Museum. However, it would not necessarily be true of fashion construed more widely as simply a desire for change.

It is in any case hardly a human desire for change that has motivated the history of Berlin and its fashion. Much to the contrary, the city's history of change has primarily been one of hardship and hard work. Here, too, Dietrich is exemplary, as the two anecdotes about her work ethos which frame the *Dietrich Icon* collection reveal. The first, by Dietrich biographer Steven Bach, narrates the rehearsals for Dietrich's successful 1968 come-back concert conducted by Burt Bacharach at Los Angeles' Ahmanson Theater, which the stage manager surreptitiously recorded and offered to his unnamed assistant, presumably Bach:

> And then I'll say, 'And here's a song from *The Blue Angel*,' and someone will begin to applaud and then I'll say 'No, no, it's not that one...' The stage manager switched the machine off and leaned heavily on the desktop. 'The speaker system feeds down here, too, you know,' he said. 'All four days of it is there on tape. Every word. All the sweat. You ever want to hear it, come on down.' 'But why?' asked the assistant. 'Because,' said the older man. '*Because*.' He sipped at his coffee, then nodded to the newspaper open to the review in the assistant's hand. 'Because it'll be proof of what happened Friday night,' the stage manager said, his voice mellow and firm. 'It'll prove what happened and how you get to be a star and how you get to *stay* a star.' I understood. Or thought I did. And went back to work. (Bach 40, italics in original)

The second anecdote is told by Dietrich impersonator James Beaman in response to a request for his favorite Dietrich story:

> My favorite Marlene story comes from a man who became a fan of mine over the years. He was a dancer in the sixties in Marlene's act in Paris. Marlene often invited the dancers and crew people into her dressing room – she had enormous respect for everyone who did the jobs that supported her show. One night, in her bathrobe, she stopped this man outside her dressing room and enlisted him in a 'job' that he would do with her every night after performance. She took him up to the stage, and he helped her go over the stage floor and pick up each and every bead and rhinestone that fell off her dress during the performance. Then she would sit in the dressing room, as he ate scrambled eggs she cooked up for him on a hot plate, and she would personally sew on each bead to her concert dress. That's the Marlene I adore – the trouper, the accessible goddess, the hausfrau in a swan's down coat. (Mayne 2007b, 375)

Dietrich is celebrated in these anecdotes for not having let success go to her head, for remaining, despite the glitzy costumes and temptations of stardom, down-to-earth – a trouper, who sewed and cooked for her fellow workers.

What is specific to Berliner Chic in these depictions of Dietrich's communitarian work ethic, in her refusal to play the imperious diva?[1] Writing in 1931 after her big breakthrough, Franz Hessel attributed it to her Berlin background: "[A]s a Prussian warrior's child she is used to discipline, instilled with a sense of punishing energy" (14). This interpretation foregrounds one of the ingredients in the soup of Berlin's past that gives it its particular flavor, or rather, to speak in the idiom of our topic, a thread that provides the historical texture of its fashion space. Unlike the other European centers of imperial power, Berlin's elites were oriented more towards military objectives than the administration of colonies, and they were destroyed later and more thoroughly (cf. P. Anderson). Part of the painful lessons of history that Berlin's past represents is a deeply developed suspicion of power, both social and political, that has become part of the city's global mystique. So strong and toxic are the associations of the city with the fascist power it briefly hosted – something perhaps most evident in popular culture, such as in the punk-rock and contemporary dystopian science-fiction imaginaries discussed in this study – it seems that once these associations have taken root, their fascination seems to make them ineradicable. The flip-side, and possible saving grace, of the resolutely and dialectically modern constitution of these fascinating forces is that they may contain an antidote for the very poison they inflict (a particularly German gift, given that *das Gift* means "poison" and comes with the philosophical pedigree of the pharmakon).[2] As we saw in reading *Aeon Flux* against *Equilibrium*, it was still possible in 2005 for a female film director from the U.S. to associate Berlin with the rootedness of the cultivated, enlightened half of the modern tradition and to depict it as providing shelter from the onslaughts of the globalized, Asian-inflected, turbo-capitalist male imaginary associated with the genres of cyberpunk and dystopian science fiction, and spaces for humans – in the first instance strong, supple women – to become who they are. On the other hand, as Alexandra Richie warns, "Berliners cannot afford to fall back on stereotypes or sentimental myths and legends about their past. Rather than alluding to kitschy images of the Golden Twenties they could perhaps ask themselves why Marlene Dietrich's grave is still regularly defaced; rather than claiming that Berlin was traditionally a city of immigrants they might protect its minorities from increasingly frequent attacks" (lix).

In this context, debates such as the vitriolic one over the Palaces on Unter den Linden, in which the "royalist" City Palace proponents won out over those of the East German Palace of the Republic, take on new shadings. The winning vision was promulgated as: "A royal palace – rebuilt by the citizens of Berlin – boasting a beautiful baroque-style facade incorporating the famous Schlüterhof and, of course, the 'King's Lodgings' in the Renaissance-part of the building at the Spree-site."[3] If one continues to read this promotional material, one finds that "This latter part will be converted into a first class hotel. The financing for this project is coming exclusively from the private sector." In the context of the history of Berlin fashion, what this means is a reassertion of the hegemonic forces challenged by Berliner Chic à la Marlene Dietrich and the Ramones fans, that is, the same convergence of imperial and entrepreneurial forces that made possible the world exhibitions, the first of which – the 1851 Great Exhibition held at the Crystal Palace in Hyde Park – was led by Queen Victoria's Saxon husband, Prince Albert. Their imaginary is akin to the Mercedes-Benz IMG Fashion Week one, at which celebrities are feted like postmodern aristocracy and underpaid helperlings (if they are paid at all) scurry around busily attending to their every whim.

One might note in concluding that the delicate balance brought about by the competing presences that champion fashion in Berlin exists within a larger national context, with which it

Figure 7.1: "Nice that we were there," graffiti on Prinzenstrasse, August 2009. (Photo: S. Ingram)

necessarily contends. While offering an exacting analysis of the neoliberal policies of Gerhard Schröder's supposedly social democratic government (1998–2005), such as its "slashing corporation and upper-bracket income tax, and rejecting any wealth tax," Perry Anderson admits that the case was not at all clear-cut: "If the long-run effect of unification has been to unleash an antithetical double movement within Germany, shifting the economy effectually to the right and the polity potentially to the left, the interplay between the two is bound to be mediated by the evolution of the society in which each is embedded." Whether the historical weight of the country's self-image as "a socially caring, morally cohesive democracy enshrined in the post-war consensus" (P. Anderson) can counterbalance its capital's new "poor but sexy" image enough to sway Berlin's financial fortunes remains a question. However, it seems doubtful that fashion of the luxe variety will eventually manage to put an end to Berliner Chic in all of its historically charged modern glory. Because of that history, it is difficult to imagine Berlin as anything other than a "uniquely politicized…historical minefield" (Ladd 3) that is not just the epitome of the modern city, but also a city of survival, an imagined environment conducive to unglamorous but appealing forms of living and moving on (Fig. 7.1).

Notes

1. Even her daughter Maria Riva's exposé of "the supposed truth behind her mother's glamorous persona" (Mayne, 2007a, 347), is not like generic *Mommie Dearest* daughter memoirs. Unlike Christina Crawford, Riva does not set out to portray her mother as a monstrous creature. Rather, as Judith Mayne has pointed out, Riva is preoccupied with Dietrich's great battle with aging and all of the tricks her mother practiced to maintain a youthful appearance. Even as an aging diva, Dietrich is portrayed not as a bitchy goddess but rather as a hard-worker, who toils and suffers for her craft.
2. Cf. Derrida's "Plato's Pharmacy."
3. On the website of the Stadtschloss Berlin Initiative (http://www.stadtschloss-berlin.de/englisch.html).

References

Abbas, Ackbar. "Faking Globalization." *Other Cities, Other Worlds: Urban Imaginaries in a Globalizing Age.* Ed. Andreas Huyssen. Durham and London: Duke University Press, 2008. 243–64.

Ackermann, Astrid. *Paris, London und die europäische Provinz: die frühen Modejournale 1770–1830.* Frankfurt am Main: Peter Lang, 2005.

Adorno, Theodor W. *Prisms.* Trans. Samuel M. Weber. Cambridge, Mass: MIT Press, 1981.

Aggio, Regina. *Filmstadt Berlin 1895–2006: Schauspieler, Regisseure, Produzenten, Wohnsitze, Schauplätze und Drehorte.* Berlin: Verlag Jena, 2007.

Ameri, Amir. "The Spatial Dialectics of Authenticity." *SubStance* 33.2 (2004): 61–89.

Anderson, Donovan. "'Literatur findet…nicht nur auf Papier statt': The Eventization of Literature in Hamburg." *German Literature in a New Century: Trends, Traditions, Transitions.* Eds. Katharina Gerstenberger and Patricia Herminghouse. New York: Berghahn Books, 2008. 39–55.

Anderson, Perry. "A New Germany?" *New Left Review* 57 (May–June 2009) <http://www.newleftreview.org/?view=2778>.

Ankum, Katharina von, ed. *Women in the Metropolis: Gender and Modernity in Weimar Culture.* Berkeley: University of California Press, 1997.

Appadurai, Arjun. *Modernity at Large: Cultural Dimensions of Globalization.* Minneapolis: University of Minnesota Press, 1996.

Aschke, Katja. "Die geliehene Identität: Film und Mode in Berlin 1900–1990." *Berlin en vogue: Berliner Mode in der Photographie.* Eds. F.C. Gundlach and Uli Richter. Tübingen: Wasmuth, 1993. 233–76.

Augé, Marc. *Non-Places: Introduction to an Anthropology of Supermodernity.* Trans. John Howe. London: Verso, 1995.

Bach, Steven. "Falling in Love Again." *Dietrich Icon.* Eds. Gerd Gemünden and Mary R. Desjardins. Durham and London: Duke University Press, 2007. 25–40.

Baer, Hester. "*Film und Frau* and the Female Spectator in 1950s West German Cinema." *Framing the Fifties: Cinema in a Divided Germany.* Eds. John E. Davidson and Sabine Hake. Oxford, New York: Berghahn Books, 2007. 151–65.

Bancroft, Alison. Rev. of *Fashion: A Philosophy*, by Lars Svendsen. *Fashion Theory: The Journal of Dress, Body & Culture* 12.3 (2008): 393–6.

Banks, Mark. *The Politics of Cultural Work.* Houndmills, Basingstoke and New York: Palgrave Macmillan, 2007.

Barth, Nadine. *Berlin Fashion: Metropole der Mode.* Cologne: Dumont Buchverlag, 2008.

Barthes, Roland. *The Fashion System.* Trans. Matthew Ward and Richard Howard. Berkeley: University of California Press, 1983.

Batchelor, David. "Chromophobia." *Color: The Film Reader*. Eds. Angela Dalla Vacche and Brian Price. New York: Routledge, 2006. 63–74.

Bauman, Zygmunt, and Lukasz Galecki. "The Unwinnable War: An Interview with Zygmunt Bauman." *open democracy* 1 Dec. 2005 <http://www.opendemocracy.net/globalization-vision_reflections/modernity_3082.jsp>.

Baute, Michael, et al. "'Berliner Schule' – Eine Collage." *kolik film* Sonderheft 6 (Oct. 2006) <http://www.kolikfilm.at/sonderheft.php?edition=20066&content=texte&text=1>.

Benjamin, Walter. "Berlin Chronicle." *Selected Writings, Volume 2, part 2, 1931*–1934. Eds. Michael W. Jennings, Howard Eiland and Gary Smith. Cambridge, Mass. and London: The Belknap Press of Harvard UP, 1999. 595–637.

—— "Berlin Childhood around 1900." *Selected Writings. Volume 3, 1935-1938*. Eds. Michael W. Jennings, Howard Eiland and Gary Smith. Cambridge, Mass. and London: The Belknap Press of Harvard UP, 1999. 344–413.

—— "Little History of Photography." *Selected Writings, Volume 2, part 2, 1931*–1934. Eds. Michael W. Jennings, Howard Eiland and Gary Smith. Cambridge, Mass. and London: The Belknap Press of Harvard UP, 1999. 507–30.

—— "The Author as Producer." *Selected Writings, Volume 2, part 2, 1931*–1934. Eds. Michael W. Jennings, Howard Eiland and Gary Smith. Cambridge, Mass. and London: The Belknap Press of Harvard UP, 1999. 768–82.

—— "The Destructive Character." *Selected Writings, Volume 2, part 2, 1931*–1934. Ed. Michael W. Jennings, Howard Eiland and Gary Smith. Cambridge, Mass. and London: The Belknap Press of Harvard UP, 1999. 541–2.

—— "Thought Figures." *Selected Writings Volume 2, part 2, 1931*–1934. Ed. Michael W. Jennings, Howard Eiland and Gary Smith. Cambridge, Mass. and London: The Belknap Press of Harvard UP, 1999. 723–7.

Bennett, Tony. *The Birth of the Museum*. London and New York: Routledge, 1995.

Benstock, Shari, and Suzanne Ferriss, eds. *On Fashion*. New Brunswick, NJ: Rutgers University Press, 1994.

"Berlin's Sony Center Sells for Bargain Price." *Deutsche Welle*, 28 Feb 2008 <http://www.dw-world.de/dw/article/0,2144,3157354,00.html>.

Bertschik, Julia. *Mode und Moderne: Kleidung als Spiegel des Zeitgeistes in der deutschsprachigen Literatur*. Cologne: Böhlau-Verlag GmbH, 2005.

Blum, Alan. "Scenes." *Public* 22/23 (2001): 7–35.

—— *The Imaginative Structure of the City*. Kingston, Montreal: McGill-Queen's Press – MQUP, 2003.

Böhlke, Michael. *In Grenzen frei – Mode, Fotografie, Underground DDR 1979–89*. Bielefeld, Leipzig: Kerber, 2009.

Böker, Carmen. "Laufsteg durch die Jahrhunderte: Die Sammlung Kamer/Ruf." *Berliner Zeitung* 4 Nov. 2005.

Bolz, Hannelore, ed. *Sie kleidet den Reichen, sie naehret den Armen: Berliner Seide und Seidenhandel [Ausstellung des Stadtmuseums Berlins, Museum Knoblauchhaus Mai 1996 bis Januar 1997]*. Berlin: Stadtmuseum, 1996.

Borchert, Angela and Ralf Dressel, eds. *Das Journal des Luxus und der Moden: Kultur um 1800*. Heidelberg: Universitätsverlag Winter, 2004.

Bordowitz, Hank, ed. *The U2 Reader: A Quarter Century of Commentary, Criticism, and Reviews*. Milwaukee: Hal Leonard Corporation, 2003.

Bordwell, David. "Film Futures." *SubStance* 31.1 (2002): 88–104.

Borgelt, Hans. *Das süßeste Mädel der Welt. Die Lilian-Harvey-Story*. Bayreuth: Hestia, 1982.

Bourdieu, Pierre. *Distinction: A Social Critique of the Judgement of Taste*. Trans. Richard Nice. London: Routledge & Kegan Paul, 1984.

Boym, Svetlana. *The Future of Nostalgia*. New York: Basic Books, 2002.

Bradby, Barbara. "Sampling Sexuality: Gender, Technology and the Body in Dance Music." *Popular Music* 12.2 (1993): 155–76.

Breen Burns, Janice. "Lock up your doubters." *theage.com.au* 17 Oct. 2005 <http://www.theage.com.au/news/creative – media/lock-up-your-doubters/2005/10/16/1129401142941.html?from=moreStories>.

Brenner, Neil, and Roger Keil. "Editors' Introduction." *The Global Cities Reader*. New York: Routledge, 2006. 1–16.

Breward, Christopher. "Couture Culture: A Study in Modern Art and Fashion." *Journal of Design History* 16.4 (2003): 351–3.

Breward, Christopher, and Caroline Evans, eds. *Fashion and Modernity*. Oxford, New York: Berg Publishers, 2005.

Breward, Christopher, and David Gilbert, eds. *Fashion's World Cities*. Oxford, New York: Berg Publishers, 2006.

Brown, Joseph. "Gianni Versace: Walking in Miami's Golden Light." *South Beach Magazine* n.d. <http://www.southbeach-usa.com/features/features1/versace/gianni-versace-1.htm>.

Bruno, Giuliana. "Ramble City: Postmodernism and *Blade Runner*." *October* 41 (1987): 61–74.

Bruns, Jana F. *Nazi Cinema's New Women*. Cambridge and New York: Cambridge University Press, 2009.

Bruzzi, Stella. *Undressing Cinema: Clothing and Identity in the Movies*. London: Routledge, 1997.

Buck-Morss, Susan. *The Dialectics of Seeing: Walter Benjamin and the Arcades Project*. Cambridge, Mass: MIT Press, 1989.

Bukatman, Scott. *Blade Runner*. London: bfi, 1997.

Burgin, Victor. *In/different Spaces: Place and Memory in Visual Culture*. Berkeley: University of California Press, 1996.

—— *Some Cities*. Berkeley: University of California Press, 1996.

Carter, Michael. *Fashion Classics from Carlyle to Barthes*. Oxford: Berg, 2003.

Castells, Manuel. *The Rise of the Network Society*. 2nd ed. Malden, MA: Blackwell Publishers, 2000.

Clifford, James. *Routes: Travel and Translation in the Late Twentieth Century*. Cambridge, Mass.: Harvard University Press, 1997.

Cooke, Paul. "Whatever Happened to Veronica Voss? Rehabilitating the '68ers' and the Problem of Westalgie in Oskar Roehler's *Die Unberührbare* (2000)." *German Studies Review* 27.1 (2004): 33–44.

Crane, Susan. *Collecting and Historical Consciousness: New Forms for Collective Memory in Early Nineteenth-Century Germany*. Ithaca: Cornell University Press, 2000.

Crary, Jonathan. *Techniques of the Observer: On Vision and Modernity in the Nineteenth Century*. Cambridge, Mass.: MIT Press, 1992.

Crimp, Douglas. "The End of Art and the Origin of the Museum." *Art Journal* 46.4 (1987): 261–6.

Czaplicka, John. "Pictures of a City at Work, Berlin, circa 1890–1930: Visual Reflections on Social Structures and Technology in the Modern Urban Construct." *Berlin: Culture and Metropolis*. Eds. Charles W. Haxthausen and Heldrun Suhr. Minneapolis: University of Minnesota Press, 1990. 3–36.

Derrida, Jacques. *Dissemination*. Trans. Barbara Johnson. Chicago: Chicago University Press, 1981.

Diederichsen, Diedrich. *Eigenblutdoping. Selbstverwertung, Künstlerromantik, Partizipation*. Cologne: Kiepenheuer & Witsch, 2008.

—— "Intensity, Negation, Plain Language: Wilde Maler, Punk and Theory in Germany in the '80s." *Sympathy for the Devil: Art and Rock and Roll Since 1967*. Ed. Dominic Molon. Trans. Tawney

Becker. Chicago: Museum of Contemporary Art; New Haven and London: Yale University Press, 2007. 142–53.

Dillmann-Kühn, Claudia. *Artur Brauner und die CCC: Filmgeschäft, Produktionsalltag, Studiogeschichte 1946–1990: Ausstellung/Filme 28.06.–09.09.1990*. Deutsches Filminstitut, 1990.

Döbler, Moritz and Miriam Schröder. "In Berlin lerne ich noch etwas." *Der Tagesspiegel* 19 October 2009 <http://www.tagesspiegel.de/wirtschaft/IBB-Foerderbank-Finanzaufsicht-Ulrich-Kissing;art271,2926891>.

Donald, James. *Imagining the Modern City*. Minneapolis: University of Minnesota Press, 1999.

Drier, Melissa. "Modemarkt Berlin." *Berlin Fashion: Metropole der Mode*. Ed. Nadine Barth. Cologne: Dumont Verlag, 2008. 24–7.

Dubow, Jessica. "Outside of Place and Other than Optical: Walter Benjamin and the Geography of Critical Thought." *Journal of Visual Culture* 3.3 (2004): 259–74.

Ebner, Claudia C. *Kleidung verändert: Mode im Kreislauf der Kultur*. Bielefeld: Transcript Verlag, 2007.

Ebner, Markus. "Junge deutsche Modefotografie." Trans. Ani Jinpa Lhamo. *Goethe-Institut online* Jan. 2008 <http://www.goethe.de/kue/des/prj/fot/por/enindex.htm>.

Eigler, Friederike Ursula, and Susanne Kord, eds. *The Feminist Encyclopedia of German Literature*. Westport, CT: Greenwood Publishing Group, 1997.

Eisler, Colin. "Bode's Burden. Berlin's Museum as an Imperial Institution." *Jahrbuch der Berliner Museen* 38 (1996): 23–32.

Eley, Geoff. "Nazism, Politics and the Image of the Past: Thoughts on the West German *Historikerstreit* 1986–1987." *Past and Present* 121 (1988): 171–208.

Elias, Norbert. *The Civilizing Process*. Trans. Edmund Jephcott. New York: Urizen Books, 1978.

Elsaesser, Thomas, ed. *A Second Life: German Cinema's First Decades*. Amsterdam: Amsterdam University Press, 1996.

—— *Metropolis*. London: bfi, 2000.

—— *Weimar Cinema and After: Germany's Historical Imaginary*. London: Routledge, 2000.

Emling, Shelley. "Big 4 fashion weeks get new company." *New York Times* 3 Oct. 2006 <http://www.nytimes.com/2006/10/03/style/03iht-Rweeks.3015966.html?_r=1&scp=1&sq=Big%204%20Fashion%20Oct.%203,%202006&st=cse>.

Evans, Caroline. *Fashion at the Edge: Spectacle, Modernity, and Deathliness*. New Haven: Yale University Press, 2003.

Evers, Bernd. "Einführung." *Die Kultur der Kleider: zum hundertjährigen Bestehen der Lipperheideschen Kostümbibliothek*. Ed. Adelheid Rasche. Berlin: SMPK, Kunstbibliothek, 1999. 7–11.

Fast, Susan. "Music, Contexts, and Meaning in U2." *Expression in Pop-Rock Music: A Collection of Critical and Analytical Essays*. Ed. Walter Everett. New York: Garland, 2000. 33–58.

Färber, Alexa. "Vom Kommen, Bleiben und Gehen: Anforderungen und Möglichkeiten im Unternehmen Stadt: Eine Einleitung." *Berliner Blätter* 37 (2005): 7–20.

Feinstein, Joshua. *The Triumph of the Ordinary: Depictions of Daily Life in the East German Cinema, 1949–1989*. Chapel Hill: University of North Carolina Press, 2002.

"Feministischer Porno-Preis 'PorYes' vergeben." *diestandard.at* 16 Oct 2009 <http://diestandard.at/fs/1254311608029/Berlin-Feministischer-Porno-Preis-PorYesvergeben>.

Fioretos, Aris. "Contraction: (Benjamin, Reading, History)." *MLN* 110.3 (1995): 540–64.

Flinn, Caryl. "The Music That Lola Ran To." *Sound Matters: Essays on the Acoustics of German Culture*. Eds. Nora M. Alter and Lutz Koepnick. New York: Berghahn Books, 2005. 197–213.

Flügge, Matthias. "Wirklichkeit als Material. Zilles Photographien." *Heinrich Zille: Berlin um die Jahrhundertwende*. Munich: Schirmer/Mosel GmbH, 1993. 7–20.

—— "Sibylle Bergemann's Photographs." *Mode – Foto – Mode: Fotografien von Sibylle Bergemann und Horst Wackerbarth*. Heidelberg: Ed. Braus, 1992. 11–15.

Franke, Monika. "Schönheit und Bruttosozialprodukt: Motive der Kunstgewerbebewegung." *Packeis und Pressglas: Von der Kunstgewerbe-Bewegung zum deutschen Werkbund, eine wissenschaftliche Illustrierte von Angelika Thiekötter und Eckhard Siepmann*. Berlin: Anabas-Verlag, 1987. 167–73.

Frey, Mattias. "No(ir) Place to Go: Spatial Anxiety and Sartorial Intertextuality in *Die Unberührbare*." *Cinema Journal* 45.4 (2006): 64–80.

Friedmann, J. "Where We Stand: A Decade of World City Research." *World Cities in a World-System*. Eds. P.L. Knox and P.J. Taylor. New York: Cambridge University Press, 1995. 21–47.

Frisa, Maria Luisa, et al., eds. *Italian Eyes: Italian Fashion Photographs from 1951 to Today*. Milan, Charta, Florence: Fondazione pitti immagine discovery, 2005.

Frisby, David. *Fragments of Modernity: Theories of Modernity in the Work of Simmel, Kracauer, and Benjamin*. Oxford: Polity, 1985.

Fritzsche, Peter. *Reading Berlin 1900*. Cambridge, Mass.: Harvard University Press, 1996.

Führer durch die Ausstellung 200 Jahre Kleiderkunst 1700–1900 im Ermelerhaus, Breite Strasse Nr. 11. Nov. 1916–Januar 1917. Berlin: Elsner, 1916.

Gaehtgens, Thomas W. "The Berlin Museums after Reunification." *The Burlington Magazine* 136.1090 (1994): 14–20.

Ganeva, Mila. "Elegance and Spectacle in Berlin: The Gerson Fashion Store and the Rise of the Modern Fashion Show in the Early Twentieth Century." *The Places and Spaces of Fashion, 1800–2007*. Ed. John Potvin. New York: Routledge, 2009. 121–38.

—— "Fashion Photography and Women's Modernity in Weimar Germany: The Case of Yva." *NWSA Journal* 15.3 (2003): 1–25.

—— "In the Waiting Room of Literature: Helen Grund and the Practice of Travel and Fashion Writing." *Women in German Yearbook* 19 (2003): 117–40.

—— *Women in Weimar Fashion: Discourses and Displays in German Culture, 1918–1933*. Rochester, NY: Camden House, 2008.

Gernsheim, Helmut. *The Origins of Photography*. London: Thames and Hudson, 1982.

—— *The Rise of Photography, 1850–1880: The Age of Collodion*. 3rd ed. London: Thames and Hudson, 1988.

Gilewicz, Samantha. "The Insider: Simon Lock, Founder of Australian Fashion Week." *Nylon* 13 Oct 2007 <http://www.nylonmag.com/?section=article&parid=555>.

Goebel, Rolf J. "Berlin's Architectural Citations: Reconstruction, Simulation, and the Problem of Historical Authenticity." *PMLA* 118.5 (2003): 1268–89.

Goos, Manuela, and Brigitte Heyde. *Kleider machen Frauen: Broschüre zur Ausstellung über Frauen in der Charlottenburger Modeindustrie nach 1945; 7.11.1990–13.1.1991, Heimatmuseum Charlottenburg*. Berlin: Bezirksamt Charlottenburg, 1990.

Greco, Nicholas. "The Berlin Wall: Bowie, U2 and the 'Urban Real.'" *The Culture of Cities: Under Construction*. Ed. Paul Moore and Meredith Risk. Oakville, Ont.: Mosaic Press, 2001. 92–4.

Greenhalgh, Paul. *Ephemeral Vistas: The Expositions Universelles, Great Exhibitions and World's Fairs, 1851–1939*. Manchester, New York: Manchester University Press, 1988.

Grossmann, Atina. "'The Goldhagen Effect': Memory, Repetition and Responsibility in the New Germany." *The 'Goldhagen Effect': History, Memory, Nazism – Facing the German Past*. Ed. Geoff Eley. Ann Arbor, University of Michigan Press, 2000. 89–130.

Guenther, Irene. *Nazi Chic?: Fashioning Women in the Third Reich*. Oxford: Berg, 2004.

Gundlach, F.C. and Uli Richter, eds. *Berlin en vogue: Berliner Mode in der Photographie*. Tübingen: Wasmuth, 1993.

Gundlach, F.C., et al. *The Heartbeat of Fashion: Sammlung F. C. Gundlach*. Bielefeld: Kerber, 2006.

Gutmair, Ulrich. "'Lost and Sound': A Book about Berlin's Techno Scene." Trans. Oliver Köhler. *Goethe-Institut online* Mar 2009 <http://www.goethe.de/kue/mus/ema/ema/akt/en4315121.htm>.

Haase, Christine. "You Can Run, but You Can't Hide: Transcultural Filmmaking in *Run Lola Run* (1998)." *Light Motives: German Popular Film in Perspective*. Eds. Randall Halle and Margaret McCarthy. Detroit: Wayne State University Press, 2003. 398–415.

Hagen, Nina. *That's Why the Lady is a Punk*. Berlin: Schwarzkopf & Schwarzkopf, 2003.

Hake, Sabine. *German National Cinema*. 2nd ed. London: Routledge, 2008.

—— "In the Mirror of Fashion." *Women in the Metropolis: Gender and Modernity in Weimar Culture*. Ed. Katharina von Ankum. Berkeley: University of California Press, 1997. 185–201.

Halle, Randall. *German Film after Germany: Toward a Transnational Aesthetic*. Urbana and Chicago: University of Illinois Press, 2008.

—— "German Film, Aufgehoben: Ensembles of Transnational Cinema." *New German Critique* 87 (2002): 7–46.

Hannesen, Hans Gerhard. *Die Akademie der Künste in Berlin – Facetten einer 300jährigen Geschichte*. Berlin: Akademie der Künste, 2005.

Harley, Ross. "Beat in the System." *Rock and Popular Music: Politics, Policies, Institutions*. Eds. Tony Bennett et al. London: Routledge, 1993. 210–30.

Hartwig, Heidi. "Ich bin Berliner!" *Heidi Magazine* Forward/Life! Issue (n.d.), 38–41.

Harvey, David. *The Condition of Postmodernity: An Enquiry into the Origins of Cultural Change*. Oxford, UK, Cambridge, Mass.: Blackwell, 1989.

Henry, Tricia. *Break All Rules!: Punk Rock and the Making of a Style*. Ann Arbor: UMI Research Press, 1989.

Hessel, Franz. *Marlene Dietrich: Ein Porträt. Mit vielen zeigenössischen Bildern und einem Nachwort von Manfred Flügge*. Berlin: Das Arsenal, 1992.

Heyden, August von. *Ein Jahrhundert der Mode*. Berlin: Bacher, 1896.

Hickethier, Knut. "The West German Film Industry in the 1950s." *Framing the Fifties: Cinema in a Divided Germany*. Eds. John E. Davidson and Sabine Hake. Oxford, New York: Berghahn Books, 2007. 194–209.

Hoch, Jenny. "Fotografiestar Wolfgang Tillmans: Ich kann über das Älterwerden nur lachen." *Spiegel online* 02.06.2007 <http://www.spiegel.de/kultur/gesellschaft/0,1518,486281,00.html>.

Honnef, Klaus. "F.C. Gundlach." *F.C. Gundlach – Das fotografische Werk*. Eds. Klaus Honnef et al. Göttingen: Steidl, 2008.

–, Enno Kaufhold, and F. C. Gundlach, eds. *Bildermode – Modebilder: Modefotografie von 1945 bis 1995*. Ostfildern: Cantz, 1995.

Huntington, Patty. "IMG takes over Australian Fashion Week." *The Sydney Morning Herald* 12 Oct 2005 <http://www.smh.com.au/news/fashion/img-takes-over-australian-fashion-week/2005/10/12/1128796550032.html>.

Huyssen, Andreas. *After the Great Divide: Modernism, Mass Culture, Postmodernism*. Bloomington: Indiana University Press, 1986.

—— *Twilight Memories: Marking Time in a Culture of Amnesia*. New York: Routledge, 1995.

Ingram, Susan. "Of Ruinous and Wasted Idylls: The Modesty of a Once-and-Future Literary History." *Hyphenated Histories: Articulations of Central European Bildung and Slavic Studies in the Contemporary Academy*. Ed. Andrew Colin Gow. Leiden: Brill, 2007. 43–58.

Jacobs, Stefan. "Berlin liegt vorn." *Der Tagesspiegel* 25.2.2010 <http://www.tagesspiegel.de/wirtschaft/Tourismus;art271,3040895>.

Jameson, Fredric. *Jameson on Jameson: Conversations on Cultural Marxism*. Ed. Ian Buchanan. Durham: Duke University Press, 2007.

—— *Postmodernism, or, The Cultural Logic of Late Capitalism*. London: Verso, 1991.

Jameson, Fredric, and Masao Miyoshi, eds. *The Cultures of Globalization*. Durham: Duke University Press, 1998.

Jocks, Heinz-Norbert. "Peter Lindbergh: Photos from a Bastardized Viewpoint." *Kunstforum International* vol. 175 (April–May 2005).

Kaes, Anton. "The Debate about Cinema: Charting a Controversy (1909–1929)." Trans. David J. Levin. *New German Critique* 40 (1987): 7–33.

Karasek, Erika. "Ein Jahrhundert Engagement für die Volkskunde." *Museum für Volkskunde: Kleidung zwischen Tracht + Mode. Aus der Geschichte des Museums 1889–1989*. Berlin: Staatliche Museen zu Berlin, 1989. 5–29.

Kelly, Lori Duin. "Measuring Up: How Advertising Affects Self-Image, and: Fashion, Desire, and Anxiety: Image and Morality in the Twentieth Century, and: Body Work: Beauty and Self-Image in American Culture (review)." *NWSA Journal* 15.2 (2003): 199–203.

Kemp, Wolfgang, and Joyce Rheuban. "Images of Decay: Photography in the Picturesque Tradition." *October* 54 (1990): 103–33.

Kimmelman, Michael. "Lively Eye on Old Berlin: Wonderful Life, Ja?" *The New York Times* 27 Mar. 2008 <http://www.nytimes.com/2008/03/27/arts/design/27zille.html>.

Klein, Naomi. *No Logo: Taking Aim at the Brand Bullies*. Toronto: Knopf Canada, 2000.

Klonk, Charlotte. "Mounting Vision: Charles Eastlake and the National Gallery of London." *The Art Bulletin* 82.2 (2000): 331–47.

Klose, Angelika. "Frauenmode im Dritten Reich." MA thesis, Freie Universität Berlin, 1989.

Koolhaas, Rem, and Bruce Mau. *S, M, L, XL*. New York: Monacelli Press, 1995.

Kosta, Barbara. *Willing Seduction: The Blue Angel, Marlene Dietrich, and Mass Culture*. Oxford, New York: Berghahn Books, 2009.

Kracauer, Siegfried. *The Salaried Masses: Duty and Distraction in Weimar Germany*. Trans. Quintin Hoare, with an Introduction by Inka Mülder-Bach. London: New York, 1998.

Krause, Gisela. *Altpreussische Militärbekleidungswirtschaft*. Osnabrück: Biblio Verlag, 1983.

Krauss, Rosalind. "Review: Jump over the Bauhaus." *October* 15 (1980): 103–10.

Krätke, Stefan. "'Creative Cities' and the Rise of the Dealer Class." Paper presented at "The Right to the City. Prospects for Critical Urban Theory and Practice" conference, Berlin, Nov. 6–8, 2008 <http://www.kraetke.privat.t-online.de/>.

Kremer, Roberta S., ed. *Broken Threads: The Destruction of the Jewish Fashion Industry in Germany and Austria*. Oxford, New York: Berg, 2007.

Kutsche, Johanna. "PorYes, das Biosiegel für Sex-Filme." *Die Zeit* 16 Oct 2009 <http://www.zeit.de/gesellschaft/generationen/2009-10/porno-feministisch>.

Ladd, Brian. *The Ghosts of Berlin: Confronting German History in the Urban Landscape*. Chicago, Ill.: University of Chicago Press, 1997.

Laughey, Dan. *Music and Youth Culture*. Edinburgh: Edinburgh University Press, 2006.

Law, Wing-sang. "Hong Kong Undercover: An Approach to 'Collaborative Colonialism.'" *Inter-Asia Cultural Studies: Movements* 9.4 (2008): 522–43.

Lähn, Peter. "Paul Davidson, the Frankfurt Film Scene, and *Afgrunden* in Germany." *A Second Life: German Cinema's First Decades*. Ed. Thomas Elsaesser. Amsterdam: Amsterdam University Press, 1996. 79–85.

Lange, Bastian. "Re-scaling Governance in Berlin's Creative Economy." *Creative Encounters Working Paper #39: Copenhagen Business School* <http://openarchive.cbs.dk/handle/10398/7981>.

Lash, Scott and John Urry. *Economies of Signs and Space.* London: Sage, 1994.

Lehmann, Ulrich. *Tigersprung: Fashion in Modernity.* Cambridge, Mass.: MIT Press, 2000.

Lehmphul, Matthias. "Sony Center: Prestige sucht Besitzer." *Tagesspiegel* 28 Oct. 2009 <http://www.tagesspiegel.de/berlin/Sony-Center-Potsdamer-Platz-Mitte;art270,2934430>.

Lehrer, Ute. "Willing the Global City: Berlin's Cultural Strategies of Inter-Urban Competition after 1989." *The Global Cities Reader.* Eds. Neil Brenner and Roger Keil. New York: Routledge, 2006. 332–8.

Lennsen, Claudia. "Women's Cinema in Germany." *Jump Cut* 29 (Feb. 1984): 49–50.

Leslie, Esther. *Walter Benjamin: Overpowering Conformism.* London: Pluto Press, 2000.

Lindemann, Bernd Wolfgang. "Bode und seine Sammler: Ein Blick auf die Sammelkultur in Berlin im 19. Jahrhundert." *Zum Lob der Sammler: Die Staatlichen Museen zu Berlin und ihre Sammler.* Eds. Andrea Bärnreuther and Peter-Klaus Schuster. Berlin: Nicolaische Verlagsbuchhandlung, 2008. 142–63.

Link-Heer, Ursula. "Die Mode im Museum oder Manier und Stil (mit einem Blick auf Versace)." *Mode, Weiblichkeit und Modernität.* Ed. Gertrud Lehnert. Dortmund: Edition Ebersbach, 1998. 140–64.

Lipovetsky, Gilles. *The Empire of Fashion: Dressing Modern Democracy.* Princeton: Princeton University Press, 1994.

Lippitz, Ulf. "Like a Rock Concert." *Zitty Modebuch* 2009, 92.

Livingstone, David. "Model walks the walk, and talks the talk." *Toronto Star* 5 May 2009 <http://www.thestar.com/printArticle/628837>.

Lux, Sebastian. "Die Erfindung eines fotografischen Stils." *F.C. Gundlach – Das fotografische Werk.* Eds. Klaus Honnef und Hans-Michael Koetzle, Göttingen: Steidl, 2008.

Maciuika, John V. *Before the Bauhaus: Architecture, Politics and the German State, 1890–1920.* Cambridge: Cambridge University Press, 2005.

Maier, Charles S. *The Unmasterable Past.* Cambridge, Mass. and London: Harvard University Press, 1988.

Maleuvre, Didier. *Museum Memories: History, Technology, Art.* Stanford: Stanford University Press, 1999.

Maron, Monika. "Place of Birth: Berlin." *Berlin Tales.* Ed. Helen Constantine. Trans. Lyn Marven. Oxford, New York: Oxford University Press, 2009. 67–80.

Marshall, William. *Film Festival Confidential.* Toronto: McArthur & Company, 2005.

Martin, Ralph. *Ein Amerikaner in Berlin: Wie ein New Yorker lernte, die Deutschen zu lieben.* Trans. Sophie Zeitz. Cologne: Dumont, 2009.

Massey, Doreen. "Places and Their Pasts." *History Workshop Journal* 39 (Spring, 1995): 182–92.

Mayerhofer-Llanes, Andrea. *Die Anfänge der Kostümgeschichte.* Munich: Scaneg, 2006.

Maynard, Margaret. "The Fashion Photograph: An 'Ecology'." *Fashion as Photograph: Viewing and Reviewing Images of Fashion.* Ed. Eugénie Shinkle. London, New York: I.B. Tauris, 2008. 54–69.

Mayne, Judith. "'Life Goes On Without Me': Marlene Dietrich, Old Age, and the Archive." *Dietrich Icon.* Eds. Gerd Gemünden and Mary R. Desjardines. Durham and London: Duke University Press, 2007. 347–63.

—— "Homage, Impersonation, and Magic: An Interview with James Beaman." *Dietrich Icon.* Eds. Gerd Gemünden and Mary R. Desjardins. Durham and London: Duke University Press, 2007. 364–75.

McBride, Patrizia C. "'In Praise of the Present': Adolf Loos on Style and Fashion." *Modernism/modernity* 11.4 (2004): 745–67.

McIsaac, Peter M. "Public-Private Support of the Arts and German Cultural Policy: The Case of Wilhelm Bode." *International Journal of Cultural Policy* 13.4 (2007): 371–91.

McLeod, Ken. "Bohemian Rhapsodies: Operatic Influences on Rock Music." *Popular Music* 20.2 (2001): 189–203.

Miklitsch, Robert. "Rock'N'Theory: Autobiography, Cultural Studies, and the 'Death of Rock.'" *Postmodern Culture* 9.2 (1999).

Mislin, Miron. "Die Morgenröte des preussischen Kunstgewerbes." *Packeis und Pressglas: Von der Kunstgewerbe-Bewegung zum deutschen Werkbund, eine wissenschaftliche Illustrierte von Angelika Thiekötter und Eckhard Siepmann.* Berlin: Anabas-Verlag, 1987. 41–8.

Moritz, Cordula. *Die Kleider der Berlinerin. Mode und Chic an der Spree.* Berlin: Haude + Spener, 1971.

Moritz, Cordula, and Gerd Hartung. *Linienspiele. 70 Jahre Mode in Berlin.* Berlin: Edition Q, 1991.

Moseley, Rachel, ed. *Fashioning Film Stars: Dress, Culture, Identity.* London: bfi, 2005.

Mundt, Barbara. "Die Textilsammlung im Kunstgewerbemuseum." *Die Sammlung Kamer/Ruf. Mode im Kunstgewerbemuseum.* Berlin: KulturStiftung der Länder, 2005. 15–20.

—— "125 Jahre Kunstgewerbemuseum. Konzepte, Bauten und Menschen für eine Sammlung (1867–1939)." *Jahrbuch der Berliner Museen* 34 (1992): 173–84.

Müller, Kai. "Die neuen Tempel des Techno." *Der Tagesspiegel* 3 Feb 2009 <http://www.tagesspiegel.de/kultur/pop/Techno-Tobias-Rapp-Watergate-Berghain-Kreuzberg-Friedrichshain;art971,2742330>.

Negus, Keith. *Popular Music in Theory: An Introduction.* Cambridge: Polity Press, 1996.

Nehamas, Alexander. *Nietzsche, Life as Literature.* Cambridge, Mass: Harvard University Press, 1985.

Newton, June, ed. *Helmut Newton: A Gun for Hire.* London: Taschen, 2005.

Opaschowski, Horst W. "Jugend im Zeitalter der Eventkultur." *Aus Politik und Zeitgeschichte* B 12 (2000) <http://www.bpb.de/publikationen/8WD8XJ,0,0,Jugend_im_Zeitalter_der_Eventkultur.html#art0>.

Orbaugh, Sharalyn. "Frankenstein and the Cyborg Metropolis." *Cinema Anime.* Ed. Steven T. Brown. London: Palgrave Macmillan, 2008.

Pacteau, Francette. *The Symptom of Beauty.* London: Reaktion Books, 2004.

"'Poor, but sexy' Berlin is a hit." *Sydney Morning Herald.* 11 Mar. 2009 <http://www.smh.com.au/travel/travel-news/poor-but-sexy-berlin-is-a-hit-20090311-8uzl.html>.

Potvin, John. "A Love that Dare not Speak its Name in Public: Clothes Come Out of the Closet." *Descant* (Fall 2007): 43–51.

—— "Armani/Architecture: The Timelessness and Textures of Space." *The Places and Spaces of Fashion, 1800–2007.* Ed. John Potvin. London, New York: Routledge, 2009.

Purdy, Daniel L. *The Tyranny of Elegance: Consumer Cosmopolitanism in the Era of Goethe.* Baltimore: Johns Hopkins University Press, 1998.

Quinn, Bradley. *The Fashion of Architecture.* Oxford and New York: Berg, 2003.

—— "'Radical' Fashion? A Critique of the Radical Fashion Exhibition, Victoria and Albert Museum, London." *Fashion Theory: The Journal of Dress, Body & Culture* 6 (2002): 441–5.

Rapp, Tobias. *Lost and Sound: Berlin, Techno und der Easyjetset.* Frankfurt am Main: Suhrkamp Verlag, 2009.

Rasche, Adelheid, ed. *Die Kultur der Kleider: Zum hundertjährigen Bestehen der Lipperheideschen Kostümbibliothek.* Berlin: Staatliche Museen zu Berlin Preußischer Kulturbesitz, 1999.

—— "Ein Modemuseum in Berlin? Zur Geschichte einer verlorenen Kostümsammlung." *Museumsjournal: Berichte aus den Museen, Schlössern und Sammlungen in Berlin und Potsdam* (Jul 1995): 15–18.

——, ed. *Frieda Lipperheide.* Berlin: Staatliche Museen zu Berlin, 1999.

——, ed. *La Fotografia di moda a Berlino negli anni trenta = Die Modefotografie in Berlin in den Dreissiger Jahren*. Milan: Silvana, 2001.

—— "Peter Jessen, der Berliner Verein Moden-Museum und der Verband der deutschen Mode-Industrie, 1916 bis 1925." *Zeitschrift der Gesellschaft für Historische Waffen- und Kostümkunde* 1995 1–2: 65–92.

—— , ed. *Rico Puhlmann: A Fashion Legacy, Photographs and Illustrations 1955–1996*, with essays by William A. Ewing and Adelheid Rasche. London: Merrell, 2004.

Rectanus, Mark W. *Culture Incorporated: Museums, Artists and Corporate Sponsorships*. Minneapolis, London: University of Minnesota Press, 2002.

Redmond, Sean. "Purge! Class Pathology in *Blade Runner*." *The Blade Runner Experience: The Legacy of a Science Fiction Classic*. Ed. Will Brooker. London: Wallflower, 2005. 173–89.

"Review: Standby for Transmission: U2's Zoo TV." *Theatre Ireland* 31 (1993): 25–7.

Richie, Alexandra. *Faust's Metropolis: A History of Berlin*. London: HarperCollinsPublishers, 1999.

Robb, David. "Techno in Germany: Its Musical Origins and Cultural Relevance." *GFL: German as a Foreign Language* 2 (2002): 130–49.

Rosen, Philip. "Introduction." *boundary 2* 30.1 (2003): 1–15.

Ross, Andrew. "Introduction." *Microphone Fiends: Youth Music & Youth Culture*. Eds. Andrew Ross and Tricia Rose. New York: Routledge, 1994. 1–16.

Roters, Eberhard. *Berlin, 1910–1933*. New York: Rizzoli, 1982.

Rowley, Stephen. "False LA: *Blade Runner* and the Nightmare City." *The Blade Runner Experience: The Legacy of a Science Fiction Classic*. Ed. Will Brooker. London: Wallflower, 2005. 203–12.

Rugg, Linda Haverty. *Picturing Ourselves: Photography and Autobiography*. Chicago: University of Chicago Press, 1997.

Sammon, Paul. *Future Noir: The Making of Blade Runner*. London: Gollancz, 2007.

Saunders, Thomas J. *Hollywood in Berlin: American Cinema and Weimar Germany*. Berkeley: University of California Press, 1994.

Schlögel, Karl. "The Black Marketeers of Bahnhof Zoo." *signandsight* 24 Mar. 2009 <http://www.signandsight.com/features/1850.html>.

Schneider, Frank Apunkt. *Als die Welt noch unterging: Von Punk zu NDW*. Mainz: Ventil, 2007.

Schönberger, Angela. "Die Modesammlung Kamer/Ruf." *Preußischer Kulturbesitz: Jahrbuch Preußischer Kulturbesitz* 42 (2005): 343–54.

—— "Die Modesammlung Kamer/Ruf." *Die Sammlung Kamer/Ruf. Mode im Kunstgewerbemuseum*. Berlin: KulturStiftung der Länder and SMB Kunstgewerbemuseum, 2005. 10–14.

Schulze, Gerhard. *Die Erlebnisgesellschaft: Kultursoziologie der Gegenwart*. Frankfurt and New York: Campus, 1992.

Schwarz, Peter. "Germany: Court Ruling on Berlin Budget Deepens Social Divisions." *World Socialist Web Site* 25 Oct. 2006 <http://www.wsws.org/articles/2006/oct2006/germ-o25.shtml>.

Schwarzer, Alice. *Alice im Männerland: Eine Zwischenbilanz*. Cologne: Kiepenheuer & Witsch, 2002.

Seabrook, Thomas Jerome. *Bowie in Berlin: A New Career in a New Town*. London: Jawbone Press, 2008.

Sheehan, James J. *Museums in the German Art World: From the End of the Old Regime to the Rise of Modernism*. Oxford, New York: Oxford University Press, 2000.

Siebel, Ernst. "Mode in den Höfen." *Die Hackeschen Höfe* <http://www.hackesche-hoefe.com/index.php?id=35>.

Smith, Roberta. "Fashion Forward (Not for the Fainthearted)." *New York Times* 22 January 2009 <http://www.nytimes.com/2009/01/23/arts/design/23phot.html>.

—— "Photography Review; Images of Fashion Tiptoe Into the Modern." *New York Times* 16 April 2004 <http://www.nytimes.com/2004/04/16/arts/photography-review-images-of-fashion-tiptoe-into-the-modern.html?scp=1&sq=Images%20of%20Fashion%20Tiptoe%20Into%20the%20Modern&st=cse>.

Sombart, Werner. *Krieg und Kapitalismus.* Munich: Duncker & Humblot, 1913.

Spieth, Angela, and Michael Oehler, eds. *Trippen.* Berlin: Trippen A. Spieth, M. Oehler GmbH, 2005.

St. John, Graham. *Technomad: Global Raving Countercultures.* London: Equinox, 2009.

Stam, Robert. *François Truffaut and Friends: Modernism, Sexuality, and Film Adaptation.* New Brunswick, NJ: Rutgers University Press, 2006.

Steele, Valerie. "Museum Quality: The Rise of the Fashion Exhibition." *Fashion Theory: The Journal of Dress, Body & Culture* 12 (2008): 7–30.

Stewart, Janet. *Fashioning Vienna: Adolf Loos's Cultural Criticism.* New York: Routledge, 2000.

Stitziel, Judd. *Fashioning Socialism: Clothing, Politics, and Consumer Culture in Germany.* Oxford: Berg, 2005.

Stratton, Jon. "Jews, Punk and the Holocaust: From the Velvet Underground to the Ramones. The Jewish-American Story." *Popular Music* 24.1 (2005): 79–105.

—— "Punk, Jews and the Holocaust: The English Story." *Shofar: An Interdisciplinary Journal of Jewish Studies* 25.4 (2007): 124–49.

Strzelczyk, Florentine. "Fascism and Family Entertainment." *Quarterly Review of Film and Video* 25.3 (2008): 196–211.

—— "Fascism – Fantasy – Fascination – Film." *Arachne: A Journal of Interdisciplinary Studies* 7.1 (2001): 94–111.

Sudendorf, Werner. "'Is That Me?': The Marlene Dietrich Collection in Berlin." *Dietrich Icon.* Eds. Gerd Gemünden and Mary R. Desjardins. Durham and London: Duke University Press, 2007. 376–84.

Sußebach, Henning. "Organic Or Bust." *signandsight* 24 Jan 2008 <http://www.signandsight.com/features/1644.html>.

Tagg, John. *The Burden of Representation: Essays on Photographies and Histories.* Basingstoke: Macmillan Education, 1988.

Thomas, Dana. *Deluxe: How Luxury Lost Its Luster.* New York: Penguin Press, 2007.

—— "Through a Camera Lens Darkly." *Newsweek* 2 Feb. 2004.

Thönnissen, Grit. "Sprung ins Graue." *Zeit Online* 21 April 2009 <http://www.zeit.de/online/2009/17/ost-mode-film>.

Till, Karen E. "Reimagining National Identity: 'Chapter of Life' at the German Historical Museum in Berlin." Eds. Paul C. Adams, Steven D. Hoelscher, and Karen E. Till. Minneapolis: University of Minnesota Press, 2001. 273–99.

—— *The New Berlin: Memory, Politics, Place.* Minneapolis: University of Minnesota Press, 2005.

Tilmann, Christina. "Wer ist Dieter Kosslick?" *Der Tagesspiegel* 2 May 2007 <http://www.tagesspiegel.de/zeitung/Fragen-des-Tages;art693,1891219>.

Tip, Edition Fashion + Design. Berlin, 2009.

Tobias, James. "Cinema, Scored: Toward a Comparative Methodology for Music in Media." *Film Quarterly* 57.2 (2003): 26–36.

Traill-Nash, Glynis. "Aussie with designs on the world." *Sydney Morning Herald* 28 April 2008 <http://www.smh.com.au/news/fashion/aussie-with-designs-on-the-world/2008/04/28/1209234714500.html>.

Vinken, Barbara. *Fashion Zeitgeist: Trends and Cycles in the Fashion System.* Trans. Mark Hewson. Oxford: Berg, 2005.

Vogtherr, Christoph Martin. "Das Königliche Museum zu Berlin. Planungen und Konzeption des ersten Berliner Kunstmuseums." *Jahrbuch der Berliner Museen* 39 (1997): 3–302.

Wagner, Gretel. "Der Sammler Lipperheide." *Preußischer Kulturbesitz: Jahrbuch Preußischer Kulturbesitz* 3 (1964): 140–7.

—— "Die Mode in Berlin." *Berlin en vogue: Berliner Mode in der Photographie*. Eds. F.C. Gundlach and Uli Richter. Tübingen: Wasmuth, 1993. 113–46.

——, ed. *Mode in alten Photographien. Eine Bildersammlung*. Berlin: Rembrandt-Verlag, 1979.

Wahjudi, Claudia. "The Knitting Avant-Gardist: Claudia Skoda has been inventing new stitches for 30 years." *Zitty Modebuch 2009–2010*. 105–8.

Waidenschlager, Christine, ed. *Berliner Chic: Mode aus den Jahren 1830–1990. Katalog zur gleichnamigen Ausstellung im Museum Ephraim-Palais 23.11.2001–Oktober 2002*. Tübingen, Berlin: Wasmuth, 2001.

—— , ed. *Heinz Oestergaard: Mode fur Millionen: Bestande aus dem Berlin Museum*. Tübingen and Berlin: E. Wasmuth, 1992.

—— , ed. *Mode der 20er Jahre [anläßlich der Ausstellung Couture, Konfektion, Varieté – Mode der 20er Jahre aus dem Berlin Museum]*. 2nd ed. Tübingen; Berlin: Wasmuth, 1993.

Waidenschlager, Christine, and Gesa Kessemeier, eds. *Uli Richter: Eine Berliner Modegeschichte, A Berlin Fashion Story*. Cologne: DuMont, 2007.

Ward, Janet. "Berlin, the Virtual Global City." *Journal of Visual Culture* 3.2 (2004): 239–56.

—— *Weimar Surfaces: Urban Visual Culture in 1920s Germany*. Berkeley: University of California Press, 2001.

Weinstein, Valerie. "(Un)Fashioning Identities: Ernst Lubitsch's Early Comedies of Mistaken Identity." *Visual Culture in Twentieth-Century Germany*. Ed. Gail Finney. Bloomington, IN: Indiana University Press, 2006. 120–33.

Westphal, Uwe. *Berliner Konfektion und Mode: Die Zerstörung einer Tradition, 1836–1939*. 2nd ed. Berlin: Edition Hentrich, 1992.

Williams, Val. "A Heady Relationship: Fashion Photography and the Museum, 1979 to the Present." *Fashion Theory: The Journal of Dress, Body & Culture* 12 (2008): 197–218.

Wilson, Elizabeth. *Adorned in Dreams: Fashion and Modernity*. Revised and Updated Version. New Brunswick, NJ: Rutgers University Press, 2003.

Winter, Caroline. "Comrade Couture: Revisiting Communist Germany's Fashion Scene." *Spiegel Online International* 6 April 6 2009 <http://www.spiegel.de/international/germany/0,1518,628632,00.html>.

Witte, Bernd. *Walter Benjamin: An Intellectual Biography*. Detroit: Wayne State University Press, 1991.

Wollen, Peter. "The Concept of Fashion in *The Arcades Project*." *boundary 2* 30.1 (2003): 131–42.

Wurst, Karin A. *Fabricating Pleasure: Fashion, Entertainment, and Cultural Consumption in Germany, 1780–1830*. Detroit: Wayne State University Press, 2005.

Wurtzel, Elizabeth. "Me2." *The U2 Reader: A Quarter Century of Commentary, Criticism, and Reviews*. Ed. Hank Bordowitz. Milwaukee: Hal Leonard Corp, 2003. 91–9.

Zika, Anna. *Ist alles eitel? Zur Kulturgeschichte deutschsprachiger Modejournale zwischen Aufklärung und Zerstreuung. 1750–1950*. Weimar: Walther Koenig, 2006.

Zinik, Zinovy. "History Thieves." *Eurozine* 27 Jul 2009 <http://www.eurozine.com/articles/2009-07-27-zinik-en.html>.

Ziolkowski, Theodore. *German Romanticism and Its Institutions*. Princeton: Princeton University Press, 1990.

Zukin, Sharon. *The Culture of Cities*. Malden, Mass. and Oxford: Blackwell Publishers, 1995.

Filmography

A Foreign Affair. Dir. Billy Wilder. Perf. Marlene Dietrich. Paramount Pictures, 1948.

Abyss, The. (Afgrunden) Dir. Urban Gad. Perf. Asta Nielsen. Itala Film, 1910.

Aeon Flux. Dir. Karen Kusama. Perf. Charlize Theron. Paramount Pictures, 2005.

Anna Boleyn. Dir. Ernst Lubitsch. Perf. Henny Porten. Messter Film, 1920.

American Psycho. Dir. Mary Harron. Perf. Christian Bale. Am Psycho Productions, 2000.

Around the World in Eighty Days. Dir. Frank Coraci. Perf. Jackie Chan. Walt Disney Pictures, 2004.

Assault, The. Dir. Fons Rademakers. Perf. Derek de Lint. Fons Rademakers Produktie, 1986.

Ave Maria. Dir. Alfred Braun. Perf. Zarah Leander, Divina-Film, 1953.

Ben Hur. Dir. Fred Niblo. Perf. Ramon Novarro. Metro-Goldwyn-Mayer, 1925.

Berlin Alexanderplatz. Dir. Rainer Werner Fassbinder. Perf. Günter Lamprecht. Bavaria Film, 1980.

Berlin Calling. Dir. Hannes Stöhr. Perf. Paul Kalkbrenner. Sabotage Films GmbH, 2008.

Blade Runner. Dir. Ridley Scott. Perf. Harrison Ford. Ladd Company, 1982.

Blonde Venus. Dir. Josef von Sternberg. Perf. Marlene Dietrich. Paramount Pictures, 1932.

Blue Angel, The. (Der blaue Engel) Dir. Josef von Sternberg. Perf. Marlene Dietrich. UFA, 1930.

Bourne Supremacy, The. Dir. Paul Greengrass. Perf. Matt Damon. Universal Pictures, 2004.

Bourne Ultimatum, The. Dir. Paul Greengrass. Perf. Matt Damon. Universal Pictures, 2007.

Buena Vista Social Club, The. Dir. Wim Wenders. Road Movies Produktion, 1999.

Cabaret. Dir. Bob Fosse. Perf. Liza Minnelli. ABC Pictures, 1972.

Cabinet of Dr. Caligari, The. (Das Cabinet des Dr. Caligari) Dir. Robert Wiene. Perf. Werner Krauss. Decla-Bioscop AG, 1920.

Carmen. Dir. Ernst Lubitsch. Perf. Pola Negri. Projektions-AG Union (PAGU), 1918.

Chinese Connection, The. Dir. Wei Lo. Perf. Bruce Lee. Golden Harvest Company, 1972.

Christiane F. (Christiane F. – Wir Kinder vom Bahnhof Zoo) Dir. Uli Edel. Perf. Natja Brunckhorst. Solaris, 1981.

Comrade Couture. (Ein Traum in Erdbeerfolie: Comrade Couture) Dir. Marco Wilms. Perf. Frank Schäfler, Sabine von Oettingen. ARTE, 2008.

Constant Gardener, The. Dir. Fernando Meirelles. Perf. Ralph Fiennes, Rachel Weisz. Potboiler Productions, 2005.

Dark Knight, The. Dir. Christopher Nolan. Perf. Christian Bale. Warner Bros. Pictures, 2008.

Death of a Salesman. Dir. Volker Schlöndorff. Perf. Dustin Hoffman. Bioskop Film, 1985.

Destiny. (Der müde Tod) Dir. Fritz Lang. Perf. Lil Dagover. Decla-Bioscop AG, 1921.

Devil is a Woman, The. Dir. Josef von Sternberg. Perf. Marlene Dietrich. Paramount Pictures, 1935.

Dishonored. Dir. Josef von Sternberg. Perf. Marlene Dietrich. Paramount Pictures, 1931.

Don't Come Knocking. Dir. Wim Wenders. Perf. Sam Shepard. Reverse Angle Pictures (II), 2005.

Downfall. (Der Absturz) Dir. Ludwig Wolff. Perf. Asta Nielsen. Art-Film GmbH, 1923.

Downfall. (Der Untergang) Dir. Oliver Hirschbiegel. Perf. Bruno Ganz. Konstantin Film Produktion, 2004.

Dr. Mabuse, the Gambler. (Dr. Mabuse, der Spieler) Dir. Fritz Lang. Perf. Rudolf Klein-Rogge. Uco-Film GmbH, 1922.

Edukators, The. (Die fetten Jahre sind vorbei) Dir. Hans Weingartner. Perf. Daniel Brühl. Y3 Film, 2004.

Equilibrium. Dir. Kurt Wimmer. Perf. Christian Bale. Dimension Films, 2002.

Faraway, So Close! (In weiter Ferne, so nah!) . Dir. Wim Wenders. Perf. Otto Sander. Bioskop Films, 1993.

Fashion Side of Hollywood, The. Dir. Josef von Sternberg. Paramount Pictures, 1935.

F.C. Gundlach: Fotograph. Dir. Reiner Holzemer and Hans-Michael Koetzle, 2008.

Girlfight. Dir. Karen Kusama. Perf. Michelle Rodriguez. Green/Renzi, 2000.

Goodbye Lenin! Dir. Wolfgang Becker. Perf. Daniel Brühl. X-Filme Creative Pool, 2003.

Handmaid's Tale, The. Dir. Volker Schlöndorff. Perf. Natasha Richerdson. Bioskop, 1990.

Harakiri. Dir. Fritz Lang. Perf. Paul Biensfeldt. Decla-Bioscop AG, 1919.

Haunted Castle. (Schloß Vogelöd) Dir. F.W. Murnau. Perf. Arnold Korff. Uco-Film GmbH, 1921.

Inglourious Basterds. Dir. Quentin Tarantino. Per. Brad Pitt, Diane Kruger. Universal Pictures, 2009.

International, The. Dir. Tom Tykwer. Perf. Clive Owen, Naomi Watts. Columbia Pictures, 2009.

Judgement at Nuremberg. Dir. Stanley Kramer. Perf. Spencer Tracy, Marlene Dietrich. Roxlom Films Inc., 1961.

Jules and Jim. (Jules et Jim) Dir. François Truffant. Perf. Jeanne Moreau, Oskar Werner. Les Films du Carrosse, 1962.

Just a Gigolo. (Schöner Gigolo, Armer Gigolo) Dir. David Hemmings. Perf. Marlene Dietrich, David Bowie. Leguan Film Berlin, 1978.

Kill Bill. Dir. Quentin Tarantino. Perf. Uma Thurman. Miramax Films, 2003.

King Steps Out, The. Dir. Josef von Sternberg. Perf. Grace Moore. Columbia Pictures, 1936.

Los Angeles Plays Itself. Dir. Thom Andersen. Thom Andersen Productions 2003.

Lost Honour of Katharina Blum, The. (Die verlorene Ehre der Katharina Blum) Dir. Volker Schlöndorff. Perf. Angela Winkler. Bioskop Film, 1975.

Love Can Be Like Poison. (Liebe kann wie Gift sein) Dir. Veit Harlen. Perf. Joachim Fuchsberger. Arca-Film, 1958.

Madame Dubarry. Dir. Ernst Lubitsch. Perf. Pola Negri. Projektions-AG Union (PAGU), 1919.

Man on Horseback. (Michael Kohlhaas – Der Rebell) Dir. Volker Schlöndorff. Perf. David Warner. Houwer-Film, 1969.

Masked Mannequin, The. (Der Fürst von Pappenheim) Dir. Richard Eichberg. Perf. Mona Maris. Richard Eichberg-Film GmbH, 1927.

Master over Life and Death. (Herr über Leben und Tod) Dir. Victor Vicas. Perf. Maria Schell. Interwest, 1955.

Matrix, The. Dir. Larry and Andy Wachowski. Perf. Keanu Reeves. Groucho II Film Partnership, 1999.

Matrix Reloaded, The. Dir. Andy and Lana Wachowski. Perf. Keanu Reeves. Warner Bros. Pictures, 2003.

Metropolis. Dir Fritz Lang. Perf. Alfred Abel, Brigitte Helm. UFA, 1927.

Miami Vice. Dir. Anthony Yerkovich. Perf. Don Johnson. Michael Mann Productions, 1984-1989.

Mildred Pierce. Dir. Michael Curtiz. Perf. Joan Crawford. Warner Bros. Pictures, 1945.

Million Dollar Hotel, The. Dir. Wim Wenders. Perf. Mila Jovovich, Mel Gibson. Icon Entertainment International, 2000.

Miss Raffka. (Fräulein Raffke) Dir. Richard Eichberg. Perf. Werner Krauss. Richard Eichberg-Film GmbH, 1923.

Monster. Dir. Patty Jenkins. Perf. Charlize Theron. Media 8 Entertainment, 2003.

Morocco. Dir. Josef von Sternberg. Perf. Gary Cooper, Marlene Dietrich. Paramount Pictures, 1930.

Murderers Are Among Us, The. (Die Mörder sind unter uns) Dir. Wolfgang Staudte. Perf. Hildegard Knef. DEFA, 1946.

O.K. Dir. Michael Verhoeven. Perf. Gustl Bayrhammer. Houwer-Film, 1970.

Ode to Cologne: A Rock'N'Roll Film. (Viel passiert: Der BAP Film) Dir. Wim Wenders. Road Movies Produktion, 2002.

Olympia. Dir. Leni Riefenstahl. International Olympic Committee, 1938.

Palmetto. Dir. Volker Schlöndorff. Perf. Woody Harelson. Castle Rock Entertainment, 1998.

Pianist, The. Dir. Roman Polanski, Perf. Adrian Brody. R.P. Productions, 2002.

Piquancy. (Pikanterie) ir. Alfred Braun. Perf. Irene von Meyendorff. Skala-Film, 1950.

Phantom. Dir. F.W. Murnau. Perf. Alfred Abel. Uco-Film GmbH, 1922.

Princess and the Warrior, The. (Der Krieger und die Kaiserin) Dir. Tom Tykwer. Perf. Franka Potente. X-Filme Creative Pool, 2000.

Reader, The. Dir. Stephen Daldry. Perf. Kate Winslet. Weinstein Company, 2008.

Rebecca. Dir. Alfred Hitchcock. Perf. Laurence Olivier. Selznick International Pictures, 1940.

Rosegarden, The. Dir. Fons Rademakers. Perf. Liv Ullmann. Central Cinema Company Film (CCC), 1989.

Run Lola Run. (Lola rennt) Dir. Tom Tykwer. Perf. Franka Potente. X-Filme Creative Pool, 1998.

Scarlet Empress, The. Dir. Josef von Sternberg. Perf. Marlene Dietrich. Paramount Pictures, 1934.

Shanghai Express. Dir. Josef von Sternberg. Perf. Marlene Dietrich. Paramount Pictures, 1932.

Silvester Countdown. Dir. Oskar Roehler. Perf. Rolf Peter Kahl. Erdbeermund Filmproduktion, 1996.

Sky Captain and the World of Tomorrow. Dir. Kerry Conran. Perf. Jude Law. Brooklyn Films II, 2004.

Sliding Doors. Dir. Peter Howitt. Perf. Gwyneth Paltrow. Intermedia Films, 1998.

Soul of a Man, The. Dir. Wim Wenders. Perf. Beck. Cappa Productions, 2003.

Spiders. (Die Spinnen) Dir. Fritz Lang. Perf. Carl de Vogt. Decla-Bioscop AG, 1919.

Swann in Love. (Un amour de Swann) Dir. Volker Schlöndorff. Perf. Jeremy Irons. Gaumont, 1984.

Tin Drum, The. (Die Blechtrommel) Dir. Volker Schlöndorff. Perf. Angela Winkler, Mario Adolf. Argos Films, 1979.

Too Many Ways to be #1. Dir. Ka-Fai Wai. Perf. Ching Wan Lau. Golden Harvest Company, 1997.

Trainspotting. Dir. Danny Boyle. Perf. Ewen McGregor. Channel Four Films, 1996.

Triumph of the Will. Dir. Leni Riefenstahl. Leni Riefenstahl-Produktion, 1935.

Trophy Wife. (Luxusweibchen), Dir. Richard Eichberg. Richard Eichberg-Film GmbH, 1925.

U2 Zoo TV Live from Sydney. Dir. David Mallet. 1994.

Until the End of the World. (Bis ans Ende der Welt) Dir. Wim Wenders. Perf. Solveig Dommartin, William Hurt. Argos Films, Road Movies Filmproduktion, Village Roadshow Pictures, 2001.

V for Vendetta. Dir. James McTeigue. Perf. Natalie Portman, Hugo Weaving. Warner Bros. Pictures, 2006.

Valkyrie. Dir. Bryan Singer. Perf. Tom Cruise. Metro-Goldwyn-Mayer (MGM), 2008.

Veronika Voss. Dir. Rainer Werner Fassbinder. Perf. Rosel Zech. Laura Film, 1982.

Voyager. (Homo Faber) Dir. Volker Schlöndorff. Perf. Sam Shepard. Action Films, 1991.

War and Peace. (Krieg und Frieden) Dir. Volker Schlöndorff. Perf. Jürgen Prochnow. Bioskop Films, 1982.

Willie Nelson at the Theatro. Dir. Wim Wenders. Perf. Willie Nelson. Road Movies Produktion, 1998.

Wings of Desire. (Der Himmel über Berlin) Dir. Wim Wenders. Perfs. Peter Falk., Bruno Ganz, Otto Sander. Road Movies Filmproduktion, 1987.

Witness for the Prosecution. Dir. Billy Wilder. Perf. Marlene Dietrich. Edward Small Productions, 1957.

Yes, Women are Dangerous. (Ja, die Frauen sind gefährlich, a.k.a. Ich zähle täglich meine Sorgen). Dir. Peter Martin. Perf. Peter Alexander. Studio Film, 1960.

Young Torless. (Der junge Törless) Dir. Volker Schlöndorff. Perf. Mathieu Carrière. Franz Seitz Filmproduktion, 1966.